Advance Praise for *Audience•ology*

"It takes about two years for my brother, Bobby, and me to make a movie. Then we show it to the world and find out whether we just wasted two years of our lives. Kevin is always at that nerve-wracking first screening, like a movie whisperer who knows all the right questions to ask the audience. Kevin's job in a nutshell is to make movies better. And he does."

—**Peter Farrelly,** Academy Award–winning writer/director

"So much of what we do as filmmakers revolves around making assumptions about what will give the viewer an unforgettable experience. Kevin serves as the last validator of those assumptions. He and his remarkable company, Screen Engine/ASI, find the line between what was intended and what actually worked."

—**Nate Parker,** actor, director, writer, and producer

"Whether you sit behind the camera or in front of it, in film school or in an office on a studio lot, or just facing a screen as a movie lover, *Audience-ology* sheds light on the value of the test screening process. The explanations are illustrated with fascinating stories that are the lore of Hollywood. I only wish this book had existed when I first started out in the business."

—**Amy Pascal,** producer and former Sony studio chairman

"The media love to gossip about who has 'final cut' on a movie. In reality, if you want a commercial hit, the audience has final cut. Getting an unbiased understanding of what the audience really thinks isn't simple. Kevin is a master in aiding in this effort, as his book so entertainingly reveals."

—**Tom Rothman,** chairman,
Sony Pictures Entertainment Motion Picture Group

"I remember our first preview of *Bohemian Rhapsody*, which took me nearly ten years to make. To say I was a ball of nerves is an understatement. When the lights came on, all I remember is seeing Kevin's big smile. He leaned over and said, 'You've got a massive hit on your hands,' and all my nerves disappeared. Kevin is truly the best in the business."

—**Graham King,** Academy Award–winning producer

AUDIENCE·OLOGY

HOW
MOVIEGOERS
SHAPE THE FILMS
WE LOVE

KEVIN GOETZ

WITH DARLENE HAYMAN

TILLER PRESS

NEW YORK   LONDON   TORONTO   SYDNEY   NEW DELHI

TILLER PRESS

An Imprint of Simon & Schuster, Inc.
1230 Avenue of the Americas
New York, NY 10020

First Tiller Press hardcover edition November 2021

TILLER PRESS and colophon are registered
trademarks of Simon & Schuster, Inc.

For information about special discounts for bulk purchases, please
contact Simon & Schuster Special Sales at 1-866-506-1949
or business@simonandschuster.com.

The Simon & Schuster Speakers Bureau can bring authors to your live event.
For more information or to book an event, contact the Simon & Schuster Speakers
Bureau at 1-866-248-3049 or visit our website at www.simonspeakers.com.

Manufactured in the United States of America

1   3   5   7   9   10   8   6   4   2

Library of Congress Control Number: 2021946374

ISBN 978-1-9821-8667-8
ISBN 978-1-9821-8678-4 (ebook)

To Joe and Catherine, and the millions of moviegoers
who continue to share their unfettered truth.

CONTENTS

CONTENTS

FOREWORD

Long before a Minion stepped into my life, I met a young focus group moderator named Kevin Goetz. I was a production executive at 20th Century Fox, and the company where he worked conducted all the research on our pictures. He and I were about the same age, career-driven, cinephiles, and in retrospect, we both had entrepreneurial spirits. Kevin tested hundreds of movies each year, not just those released by Fox but movies from all the major studios. He always brought a well-informed perspective when we chatted about our films. It would be the beginning of our thirty-year friendship.

By 1996, I was running Fox's animation division, and soon thereafter, my colleagues and I began kicking around the idea for a film set against a prehistoric backdrop. After seeing some clips of spectacular CG animation from Blue Sky Studios, I established a relationship with its groundbreaking creative team to produce the film for Fox. *Ice Age* was born.

The audience testing that Kevin led on *Ice Age* resulted in two realizations that would change the course of my career. As we began to contemplate the release of *Ice Age*, we were still recovering from a massive financial loss of our previous animated film, *Titan A.E.* Feeling anxious, we took the film to other studios and looked for a partner to reduce our risk. While most of the town turned us down, we had one viable potential partner ready to start discussing a deal when we had that first preview. While the audience feedback was mixed, it was sending us a clear signal that this was not the right moment to be ruled by our anxiety.

The second realization was tied to the audience resistance that resulted in the "mixed" reaction. It's important to point out that the entire existence of Fox Animation and Blue Sky Studios rested on the shoulders of this movie pleasing its audience.

My team and I were very excited about a bold choice that we made to create a memorable and emotional end-of-second-act low moment. We killed off Diego, the saber-toothed tiger, one of our three main characters. When we took *Ice Age* out for its first test drive, we were surprised that the audience completely rejected this choice. To put it mildly, Diego's death stopped moviegoers in their tracks.

Kevin was at that early preview, and after the film was over, he assembled a focus group of parents and kids selected from the larger audience to stay behind and discuss what they had just seen. He quickly got feedback that the overwhelming majority of the focus group was not prepared to accept the death of a beloved character.

When Kevin dismissed the group, we gathered for his debrief. I will never forget how succinctly and sensitively he presented his findings, using the focus group's comments to provide essential insights about how our movie had played. He then presented us with what felt like an impossible challenge: to cut our precious death scene but make absolutely certain that we found another way to bring emotion to the conclusion of Diego's storyline.

Without that screening and the guidance Kevin provided, Fox would have sacrificed billions of dollars of revenue to a partner, and we would not have made a film so well liked that it spawned four sequels. Kevin earned a tremendous amount of credibility that day, effectively becoming a part of our Fox team.

Sometimes the lowest points during the movie research process inspire ideas that become highlights of the film. And that is exactly what happened with *Ice Age*. Like others who recount their stories in the pages ahead, I have a deep respect for the testing process and consider it an important step in filmmaking. What we learn from this type of research can validate what we already suspect or can propel us into entirely new directions. Either way, an early test screening allows us to make informed choices. Sometimes it's as simple as changing a music cue, tightening a scene, or substituting alternate jokes for ones that don't land. Other times, as some of the chapters in *Audience-ology* point out, we are faced with big decisions, like recrafting an entire sequence or even rewriting the end of our second act.

Out of our disappointment in learning that we couldn't kill off Diego, we were prompted to come up with one of the most memorable scenes in the film, where the vicious saber-toothed tiger plays peekaboo with the baby as he is being carried off with his family. To this day, Kevin is quick to point out that we would have had a good movie under any circumstances, but I'm convinced that these changes became the difference between a one-off film and a beloved franchise.

Ice Age would become a pivotal point in my career, and a few years after its release, I founded my own company, Illumination Entertainment. Kevin's star was rising on a parallel path. He had become the preeminent market researcher in the movie industry, and a year after I opened my door, he launched his own company, which now conducts most of the test screenings in Hollywood. We've remained friends and close confidants to this day, and I would never make a film without his involvement. He weighs in on my biggest decisions about ideas, stories, and characters. I showed him early renderings of the characters in *Evil Me*, the movie that would solidify Illumination's stature in the world of contemporary animation when it was released in 2010 as *Despicable Me*.

I can trust Kevin to tell me the truth, even when I don't want to hear it. I chafed at his advice after *The Secret Life of Pets* was first tested. These screenings can be personally very challenging. That afternoon, the previous three years' worth of our team's work was about to face three hours of evaluation. I was feeling particularly sensitive and craved affirmation for the film. On the surface the testing was fine, but Kevin felt that the movie's playability could be improved. So he relentlessly dove deep into the focus group discussion, looking for a key to unlock yet-to-be-realized potential. In the debrief that followed, he brought his hallmark honesty. I wasn't prepared to hear it. It was one of the rare moments in our relationship when I couldn't accept the constructive criticism. Friendship aside, Kevin was undeterred from his mission to help make each of our films as strong as they can possibly be.

Later that night, when I got home and thought it over, I sent Kevin an email acknowledging he was right. He helped the movie tremendously. I called him on the eve of our opening day to thank him—it went on to gross more than $100 million over its first weekend—because I wanted to make sure he knew how much I appreciated his contribution to the film.

Illumination has made ten movies, and Kevin has played a pivotal role in helping each of them be successful. However, our conversations are never about improving box office. The conversations are about improving the movies. The audience data is valuable, but hearing those reactions through Kevin's lens is invaluable.

As wonderful a tool as test screenings are, Kevin has elevated them with his filmmaking acumen. He's produced his own movies, understands the production process, and speaks the film language. Time is always our biggest enemy, even more so than money, because we're locked into release schedules. When Kevin conducts research, I'm not just getting a laundry list of grievances from the audience. He is going to synthesize the feedback into themes and hierarchies so the Illumination team can prioritize our precious resources on fixes that will truly improve audience satisfaction.

Kevin Goetz is the perfect person to write a book about how feedback from everyday moviegoers participating in test previews has helped turn good movies into great ones, profitable ones into blockbusters, and little gems into classics. He is attuned to the audience's willingness to suspend disbelief, and he has an uncanny sense of where and when a film might veer off course. He gets inside moviegoers' heads and hearts and can articulate their feelings even when they have difficulty finding the words. I trust that he will always offer constructive, prescriptive advice. After all, he is the doctor of audience-ology.

—**Chris Meledandri**
Founder and CEO, Illumination

AUDIENCE·OLOGY

INTRODUCTION

In the spring of 1994, I made the second unluckiest bet in Hollywood history. It was with John Goldwyn, who is, well, a Goldwyn. His grandfather was the "G" in MGM, one of the architects of early-twentieth-century Hollywood. His father was the famous independent producer and distributor, a stately man who ran the show at the Samuel Goldwyn Company well into his eighties. Pedigree notwithstanding, John Goldwyn is an accomplished production executive and producer, but this was decades ago when he was working at Paramount Pictures, and the wager took place as we stood outside a movie theater.

To be clear, this was the *second* unluckiest bet in history. The absolute unluckiest bet had occurred almost twenty years prior, when a young director became convinced that his new science fiction movie was a disaster and would bomb. He bet his friend Steven Spielberg, who was working on another sci-fi film, *Close Encounters of the Third Kind*, that Spielberg's movie would make more at the box office.

It would have been an excellent bet, a surefire winner, except that the frustrated filmmaker's name was George Lucas.

And his movie was a little passion project called *Star Wars*.

My bet with John Goldwyn in '94 wasn't nearly so rich. It wasn't *Star Wars* money. In fact, it was only for a dollar, a lonesome buck. But it was similar to George Lucas's bad wager in two ways: first, it was also a bet over box office revenues. I had wagered that a new movie from Paramount Pictures, where John was the head of production, would not make more than $200 million at the box office. At the time, only a few movies had ever earned that kind of money. Even Spielberg's latest *Indiana Jones* movie hadn't quite busted through the $200-million barrier, and while I liked Paramount's new film, I thought my bet was safe.

But there was a second reason my unlucky bet was like Lucas's. Both of us broke a cardinal rule of the movie industry, a rule that given my particular place in that industry, I should have followed to the letter.

The rule is this: don't pass judgment on a film before an audience has seen it.

After all, John Goldwyn and I didn't make our bet on any old night. It was *screening night*—the night that a test audience of real, live people would see the picture for the first time. And when John and I shook hands and sealed my very bad wager, those audience members still had their asses parked in the theater seats. The credits had yet to roll. They had yet to fill out the comment cards that I would pass out after the preview, cards on which they'd assess the movie and give the studio its first sense of whether it had a hit.

I remember that night clearly, just like every other night when I'm present for the birth of a motion picture into the world, the moment at which the film leaves the director's hands and becomes the property of the audience. I remember the studio heads shuffling into the back of the theater, anxiously wringing their hands. The executives had believed this movie—and I quote—"had Oscar written all over it" from the time they'd first read the script. But I was skeptical because I had heard similar sentiments plenty of times before. People close to a film can get caught up in their own delusions of grandeur. And what about that title?

"That is one of the strangest titles I've ever heard," I thought as I continued to chat with John. "What does that even mean?" I asked him. But he was unflappable, insisting that the movie was something special and destined to be a hit. We were about to see if moviegoers agreed.

I recall the director storming out of the theater, fearful that if the response wasn't as strong as he hoped, the studio might change his movie—his baby—based on the feedback. He had believed in this picture so fully that he'd even deferred a large portion of his own salary so the studio would have enough money for the production costs.

Then there was the moment when the lights dimmed, the projector whirred, and the screen lit up with the moving image of a feather floating down onto a park bench, where two people sat, including the simple-minded yet bighearted character who was about to transport us through rock and roll, Vietnam, and Ping-Pong diplomacy in China.

Most of all, however, I remember what happened after the screening, when it was time to do my job. I was conducting a focus group of twenty moviegoers who had stayed behind to talk about the film. At one point, an older male participant raised his hand and said, "I've seen God tonight, and his name is Forrest Gump."

The picture, of course, became a smash success with audiences and critics alike, earning six Oscars, including Best Picture and Best Director for Robert Zemeckis. *Forrest Gump* went on to make $330 million at the box office in the United States alone—and lost me a buck.

This is not your typical book about the movies.

You won't find stories here from the director's chair or from the star's trailer or from the chic lunch spots in LA, where gossip is served up faster than a forty-four-dollar McCarthy Salad at the Polo Lounge.

This story takes you to one of most secretive places in Hollywood—a place where famous directors are reduced to tears and multimillionaire actors reduced to fits of rage. A place where dreams are made and fortunes are lost.

It's told from the back of the movie theater at the end of the night, set when the lights are on and the projector is off and the popcorn is stale. It's the chronicle of how people—real people, like those gathered for the screening of *Forrest Gump*—have, a few hundred at a time, written and rewritten America's cinematic history by showing up, watching a rough cut of a new film before anyone else has seen it, and giving their unfettered opinions so directors and studios can salvage their blunders or, better yet, turn a good movie into an all-time classic.

For more than thirty years, I've been at the center of what Hollywood calls the movie research industry. My firm, Screen Engine/ASI, which I founded in early 2010, conducts research for nearly two-thirds of all movies that are tested and widely released in America. More than anyone else, we sit between the filmmakers and the audiences, just as doctors sit between patients and their test results. I am, as the *Los Angeles Times* once called me, "the doctor of audience-ology."

My firm tests. We diagnose. We prescribe a remedy. Occasionally we must break the news that the patient is dead on arrival.

On the best nights, of course, no remedies are required. Some nights are *Forrest Gump* nights, evenings of relief when the audience is all grins and thumbs-up and the directors and studio heads can breathe again. Then they go pop a bottle of Dom Pérignon.

But most nights aren't like that. Most nights the audience watches a new film and finds flaws. They spot the rough edges and plot holes that the filmmakers cannot see—or, sometimes, don't want to acknowledge—and it's my job to interpret that audience feedback and to convey it honestly. I help filmmakers and movie execs confront the flaws and recommend ways to fix them.

Imagine a *Fatal Attraction* where Glenn Close dies by suicide, or *The Martian* without seeing Matt Damon return to Earth, or *Jaws* without one of its signature scares—the moment that Richard Dreyfuss dives into a sunken ship, only to have the severed head of one of the shark's victims pop out. All those things happened (or didn't) in the original cuts, and it was audience feedback that led filmmakers to sand those rough edges. They edited the scenes, sometimes even reshooting them altogether, and made better pictures as a result.

America's movie catalog would be much different—and objectively, much less polished—if not for film-screening research. You're about to read how and why.

This book takes you inside the real, raw Hollywood before the makeup and airbrushing is applied. But the reason I've written this book is not just to tell the secret stories about the movies that you know and love. I wrote this book because the principles and practice behind a film test screening aren't just a Hollywood phenomenon. The reliance on data and analytics in decision-making is happening everywhere—from the marble-lined hallways of Washington, DC, to the grass-and-chalk fields of professional sports.

Over the past twenty years or so, we've watched data upend whole industries where emotion, not evidence, once drove decisions. In politics, Nate Silver has become a household name by building an analytic model that synthesizes polling data to predict who will win an election. Then there's the author Michael Lewis, who coined the term "moneyball" to describe how statisticians found inefficiencies in the baseball free agency market—and picked up top talent at a low cost.

We often see filmmaking as something separate and apart from this trend of data-driven decision-making. We like to think of directors as auteurs and their films as wonderful, original pieces of art that have sprung, fully formed, from their minds. Some are something close to that. But most films can benefit from an intensive process of viewer testing, analysis, and analytics-driven editing. And that includes movies that have captured awards from the world's most prestigious avant-garde film festivals.

This isn't to say that everyone loves screening their movies or that it's a practice without controversy. The visionary filmmaker Ang Lee, who directed *Brokeback Mountain* and *The Life of Pi* and won Oscars for both, once quipped to me that "Picasso never audience tested his paintings," and he is right about that. Picasso never changed a canvas from red to blue, or a squiggle to a straight line, because a group of museumgoers told him to. And I'd never suggest that Lee, who might be the closest thing we have to a modern-day Picasso, should compromise his vision either.

But I'd also tell Lee something else. I'd tell him—and all his fellow directors—that we live in a different time and work in a different medium than Picasso. The films we make cost millions upon millions of dollars, while Picasso's art supplies cost a couple of pesetas. Had Pablo's paintbrushes cost a fortune, and had he stood to lose his shirt—or even his entire career—with a single bad stroke, he might have loved to know if one particular painting wasn't really capturing his audience. Not to mention, if Picasso didn't like his work, he could stick the canvas in the back of his closet.

Today, that's what filmmakers and studios use the film screening process for—to see if it's having the intended impact. To see if a particular joke lands. If a chase scene is just a hair too long. If one ending is better than an alternate version that the director just happened to capture on film. All of these questions can be answered through test screenings. They can be tested, measured, empirically proven. Because there is wisdom in crowds, and even the most talented directors and seasoned executives can learn something from them. Just ask the guy who was unsure if *Forrest Gump* would be a smash hit.

In other words, while my hope is that anyone interested in Hollywood will find entertainment and education in these pages, I also hope that movie industry insiders—and those who aspire to join the industry—will see this as a how-to manual.

The film screening process can be a mysterious and anxiety-inducing thing. There is no "Screening 101" class in film school. Many directors walk into our screenings not knowing what to expect—or even why they're there. They come in blind, after having spent years crafting their pictures, after they've raised them like expensive children. And then, over the span of two hours at some random mall movie theater, they're asked to give up their children to a bunch of perfect strangers so the strangers can rate them and say whether they're worthy enough to be part of the world.

I've witnessed grown men and women cry over this. I've seen fists go through walls and filmmakers vomit in the parking lot when nerves got the best of them at test screenings.

The truth is, these screenings will always be an anxiety-inducing process, a panic attack by way of feedback, and this book is not going to change that. My hope, though, is that I'm able to show why this type of research is worth such pain and agitation, why gathering data to make informed decisions is very necessary.

After all, more than thirty years in this business have taught me one thing above all else: films, and maybe everything else, can be improved by listening and thoughtfully considering the opinions of the paying public.

finally, before we begin, I need to describe my methodology. You will notice that many of the stories are told through the lens of others.

You see, my work is conducted with the utmost confidentiality. I'm like a doctor in that way, too—I adhere to my own version of the HIPAA regulations. I reveal the results only to the small group of filmmakers and top-level studio executives who have entrusted me to conduct their previews. Even when I visit colleges to lecture about my work, I don't reveal details. As a general rule, I rarely mention specific films and never reveal test results, which is a minor problem when you're writing a book that is about specific films and their test results.

So I faced a dilemma. How was I going to write this book? Would it be hundreds of pages without a single story or name? Would I have to redact the whole damn thing? Was this going to look like some declassified CIA document with every other word blacked out?

Thankfully, I came up with a solution to my confidentiality problem. I did something that doesn't tend to come naturally in Hollywood.

I asked. And I listened.

This book is possible only because of the generosity of my friends and colleagues who sat down to share their perspectives. It's the product of more than a hundred candid interviews with some of the industry's most successful directors, producers, and studio executives. I sat with each of them to capture their experiences with the process, and I wound up with a treasure trove of never-before-told stories about beloved films. You will find in these pages the stories of how *Titanic* premiered to a shocked audience, how a song about a pizza pie changed movie history, and how the first showing of *Gone with the Wind* was really an exercise in mass kidnapping.

What you're about to read is movie history, although it isn't told from start to finish. It jumps around. Time goes backward, then forward.

Actors are grizzled veterans, then they're ingénues. Hollywood is filming in thirty-five millimeter, then IMAX. The glue that holds the story together, the through line, is not time but a common theme. It's the idea that cinema is a product of both auteurs and audiences, of both art and business.

It's that combination—the marriage of numbers and pictures—that has built something beautiful. It's created that magic in the dark that we call the movies, and for me the story begins about a dozen years before writing this.

1.

FINDING MY "AND"

In February 2010, I pulled my car into a Staples parking lot and asked myself, *How the fuck did I get here?*

This wasn't a literal question. By then my skills navigating the 405 Freeway were pretty well honed. Rather, it was existential, like something you might say a moment after leaping off a cliff, when you first realize that you're airborne and only two options exist: fly or go splat. That was the kind of day I was having. This Staples parking lot became my setting for some deep self-reflection.

For the previous seven years, I'd been working at a company called OTX. It was the premier film-testing company in the world, and I'd helped make it that way. I was brought in to build out their nascent Motion Picture Group and was responsible for everything from orchestrating the film screenings to soothing A-list directors and studio heads when the results weren't great. The job came with the usual perks, including a big salary.

The OTX job was a good job. A great job. But just a few days earlier, I had given it all up. I'd said goodbye, turned in my corporate AmEx card, and walked out the door into the wild unknown of Hollywood.

As great as things had seemed on the surface, OTX had changed. The owners had sold the company to a billion-dollar conglomerate. Everybody's job was up for renegotiation. And while the conglomerate wanted me to stay on and offered me a fair-enough contract, I knew I was facing a "now or never" moment to see if I had what it took to start my own firm. So I gave up the comfort and cushiness of that job, liquidated all my bank accounts, emptied my 401(k), and started my own film-testing firm out of my living room. I called it Screen Engine.

There's an oft-quoted line in *Field of Dreams*—"If you build it, he will come"—and indeed, people came. I'd spent years developing relationships with directors and studios, and when I established my new company, they stood with me. The vast majority of my clients followed me from OTX to Screen Engine.

Within two weeks, Screen Engine had outgrown my living room (much to the delight of my labradoodle, Kugel) and we moved into a two-hundred-square-foot shared office space on Wilshire Boulevard in Beverly Hills. It had that crucial 90210 zip code. We were a team of six at that time, writing emails on the floor, taking meetings in the hallway because we didn't even have a suitable conference room. We were overworked and under siege. Because, in addition to trying to serve all the clients that it had taken a much larger firm to serve, someone else showed up at our door: lawyers.

You see, big companies don't take too kindly to losing clients, and they'll fight—often with an army of attorneys—to keep you from taking them. Fortunately, I had never signed a noncompete and was legally free to work with my old clients (I play hard, but I play fair). But that didn't stop my former employer from serving me with a stack of paperwork so big that there's now probably a soccer field somewhere in Brazil that used to be a lovely rain forest.

My job as CEO was to put on a brave face for our team and keep them focused on doing great work for our clients. But the truth was, I was scared as hell—scared of losing my company, my savings, and the respect of my peers that I had worked so hard to build.

But if I'm being honest, the risk and uncertainty were also thrilling. After getting bored working in an increasingly corporate environment, every day at Screen Engine was a shot of adrenaline. I was exhausted, but I leapt out of bed every morning ready for battle.

Even everyday tasks like buying office supplies for the new company seemed like a thrilling adventure.

Which is how I ended up in that Staples parking lot in the winter of 2010 with that all-important question: *How the fuck did I get here?*

Oh, and on which aisle does Staples keep the printer ink?

I've never wanted to buy into astrology, the whole idea that how the stars align when you're born dictates who you become. But I do think that's why I am the way I am. I don't have a better explanation. I really don't.

I was born in Brooklyn in 1962, a year and a place where the stars aligned. It was the year that *Lawrence of Arabia* hit the big screen, when *Cape Fear* premiered, and when Stanley Kubrick took on the Hollywood censors and turned *Lolita* from a book into a film.

Brooklyn was where Mel Brooks was born, where Eli Wallach, Rita Hayworth, Barbra Streisand, and Woody Allen all grew up, just to name a few. Eddie Murphy was born not far away—and just over a year before me.

Years later, in college, I would have an argument with a sociology professor who claimed that behavior was learned—that you grew into your passions, you weren't born with them. "Au contraire," I said. I'd known that I belonged in show business from my first moment of consciousness.

When my mom went to buy clothes for us kids, I always asked for something that looked like a costume. When my brother locked himself in his room and pretended he was a baseball announcer, I retreated to my room, which was outfitted with a dance barre and mirrors, and practiced my Oscar acceptance speech. I have only one memory of the third grade: playing the garage mechanic in the school play, *Chitty Chitty Bang Bang*. (Did that role even exist in the movie?)

Indeed, if there's one element of my early life that foreshadowed who I'd become, it's this: an urgent, overwhelming desire to perform.

My parents didn't exactly encourage my passion for acting, singing, and dancing. Far from it.

But in the early 1970s, my dad took me to see *Pippin* on Broadway and I remember thinking, "This is what I want to do."

A year or two later, we went to see *A Chorus Line* and I knew, "This is what I *have* to do." It was life changing.

While my father was somewhat supportive, my mother wasn't having any of it, and early on, I'm sure she hoped it was a passing obsession. I can't exactly blame her; she certainly didn't envy the lives of parents of child actors. Who wants to take a day off work so they can take a kid to Manhattan so he can belt out "What I Did for Love" from *A Chorus Line* to some power-drunk casting director? Not my mother.

When I was in elementary school, my parents moved us across the Hudson River to what they called "the country," but was actually just the town of East Brunswick, New Jersey. Unfortunately for them, the move outside New York didn't change my show business aspirations. It didn't dampen my desire to be under bright lights. It only intensified it.

Our new house, it turns out, was located a few blocks away from some young aspiring actors, like my friend Metoka Singletary and the Munk brothers: David, Jonathan, and Robbie. All three Munk brothers regularly appeared in commercials (and Jonathan would eventually land a significant part in *Annie Hall*, playing the child version of Woody Allen's character). This immediately made them my idols, and even better, they introduced me to their manager, Delores Reed, who wanted to sign me.

I was once told that the great Shakespearean actor Laurence Olivier said something like, "It's not enough to have talent. You must have a talent for talent." Even at an early age, I instinctively understood that to get what you want, you have to be both talented *and* aggressive. Maybe even a little reckless.

This is how, when my mother refused to sign the papers allowing me to work with the manager, I made the most fateful decision of my fifteen years. I pursued the only option left for a minor who had saved every dollar he ever earned: I ran away from home.

Well, I ran away . . . *for the day.*

During the summer of 1977—the Summer of Sam—I left my house

without telling my parents and hopped a bus to New York. I found a photographer to take my headshots and signed up for a "turn class," which literally taught you how to turn like a dancer—or "spot," in the parlance of choreographers.

Let me tell you something: nonstop spinning is a terrible thing to practice when your only ride home is the Suburban Transit bus on the potholed Jersey Turnpike. (Luckily, my school Spanish teacher, Ms. Mark, happened to be on the bus, too, and she took care of me and my spinning-induced nausea.)

When I returned home that evening, I found my parents worried and pissed off. But they were also resigned. They now knew that I was serious about this "performing thing," that it wasn't just a passing phase. And it wasn't long after that I asked my mom to sign papers from a new talent manager who wanted to represent me.

I remember it clearly: it was 6:30 a.m., before school, when I walked into my parents' bedroom, after weeks and weeks and weeks of nagging my mother to sign the contract. She lifted herself from the bed, grabbed the papers out of my hand, and signed them without looking. The signature was almost illegible; it went up the side of the page. But it was enough.

That's how I became a professional actor: with the signature of my half-asleep mother who'd made me earn it. And in retrospect, I'm grateful to her for that.

By the time I'd reached my late teens, I was acting like I was breathing. I just did it. All the time.

My manager was a tough old broad named Barbara Jarrett. She represented young actors like Brooke Shields, Lori Loughlin, and Elisabeth Shue, and with her representation, I landed all sorts of commercials.

There was Stridex, the pimple medication, which thankfully was a radio spot. ("Oh, Romeo, Romeo, wherefore art thou Romeo?" "I'm here . . . *but I'm with pimples!*")

There was McDonald's. (To my buddy, regarding the pretty cashier who'd given me extra fries: "I think she likes me!")

Then, there was Sure deodorant, and on and on.

My parents had changed their tune, too. Their reluctance to let me follow my passion was long gone, and they were now my staunchest supporters, loving that I balanced being both a student *and* a working actor. What parent doesn't want their kid to learn the value of a hard-earned dollar?

When it came time to think about college, I was more interested in going to Broadway. My parents insisted that I continue my education. Fortunately, my high school mentor, Elliott Taubenslag, suggested that I do both by applying to the prestigious Mason Gross School of Arts at Rutgers, which coincidentally was only thirty minutes away from my home in East Brunswick. I figured that at the very least, I could keep my parents happy and skip class whenever I wanted to head into NYC to audition and get to work.

Mason Gross was, and is, one of the finest schools for acting in the country. Prospective students don't only send in an application, they audition—and I'll never forget mine. The late William Esper, the legendary acting instructor, watched my performance, and after it was done said, "You know, Kevin, if you come here, you won't be able to audition in New York." The curriculum, he said, was so intense that there'd simply be no time to even hop the train from Rutgers to Manhattan. I rolled my eyes—or at least, I thought about rolling my eyes—as I said, "Sure, I understand," in a way that sounded a lot like, "Oh yeah. Right, buddy." But it turns out that Bill was right.

Mason Gross was an intense place, full of competition, which only served to heighten my determination to be the best. In my junior year, for example, I lost out on a part in a mainstage production. The play was *Crimes of the Heart*. I'd lost the lead to a sophomore, and I recall tracking down Kathryn Gately, my acting teacher. Kathryn was a master instructor who was to become one of my lifelong mentors, and I vented to her about not getting the lead, not knowing what she might do next. She marched into the office of the administrative head of the Theater Department and told her, "I don't think this school wants to make an enemy out of Kevin Goetz!" (This didn't help me get the part.)

Rutgers also introduced me to like-minded people, like Lorraine Gauli. She had grown up forty-five minutes north of me in a little New

Jersey town called Glen Ridge. She was a marvelous actress, and like me, she was already a professional by the time she'd reached college.

Lorraine also had a sharp eye for new talent. At her high school, she saw a production of *Guys and Dolls* featuring a friend of hers who was also on the wrestling team. Lorraine had been a cheerleader and knew the kid was a quality athlete, but when she saw him on stage, she instantly recognized that he had serious talent and introduced him to her manager, Tobe Gibson.

Later on, the young wrestler-turned-actor would thank Lorraine in her high school yearbook, which she showed me. "Good luck in your career! I know you'll make it. I hope to be seeing you up there in lights one day. Good luck. Love ya, Tom," he wrote right above his name, Thomas C. Mapother IV.

A couple of years later, Tommy Mapother would make his way to California and change his last name to Cruise.

By the time I was twenty-one, I was out of college and living in Manhattan. I had almost a decade of acting under my belt, and while I still loved show business more than life itself, performing does lose some of its shimmer once you've faced down one thousand different casting directors and learned that your career really is in their hands. I didn't like giving up that kind of control. Plus, coming home to a roach-infested West End loft was not the kind of life I'd aspired to.

I had first moved in after college with an actor, PJ Wilson, a super-cool guy who had recently landed a part in the Broadway musical *Oh! Calcutta!* which was performed completely in the nude. Thankfully, PJ was kind enough to don a robe while rehearsing in our tiny studio apartment, but the robe still left little to the imagination (his balls were basically swaying in my face). Between that and the endless roaches, it was enough to make me find a new place to live.

This is how I landed my apartment on the Upper East Side.

More important, it's how I found the video store.

I had queued up a steady stream of auditions during most of my weekday hours and was acting regularly, but I still needed a part-time job to make rent. One night, I saw that Video Hut near my apartment was looking for a weekend manager. It wasn't exactly my dream job, but it was convenient, and at least I'd be surrounded by movies while I worked there. I walked into the store that night and walked out with the job.

Most of my time was spent restocking shelves and rewinding copies of *Trading Places* and *Gremlins*. Not exactly intellectual work. But after about a week, I had a revelation: I decided that if I was going to work at that video store, I was going to be the greatest goddamn video store employee the world had ever seen. In fact, I wasn't just going to work there. *I was going to try to buy the store.*

My logic was sound. Customers liked me. I always had a good movie recommendation, and I thought I could juice business more than the current owner, who was largely absent. He showed up just long enough to pay me and make sure no one had stolen from the register. Plus, I always had an entrepreneurial streak. In high school, I became the youngest member of the East Brunswick Chamber of Commerce when I opened my own after-school dance studio, Jazz Arts Studio, which was first located in a preschool and then in the local Unitarian Church. At one point, we had dozens of students. I taught classes, hired instructors, made payroll, had insurance, everything.

I used those skills to write a business plan for the video store. I surveyed customers to learn how I could improve the service. I had grand designs about what a movie rental place could be, and I thought that when I told the owner of my plans, he would be so impressed that he'd accept my offer on the spot.

Here's what happened instead: He fired me. He snickered at me and kicked me out the door.

It turns out I had become an expert on the business, and my offer was so well thought-out that he didn't want me around anymore. I went from being just another employee to being a threat.

But I came away with a lesson, one far more valuable than the ownership stake in a mom-and-pop video store, which went out of business just a few years later. (Thanks, Blockbuster!)

I loved the thrill of being an entrepreneur. I loved the stress and excitement of starting a new enterprise almost as much as I loved acting. This passion for entrepreneurship would continue throughout my life, although in 1986, I didn't know it yet. I wasn't even sure what to do with my newfound love of business. My thoughts were elsewhere.

After leaving the video store, I performed in a slew of plays, including *Hello, Dolly!* at the Bucks County Playhouse and an Off-Broadway musical called *The Second Hurricane*, where I met the great Aaron Copland, who'd composed the score. But I also knew it was time for me to move on, to head in a new direction, and to fulfill my destiny. I packed my bags and moved to California.

In my mind, my early California days play like a movie montage—like that interlude of cut scenes in *Rocky*, where Sylvester Stallone is training to fight Apollo Creed, hitting the punching bag, running in the snow, then climbing those iconic steps of the Philadelphia Museum of Art.

My first months on the West Coast were a lot like this, except instead of working out, I was working at a hodgepodge of strange and random jobs. I landed first on California's Central Coast, in Oceano, a beach town near San Luis Obispo, where I'd won a four-and-a-half-month contract to perform in a local theater, the Great American Melodrama. It wasn't my dream job, but it was a means to an end. I knew it was just a stopover that got me to California, and closer to the auditions that would launch my Hollywood debut.

In Oceano, I met the Suttons, a bighearted family who took me under their wing. The father, Bill, taught me how to drive a stick shift, a skill that I'd use a couple of months later when I headed south on US-101 in my recently purchased preowned Mercury LN7. I heard that one of my fellow company members from the Melodrama had an open room at an LA apartment—and, more important, that rent was only $172 a month.

As cheap as rent was, though, I still needed some extra cash to afford my other expenses. The movie gods don't exactly pay you to audition in LA, and so I took the first paying part-time job I was offered, which was catering. I served lunch every day to Michael Milken, the "Junk Bond King," who later went to jail after being indicted for fraud and racketeering. Milken kept East Coast hours, so I served him his special Pritikin Diet lunch every morning at 10 a.m.

Catering, however, wasn't enough to pay the bills, so I took the next survival job I was offered: I sold typewriter ribbons over the phone. I lasted approximately seventy-two hours in the job and quit once I learned that I had to (1) be there every morning at 6 a.m. and (2) ring a stupid bell to announce whenever I'd made a sale. For this reason—as well as a general lack of demand for typewriters—I never sold a single fucking ribbon.

The jobs kept coming. I next worked at an answering service, where I'd take messages for people who were too busy, or important, to respond to their pagers. I was getting a little closer to the entertainment industry, as one of the service's clients was the soap opera star, Deidre Hall. The place was so run-down and the phones were so grimy after hours of use that everyone working there became a germophobe. After spraying my station with Lysol for the hundredth time, I started looking for a better survival job.

I was in luck. I reached out to my old friend Metoka, who'd lived a few houses down from the Munk brothers back in East Brunswick. She was a dancer and an actress, too, and she'd told me that in order to make ends meet she'd taken a job with a company where, in her words, "they test movies."

I had no idea what testing movies meant. Did I have to make sure that the projector was functioning correctly? Did I have to figure out what to rate the movie, PG-13 or R? Who the hell knew?

What I did know, however, was that Metoka's part-time gig at National Research Group, or NRG, paid a minimum of four hours of wages for every job, plus the time it took to travel to a given theater anywhere in the LA area. That was enough for me.

I began my career in film testing in the most unassuming way possible, working my way down a line, outside a movie theater, with a clipboard in my hands, checking in filmgoers.

It was pretty clear from the get-go why they were there and what this whole film screening process was about. For one thing, I knew that the audience was there to give feedback because it was my job to hand out questionnaires, each of which read, "Please give us your thoughts about the movie."

I also knew they were watching an early cut of a film because every screening would begin with a similar spiel, delivered by one of the NRG senior executives. "You're about to see an unfinished movie," they'd tell the audience. "You may notice that the color and sound aren't perfectly balanced. The music is temporary. Just know that when the movie is officially released, it will all be technically perfect."

About three or four times a week in '87, this is how I spent my nights, as the charming face who would greet these kind moviegoers. It was a stress-free job until about a year or two after my first screening, when I received a promotion. The heads of NRG, Joe Farrell and Catherine Paura, needed me to moderate a focus group after one of the films we were testing.

Focus groups are an important part of the film screening process. They help studios figure out *why* their movies are good or bad—and not just *if* they're good or bad.

Assembling a good focus group takes skill. Before the audience enters the theater, a "focus group puller" will identify people in line who fit certain desired demographics. If, for example, the movie's target audience is mostly females between ages eighteen and forty-nine, the puller may tap about fourteen women dispersed by their ages, and only six men to sit in a twenty-person focus group. They're asked to sit close to the aisles to gain easy access. After the film is over, these people are offered a small incentive, typically a free pass to see a movie currently playing at the same theater, to stay and participate in a thirty-minute discussion with a moderator. Everyone in the theater fills out a questionnaire, but only these individuals are asked to dig deeper into what they liked or disliked about the film.

Moderating a group like this is more art than science; at least that's how I first saw it. You had to be careful not to open with too many negative comments about the film, lest the filmmakers (who are usually watching from the back of the theater) get upset. But you also had to devote enough time to the film's flaws so the studio would have enough information about what specifically was wrong.

Moderating, in other words, was a precarious high-wire balancing act, and slipups could lead to death, at least of one's career. This is probably why I don't remember too much about one of my first moderating sessions. I was stressed. I had trained tirelessly for the night. Both Joe and Catherine rehearsed me. But to this day, I really only remember the movie's title—*The Beast*, a film about the Soviet Union's invasion of Afghanistan.

The truth was I had no experience that qualified me to moderate a Hollywood focus group. The stakes were extremely high, which made me nervous but also exhilarated. It was baptism by fire.

I accepted the challenge and kept moderating, even after *The Beast*, because I was aware of what skills I did have. I leaned into my acting technique and the comfort I had performing in front of people since I was a boy, and for some reason, those people trusted me—and wanted to open up. I knew I could deliver criticism gently and praise genuinely. And if all else failed, I knew I could use my acting skills to play the part of a focus group moderator until I actually mastered the art. Within the year, studios started to request me to moderate their post-movie discussions. A year after that, I was often requested, even over my bosses.

Here's the funny thing about my experience with film testing in Hollywood: for years, no one seemed to care—or even know—that it wasn't my full-time job.

In fact, it wasn't even my main job. I worked at NRG for roughly sixteen years, and all throughout that time, I was still auditioning, still acting, and I even managed to open a professional theater on the Central Coast of California.

Together with my friend and mentor Anet Carlin, whom I'd met at the Great American Melodrama playhouse near San Luis Obispo, we discovered an old black box theater on the local campus of Cuesta College and decided to fix it up. The project allowed me to flex those entrepreneurial muscles again. Anet and I raised money from the school and from ads in the playbill, bringing actors and artists together in what would become a huge source of pride for me. I remember that on opening night, as the theater filled to capacity, I walked out through the scene shop to the loading dock, where I could be alone for a few minutes. I had a role in the first production, and I was going through my emotional preparation when it suddenly occurred to me that it was a year to the day since Anet and I began this endeavor. Looking up at the stars, I thought, "Wow. We actually pulled it off."

In fact, by the new millennium, I also had a nice business producing TV movies, too. My production company was named BBMG—Brooklyn Boy Makes Good—courtesy of my mother. She had seen Joan Rivers on television talking about how she had named her own production company and noticed that it was also an acronym, PGHM, although neither of us knew what it stood for. Years later I met Joan and she told me: Please, God, Help Melissa! (referring to her daughter).

Anyway, I had decided I wanted to produce a movie back in 1993, and it took me five years to make one. Then the business took off. Between 1998 and 2001, I had made five films in three years, one of which, *Wild Iris*, earned Laura Linney an Emmy for her performance as a woman whose husband had died by suicide. Gena Rowlands was also nominated for an Emmy in that same film.

I had always seen my work at NRG as just another line on my résumé, another word after a hyphen. I was Kevin Goetz, the actor-producer-moderator-film testing pro. (Try fitting that on a business card!)

Some people may look at all those hyphens and see a man who doesn't know what he wants, but I knew exactly what I wanted. I wanted to do everything, or at least I thought so. I loved those hyphens and all the jobs attached to them. I loved that I was still pursuing my old childhood passion for performing and art, and my newer passion for business and consulting. It never occurred to me, however, that I didn't have to pursue each of those passions piecemeal. I never realized that one job could bring me the same level of joy as many different ones. That was all about to change.

By 2002, the big research firm Nielsen had acquired NRG, and my old bosses, Joe and Catherine, were stepping down to enter into a producing deal at Disney. This left an opening at the top of the firm. Initially, Nielsen hadn't considered me for the job, and I hadn't thought about taking it. After all, I was now a producer and on a roll.

A year later, a call from a headhunter changed the course of my life. "We've been calling around, trying to find someone to run NRG for Nielsen," the recruiter told me. "Is it true that you actually work there? Everyone we call mentions your name."

It turns out Nielsen wasn't the only company looking for someone to head this corner of their business. There was a perfect storm happening in the industry—NRG had a near monopoly in the movie research business for more than two decades. Joe Farrell had seen to it that people trying to enter the business wouldn't get very far, so when he and Catherine Paura opened the door, everyone was trying to get in on it. In addition to Nielsen, I also spoke to our competitors at a company called MarketCast, and then, finally, with a woman named Shelley Zalis, who two years earlier had founded her own research firm, OTX, which was one of the first to conduct research online.

Shelley is a sharp businesswoman, a real go-getter. And even though her reputation as such preceded her, I didn't expect the speed with which she would act to build her business. A friend whose name is, appropriately, Bruce Friend had offered to connect us, and he left Shelley a phone message suggesting that we meet. Within five minutes—literally—of Bruce calling Shelley, she'd called me and set a lunch the next day. In less than twenty-four hours from our first phone call to the time we finished our salads at Off Vine, she'd met me, sized me up, and offered me a job as the executive vice president of OTX's new test screening business.

There's a scientific theory that contends there are infinite universes. We can imagine a universe where we elected Hillary Clinton president, where the Roman Empire never fell, or where Jurassic Park is a real thing. There is, if we're to believe the scientists, a universe for every conceivable possibility. But for the life of me, until 2002, I could not have conceived of a universe where I was not first a performer. No matter what the science said.

I was excited about the OTX job, but there was a part of me—a large part—that was scared, unmoored even. I was about to embark on a new job, a full-time one that would pull me away from the old passions that once stirred and sent me to Hollywood. Acting was the only thing I ever imagined doing with my life. From the time I could speak, the stage was where I felt most like myself. It was my identity. Realizing I wanted a break was almost an existential crisis. If I wasn't Kevin Goetz, actor, singer, and dancer, who was I?

I asked that question until I had a realization during my first weeks on the job at OTX. It was the first time in my life that I was single-focused. I realized that I didn't have to adhere to some forty-year-old notion of who I was, that I could combine the two things I loved—art and business—in a way that I never before dreamed and still find that same level of satisfaction I'd first enjoyed on the stage performing in *Chitty Chitty Bang Bang* or writing the business proposal to buy Video Hut.

Except now, my joy was doubled, because those pursuits had been combined.

There are few things as unnerving as receiving a phone call from the dean of your college—even if you'd been graduated for thirty-plus years. Fortunately, Dean George Stauffer and I were friends. I'd met him a couple of years prior, when I made a sizable donation to my alma mater. In 2013, I donated a new, state-of-the-art rehearsal studio to Rutgers University—the Kevin Goetz Studio for Theater and Dance that now sits squarely on the Mason Gross School of the Arts campus.

In college, the names of the buildings around campus became a kind of shorthand for my friends and me. We never said we were "going to class." Instead, we were meeting "at Vorhees" or rehearsing "at Levin." Today, I'm really proud to say that the latest group of Mason Gross students are now talking about rehearsing "at Goetz."

All that said, Dean Stauffer's call in early 2016 still took me by surprise: Would I deliver their commencement speech? I told him I would and that it would be an honor, but I was worried. I needed to find words to inspire these young people. *What would I say? Should I be funny? Should I be serious?*

Commencement speakers always tell students that graduation day is about them, but the truth is, it's a lot about the commencement speaker, too. When you prepare a speech like that, it forces you to reflect on your life, to draw lessons from your experiences. I spent weeks on my speech.

I wrote about how happy I was that my husband, Neil; my father,

Louis; and my sister, Lisa, were all there. I wrote about how grateful I was that one of my oldest friends, Valerie, who'd taught me the value of being single-focused, had come. And I wrote about how much I missed my brother, Peter, and his family, who couldn't make it that day, and how proud my late mother, Rhoda, would've been if she could've made it, too.

I wrote about the friends I'd made at Mason Gross, including my roommate, Joe, as well as Andrea, Roger, Mike, Colleen, and, as I mentioned earlier, Lorraine—or "Rainie"—who grew up to become a successful lawyer.

I told the "Don't make an enemy of Kevin Goetz" story and shared my video store experience, which got some laughs.

I described what happened when I went out to California, produced that play, started my career in film research, and felt the same thrill of entrepreneurship that I had felt in the video store. I told the audience how afraid I had been of that feeling. How afraid I was of no longer being an actor first.

Then something shifted after I began my film research gig. I realized that I was an artist in a different way, that it took the same level of creativity to fix a movie as it did to direct one or act in one. And that gave me solace.

"If I'm being totally honest," I said, "if someone told twenty-one-year-old Kevin that this is what fifty-three-year-old Kevin would be doing, I'd probably be disappointed, maybe even devastated, because it doesn't jibe with the very specific vision I had for my life. It's easy to get stuck, especially for artists. I implore you to keep an open mind and heart.

"There was a great lesson in that," I continued. "Find your *and*. I'm an artist *and* an entrepreneur," I told the graduates. "That's what I was always meant to be. And even if I didn't always see it, there were signs all along the way."

2.

LOCKED DOORS, SEVERED HEADS, AND THE EARLY HISTORY OF TEST SCREENINGS

M ovie research has been around almost as long as the movies themselves, and while many of the practices and principles of the business have changed over the last century, you can't understand the modern film screening process without understanding first where it came from.

I love history, especially art history. In college, I was enraptured by a course that took me from the ancient cave paintings in France to the works of Jackson Pollock. Yet I'm not an expert in art history, not even if we're including movies in the curriculum. We need qualified guides to walk us through all the progress and change in movie research history— which is why I'm grateful that I had access to two descendants of Hollywood royalty a few years ago: Richard Zanuck and Samuel Goldwyn Jr.

The morning fog was starting to burn off as I made my way up into the hills above Sunset Boulevard. Driving along the winding canyon road, my car rose above the mist and the congestion of the city below.

The traffic thinned, and soon I passed only the occasional gardener, a jogger, a uniformed housekeeper walking a small dog. At the summit, the puffy blanket of moisture rested below, and the view above it cleared to reveal the magnificent homes dotting the surrounding hilltops. I entered the private enclave, announced myself at the guardhouse, and passed through after my name was checked against the guest list.

When you get to a certain status in Hollywood, you don't rush into the office for a 9 a.m. meeting.

Morning meetings are brought to you.

And on this morning, I was bringing myself to meet Richard Zanuck at his home to discuss screening research. As the gates to his tree-lined driveway opened, I felt that I was about to get a glimpse into Hollywood history.

Dick Zanuck and I had become acquainted when I conducted pre-views for a couple of his films, but we had never spoken at length about the process of testing movies. I anticipated a robust conversation and hoped he would regale me with stories from his impressive roster of films. An accomplished producer and executive with movies like *The Sound of Music, Jaws, Driving Miss Daisy, Road to Perdition, Charlie and the Chocolate Factory*, and *Sweeney Todd: The Demon Barber of Fleet Street* to his credit, Dick was also the son of one of the early titans of the movie business.

Dick's father, Darryl Zanuck, arrived in Hollywood in the 1920s and spent several years churning out scripts for the four Warner brothers, most notably collaborating on the *Rin Tin Tin* series of pictures. He soon distinguished himself as a leading force at Warner Bros., shaping its film slate for several critical years during the infancy of color and sound. In 1933, with many successful movies to his credit and financial backing from Louis B. Mayer and Joseph Schenck, Zanuck left Warner Bros. to establish his own studio, Twentieth Century Films. Two years later, he absorbed a nearly bankrupt giant called Fox Film Corporation and the combined entity became Twentieth Century–Fox.

Zanuck Sr. ran the studio for decades and is often regarded as the "last mogul standing" because his career endured longer than that of any of the studio heads of Hollywood's golden age. He passed away in 1979, and I wondered if his son, himself in his seventies on the morning of our meeting, would remember much about his father's views of movie screening research.

Several months earlier, I had had the opportunity to speak with Samuel Goldwyn Jr. (father of John Goldwyn, with whom I made that very bad bet about *Forrest Gump*), who shared some of his memories with me. Sam was also second-generation Hollywood royalty, the son and namesake of Samuel Goldwyn, who, like Darryl Zanuck, was one of the founding fathers of the industry.

I remember being surprised to learn that based upon screening research, the elder Goldwyn had changed the ending of the 1939 masterpiece *Wuthering Heights*.

Sam Jr. told me that his father and the film's director, William Wyler, had argued about the final scene in the picture, which originally showed Cathy (played by Merle Oberon) dying in the arms of Laurence Olivier's Heathcliff. Goldwyn felt certain that an epic romantic movie should not end so darkly, but Wyler fought to keep the last scene intact. An audience screening was arranged to settle their dispute. The test audience unequivocally disliked the ending, and Goldwyn prevailed.

At his insistence, a different ending was shot, one in which a bereaved Heathcliff, believing that Cathy's spirit is calling to him, runs onto the moors in search of her. The new scene was substituted for the original ending even though Wyler was never comfortable with the change. Sam Jr. informed me that on many occasions, Wyler retold the story of how his father had forced the new ending upon him. "Your father was right because the picture was a hit," Wyler would say magnanimously.

What is perhaps even more astonishing than the use of audience feedback to improve *Wuthering Heights* is that screening research has been around nearly as long as movies themselves. From the earliest days of silent film, silver-screen clowns Buster Keaton, Harold Lloyd, and Charlie Chaplin would often preview bits and pieces of their upcoming movies to see how well their jokes played to an audience. Veterans of vaudeville, they knew the value of perfect timing and were able to gauge the audience's laughter to determine if they were on the right track. Lloyd is credited as the earliest pioneer of the screening process, and there is evidence that he began testing his sequences in 1919 or 1920. There is no doubt that Lloyd was a gifted filmmaker, but he was also a shrewd businessman who used rudimentary research techniques to craft crowd-pleasing comedies that would eventually earn him a fortune.

As a child, the Nebraska-born Lloyd performed in stage plays in the Midwest, an experience that would later serve to give him a foothold in the emerging motion picture business. His family moved west, eventually relocating to San Diego, where he attended high school and then acting school. In 1913, at the age of twenty, Hal Roach (who would later produce the iconic Laurel and Hardy pictures) gave Lloyd his first break, a tiny part in a silent film called *The Old Monk's Tale*. The enterprising Lloyd soon established himself as Roach's protégé, and within a few short years, he was writing, directing, and starring in his own films. In front of the camera, Lloyd was a talented comedian, the bespectacled character dangling from a clock tower high above the city streets in *Safety Last!* But behind the lens, comedy was serious business to Lloyd, who did everything possible to make his pictures successful. Early in his career, he began to develop his own testing methodologies.

In an interview two years before his death that was featured in the 1969 fall edition of *Film Comment*, Lloyd reminisced about those very early tests. "Even back in the one-reel days, I would take a picture out to a theater when I knew the picture wasn't right. And the manager used to always have to come out and explain what was going on. When we were doing two-reelers, he came out in white tie and tails to do it, and it was quite an event for him, and the audience would listen attentively."

Regardless of the fanfare surrounding those early previews, what really mattered to Lloyd was the audience's laughter, and he invested great energy in observation and evaluation of it. He was the first person to attempt to make the screening process "scientific" by plotting the timing and intensity of the laughter on huge graphs. He would then use the charts to recut his films, eventually becoming so proficient at it that his films became laughter-generating machines. His efforts paid off; during the 1920s, Lloyd earned millions and established himself as one of the most successful filmmakers of his time.

Harold Lloyd was not alone in the endeavor to use screening research to finesse movies. Charlie Chaplin took footage into Hollywood where he had arrangements with theater owners to play scenes from his works in progress, either before or after the regular feature. Standing in the back of the auditorium, he would listen to the audience's laughter and then run back to his studio where he would make adjustments according to what he had learned.

Keaton, too, would modify his films based on the results of screening research. For his film *The Navigator*, Keaton completed an elaborate underwater sequence in which he played a traffic cop directing schools of fish, a highly unusual production feat in 1924. When he screened it and moviegoers were too flabbergasted to laugh, Keaton scrapped the entire scene.[1]

The incidence and intensity of audience laughter is still the very best way to evaluate the performance of a comedy, as those specializing in this most popular genre know only too well. Technology now allows us to capture moviegoer laughter using digital audio recorders or high-definition, night-vision cameras, which are often strategically placed in theater auditoriums on the night of a test screening. Modern surveys ask a number of different questions to establish quantifiable data on how well the humor plays. Even so, I often station notetakers in the audience who jot down the big-laugh moments during the test preview of a comedy. I wonder if they realize that Harold Lloyd was doing the very same thing a hundred years ago.

By the early 1930s, test previews of comedy sequences gave way to full-length movies being previewed before theater audiences who would then fill out surveys at the request of studio chiefs. Postcard-size with only a few questions on them, the earliest questionnaires provided enough feedback for the studio to determine whether a film was ready for release. Film archives are chock-full of examples of movies from that period that were taken to outlying areas of Los Angeles to be tested before the public.

In addition to identifying what worked or failed, previews often resulted in the discovery of new talent. A silly Depression-era film titled *Stand Up and Cheer* generated harsh feedback from its test audience, but the adorable five-year-old featured in the picture won accolades from moviegoers. That child was Shirley Temple.

When the survey cards from the screenings of the 1936 film *Girls' Dormitory* revealed that moviegoers were enamored by the "good-looking boy"[2] featured in a single scene, studio executives at Twentieth Century–Fox Film Corporation took note. They gave the unknown actor, Tyrone Power, a leading role in his next film, *Lloyds of London*, and he went on to become a matinee idol.

As folklore has it, both Clark Gable and Joan Crawford also graduated from the back row to major stardom by virtue of highly positive preview cards.

In *Big Broadcast of 1938*, a new comedic actor named Bob Hope was featured in several early scenes that didn't play well to the test audience. Moviegoers were unfamiliar with his style of humor and didn't find it particularly funny. But in one of the film's later scenes, the audience roared with laughter at his antics. So Paramount, recognizing that audiences might need a different introduction to his brand of humor, reordered the scenes to put his big laugh scene before the others. At the next test screening, moviegoers found Hope to be funny all the way through.

There is, of course, the famous story about the first test screening of *Gone with the Wind* in 1939, the same year as the release of *Wuthering Heights*. Much has been written about David O. Selznick's decision to take the still unfinished *Gone with the Wind* to Riverside, California, where it was shown to an audience at the Fox Theater. With great secrecy, Selznick had prearranged that the theater manager would announce the special preview following the regular feature film, but the title was not to be disclosed. Moviegoers could choose to leave the theater before the preview began, but those who committed to stay were told that there would be no readmissions once the film started.

Legend has it that the doors of the theater were locked, the lights went down, and the audience nearly fell out of their seats as *Gone with the Wind* flashed across the screen. There had been huge anticipation of the movie because Margaret Mitchell's thousand-page novel had been a bestseller, and the lucky Fox Theater patrons were thrilled to be previewing it. Enraptured, they hardly moved throughout the nearly four-hour screening, and in the surveys they completed afterward, begged the filmmakers not to cut a single frame from the movie. Sam Goldwyn Jr. remembered hearing the story directly from David O. Selznick and his wife, Irene, the former telling him that he stood in the back of the theater and watched people go to the bathroom to make sure they came right back. He maintained that the doors to the theater were never actually locked.

Many of the early studio moguls used screening research, at least occasionally, as a first line of defense to make sure their investment in a picture would reap returns at the box office. Darryl F. Zanuck was no exception, as his son would confirm during our morning meeting. He told me that his father would sit with an audience while they watched a movie and sense whether they were enjoying it. He knew if they seemed restless, and from his own perception of their reactions, he was able to pinpoint the places in a film that needed to be reworked. A bit of firsthand observation was all these studio heads needed to validate their instincts for what pleased moviegoers.

Toward the end of the 1930s, famed political pollster Dr. George Gallup saw an opportunity to transform the movie business from one based largely upon gut decisions into a more scientifically enlightened one. Leveraging his experience and celebrity in the political arena, Gallup developed an empirical formula for movie concept testing, and for a while he had the ear of some of Hollywood's biggest studio heads. The researcher, who was based in Princeton, New Jersey, made multiple trips to California during the 1940s to pitch his survey-based techniques. He explained that the same methods used to predict presidential election results could also be implemented to probe the ticket-buying public for their opinions on stories, stars, and even film titles.

Gallup's ideas intrigued some, especially once he partnered with David Ogilvy, a dynamic young advertising genius who had immigrated to the US from Great Britain in 1938 (and who would later go on to become one of the most successful agency principals in the history of advertising). Together, the two traveled repeatedly to Hollywood to sell research studies to the studios. For a time, Walt Disney and independent producers Samuel Goldwyn and David O. Selznick embraced Gallup and his methods. Yet when push came to shove, many rebuffed expertise from outside sources. Darryl Zanuck, Louis B. Mayer, and Jack Warner preferred to rely on their own astute judgment to choose material, cast stars, and assign titles to the pictures they made.

In the 1950s, another independent research analyst, Albert Sindlinger, emerged on the scene and established contracts with some of the big studios, Columbia among them, to conduct surveys that measured interest in film concepts. For a while, Sindlinger and Gallup competed for broad-based studies that promised to shed light on box office slumps, the threat posed by television, and solutions for luring prospects out of the house and into the theater. Both pitched proposals for movie ad testing and title tests as well. But in the end, neither Gallup nor Sindlinger were successful. It would be two decades before any outside research company would gain traction within Hollywood. The studios kept a tight hold on their own research efforts, which consisted of test previews and little else. Only recently, in the twenty-first century, have studios embraced concept testing as a protocol.

Between the 1930s and the early 1970s, screening research underwent only subtle changes. The questionnaires became longer; more details were probed regarding the stars, the scenes, confusion, and pacing. By the 1950s, the surveys also asked moviegoers to provide their gender and age, a move toward distinguishing a film's appeal by audience segment. Recruitment to test previews also changed. The earliest screenings of films substituted the picture that was being tested for the second movie of a double feature, and the theater manager announced it to the audience, often to their surprise. Later, the main feature was billed with an *announced* preview—listed on the marquee and/or in a newspaper ad—and moviegoers knew before entering the theater that they would be among the first to see the new film. As the concept of double features became obsolete, moviegoers were invited to attend special previews and studio publicity departments worked with theater owners and local media outlets to fill the auditoriums.

Then, in the mid-1970s, the industry experienced a number of changes that would catapult screening research into widespread use and force the process to become more stringent and principled. First, studios began releasing movies simultaneously in many markets across the

country, a departure from the "platform release" schedules of earlier decades when a film would open in only a handful of big cities and slowly,
over many months, the prints would be cycled into smaller markets and
eventually, everywhere. With the advent of national release schedules,
studios issued enough prints to cover most or all of the country at one
time. They began marketing movies more broadly to cover their wider
distribution patterns, tapping into network television as the most effective advertising medium to open a picture. Then, new digital technolo-
gies were developed that allowed movies to feature special effects like
never before.

The combined impact of these advances greatly increased the cost of
producing and distributing films, and consequently, studios were more
motivated than ever to test the water before jumping in.

On a rain-soaked afternoon in the spring of 1975, a group of filmmakers and MCA Universal studio executives sat in a Dallas coffee shop
having lunch and debating whether to cancel the test screening of a film
that was scheduled to occur that evening at the Medallion Theater. One
of the execs in the group was Dick Zanuck, who relayed this story to
me as we sat in the library of his home many years later, surrounded by
books, awards, and movie memorabilia. Dick, who was the film's producer, had flown from Los Angeles to Dallas that morning, and as he sat
with the director and the president of the studio, Sid Sheinberg, he could
sense that everyone was on edge. He was cognizant of how much was
riding on this picture.

The studio had not had a major hit in a long, long time. Zanuck himself was just three years into his own independent production company
with partner David Brown, a collaboration that had already seen success
with the 1973 hit *The Sting*. The director of the film set to be screened that
night, twenty-eight-year-old Steven Spielberg, was a virtual unknown,
having worked on a few television series (Rod Serling's *Night Gallery* and
Marcus Welby, M.D.). His first endeavor as a director, on a film called *The
Sugarland Express*, which Zanuck/Brown Productions and MCA Universal had released the year before, had produced very modest box office

results. Now, looking through the windows of the coffee shop at the torrential downpour, the group doubted if an audience would show up to preview their latest project.

Back in the mid-1970s, screenings were arranged through studio publicity departments. A popular local radio station would be contacted, one of their disc jockeys would mention the time and place of the screening, and the studio would hope for the best. There was nothing scientific about balancing the audience demographically or confirming the attendance of the prospective moviegoers. The theater manager and the publicity department handled all the details, such as they were, and radio listeners who were intrigued by the film's title or stars would just show up at the announced time and place.

On that day of inclement weather in Dallas, it was understandable that the group wondered if the theater would fill. So much of the process in that era was left to chance. But after checking the forecast and considering their options, the filmmakers and studio executives decided to go through with the screening as planned. They finished their lunch and headed back to their hotel to wait until evening.

Zanuck and Brown had purchased the rights to a book called *Jaws* when it was still in manuscript form—a daring move considering its author, Peter Benchley, was a first-time novelist. Months before the book was published by Doubleday in 1974, the producers sealed the deal based on what they believed was a terrific story that would translate well to the big screen. They worked with the author and publishing company to design the book's cover art, which they planned to carry through to all of the marketing materials for the film. The chilling visual of a shark ascending through the depths of the ocean toward a swimmer above would become the iconic artwork for both the book and the movie.

The book debuted in February 1974 with an initial run of thirty-five thousand copies, which flew off the shelves so quickly that it went into a second printing before the month was out. It soon earned a place on the *New York Times* bestseller list, where it stayed for forty-four consecutive weeks. During the summer months of 1974, *Jaws* kept beachgoers riveted to their blankets and too frightened to venture into the water. By the time the film was ready to be screened on that rainy day in Dallas, the paperback edition was ubiquitous. The cover art was even more provocative than on the earlier hardcover version, the shark bearing razor sharp teeth as it menaced the now naked swimmer.

On the evening of the screening, Zanuck met the group in the hotel lobby where they climbed into cars that would take them to the theater. The weather had not improved. "It was a driving rain; we couldn't see five feet," he recalled. The car made its way through the flooded streets, and as they approached the theater, Zanuck remembered looking through the windshield and wondering if he was seeing a mirage. As the wipers worked furiously to clear the pounding rain, he saw a huge crowd assembled.

"There was nothing but people. It was like arriving at a major sporting event," Zanuck recounted. The astonished group got out of the cars and made their way through the crowd. More than three hundred people had to be turned away that night, and the auditorium seemed to burst at the seams. Because of the popularity of the book and the radio announcement, the place was packed.

Zanuck remembered taking a seat next to Spielberg, who was very nervous. "We were both scared," he said. "Spielberg was just a kid. We had never seen the picture with any kind of an audience. And having lived through the nightmare of making it, we didn't know if it would play."

The production had been difficult. A mechanical shark, which the production team had nicknamed "Bruce," was temperamental and refused to work most of the time. When it did function, the crew would burst into laughter because it looked so phony. Now, sitting with an audience, Zanuck and Spielberg wondered if they would get the same reaction.

"We had high hopes, but we didn't know if an audience would say, 'Oh for God's sake, it's a big rubber dummy.' The shark could have been a huge disastrous mistake and the whole thing would have been laughable."

Zanuck clearly remembered the first screams. The enormous shark is suddenly revealed, then Roy Scheider (playing Brody) announces to Robert Shaw's Quint, "You're gonna need a bigger boat." The Dallas test audience never heard that classic line. They were too busy screaming, and the noise completely obliterated the dialogue. Zanuck and Spielberg clutched each other's arms, and in that instant, they knew the audience bought the shark. It was credible. It was the terrifying monster they'd hoped it would be. For the remainder of the film, there was a constant flow of people in and out of the theater, and not to buy popcorn and candy. Many *had* to leave for a few minutes, just to calm down and compose themselves. A few vomited. *Jaws* was graphic, gruesome, and disturbing, and to a 1975 audience, it was unlike anything they had ever seen before. Zanuck was thrilled.

For the most part, the movie played very, very well in Dallas. There was one scene that caused the audience to jump, but Spielberg thought it should have been even more frightening. Zanuck recalled, "It was very interesting, because the way he had shot it originally, Dreyfuss is diving down along the side of an abandoned boat at night and he's got an underwater light. He's looking along the hull and he comes across the head of the guy who was the captain of that ship. It got a good response, but we expected more." Spielberg had an idea of how he could enhance the scene to make it more powerful.

The following day, the group returned to Los Angeles. Spielberg got right back to work, mapping out a plan to reshoot the underwater scene. In order to keep costs down, he proposed using the swimming pool of his editor, Verna Fields, who agreed. With the crew assembled in her backyard, the sun setting in the west, a gallon of milk was poured into the water to make it just murky enough to look like Nantucket Sound at night. The boat prop was lowered to the bottom, and Dreyfuss climbed into the water. Zanuck explained, "So what he did in the pool, he had the same shot—Dreyfuss diving along the side of the boat—you see the hole, it's an *empty* hole and then the head floats in. That little bit of movement was all they needed."

Lew Wasserman, then chairman and chief operating officer of MCA, had not been available to attend the first screening of *Jaws*. Everyone involved wanted Wasserman to experience the audience's reaction to the film, just as they had in Dallas. So a few weeks after the reshoot in the pool, the studio executives arranged for a second test screening in Lakewood, California. The film played just as well as it had in Dallas, with the exception of the scene that had been reshot. Moviegoers were riveted as that moment unfolded. Dreyfuss's character dives along the side of the ship, discovers the gash in the boat's hull, and shines his light into the gaping hole. The camera lingers for a moment on the blackness within. Then, suddenly, the corpse's head floats into view, one eye bulging in deathly terror, the other eye missing altogether, the socket crawling with crabs. The theater erupted.

"I'm telling you, the reaction to the whole film was just thunderous!" exclaimed Zanuck. When the movie was over, Wasserman assembled the group in the theater manager's office and turned to the head of distribution, who had flown in from New York to attend the preview. Zanuck recalled Wasserman saying, "How many theaters do you have?" The distribution person admitted that since the first screening in Dallas, he had been unable to return the flood of calls that he had received from exhibitors across the country, clamoring to book *Jaws* into their theaters. But he proudly announced that he was up to six hundred theaters. The group was dumbstruck. A film had never opened in so many theaters. Ever the brilliant businessman, Wasserman retorted, "Cut half of them! I don't want this picture playing in Palm Springs. I want Palm Springs moviegoers to have to drive to Los Angeles to see it."

Jaws stayed in theaters as the number-one picture for the entire summer of 1975. Wasserman's efforts to limit its release went only so far—it opened in 465 theaters, the broadest distribution for a film in motion picture history until that time. It was the first summer blockbuster, and the prelude to what is now called the "tentpole," those huge moneymaking films that support a studio's annual slate of releases, which inevitably include others that are much less profitable.

Indeed, Hollywood by the 1970s was fast becoming an industry with huge assets, not unlike the professional sports industry, with its enormous contracts and multibillion-dollar stadiums. And much like in that industry, there was so much cash at stake in the movie business that, at least financially, it made sense to test product six ways to Sunday.

The data didn't supplant the artistry, but it did open up a seat at those big boardroom tables that you can find in so many Hollywood studios, tables where execs had once green-lit or killed films based on gut instinct alone. Now there was a place setting for another type of decision-maker, one who would have to take into consideration the art and the science. Someone who was as much MBA as MGM.

It was a seismic shift.

A little aside before we move on. In the summer of 2018, I vacationed on Martha's Vineyard. I was there over July Fourth and my buddy Kevin and I decided it would be a kick to go see *Jaws*, which is featured as an annual revival showing in a local theater to commemorate the holiday. It was fun to watch it again, this time recognizing many of the locales where the filming took place, now that I was familiar with the Vineyard. During the scene when the corpse's head comes into view and the crab crawls out of the eye socket, I watched as nearly the entire current-day audience jumped. Hell, I'll admit it—even knowing full well what was about to happen and how it had been orchestrated as a reshoot in Verna Fields's backyard pool, I jumped, too!

3.

THE LIGHTS IN MINNEAPOLIS

Test screenings, whereby several hundred people are brought into a theater to see an early cut of a film, require a well-choreographed and experienced staff who manage all facets of the operation. I'm lucky to have a company filled with experienced and dedicated professionals who can handle these complex projects.

The process begins with a phone call from a studio executive, usually the head of research but sometimes the production executive assigned to the film or, on occasion, the president of marketing, distribution, or acquisitions. The caller communicates that postproduction on a film is being completed and a first cut is ready to be screened before an audience of regular moviegoing folks. We discuss the anticipated appeal, perhaps similarities to other films and the audiences those pictures attracted when they were in release. Such considerations are important in defining the audience composition of moviegoers we will recruit to the test preview.

For nonstudio films, those produced by independent production companies, the producer, the postproduction supervisor, or sometimes even the director will contact us to arrange a screening. Very often these previews are conducted in the hope of getting positive audience feedback that can be used by the filmmakers in their efforts to secure distribution deals for their movies that were paid for and produced independently but have yet to find studio backing.

Regardless of who from the studio or production company contacts me, that phone call sparks a flurry of activity within our company because the window of time that we have to plan a screening is more often than not very short. These projects are initiated about a week or two in advance of the desired screening date, so everything that occurs from the time we hang up the phone until the night of the preview happens at warp speed.

The details are mind-boggling and the process is extremely labor-intensive. In fact, it's a lot like throwing a very elaborate party or wedding. Venues are considered, a room is rented (actually, a theater), invitations are carefully crafted, guests are invited, and RSVPs are counted. In situations where a high-profile film is being tested away from the glaring lights of Hollywood, or when the studio wants to get a read on how it plays in Middle America, the preview is held in a distant locale. In this scenario, travel arrangements are made for the core screening staff who must transport all the materials and equipment needed, including the questionnaires (paper or electronic tablets for every attendee), audio recording devices, biometric wristbands, walkie-talkies, signage, laptops, portable printers, and confidentiality agreements that each audience member is required to sign. An advance team is sent ahead to take care of the details that cannot be handled from afar, like coordinating physical logistics at the theater, making sure security is in place with metal and wireless detection, and setting up night vision/infrared cameras to gauge audience reaction. Every line item is tracked and a budget maintained. There are always small crises along the way, but as with weddings, when the big day arrives, the event itself must be flawless.

Most of our recruiting is done via online methods, principally through our internal database of several million moviegoers as well as other social media metrics. We may also deploy a team of field recruiters, who directly interact with patrons, or "intercepts," in front of movie theaters and in malls within close proximity to where the event will be held. Meanwhile research and operations personnel work from the Los Angeles office to manage all other aspects of the project. The recruiters are armed with a concise, well-worded description of the film that is designed to entice targeted prospects to the screening. This description is known in the industry as the "recruit paragraph." The recruiters carry stacks of invitations that they hand out with the specific theater, date, time, and RSVP instructions. People are then directed to our website to confirm their attendance and answer a battery of questions principally designed to prevent security breaches. Meanwhile, the questionnaire that will be distributed to attendees after they see the film is developed and sent to the studio for approval.

The planning efforts and attention to detail finally pay off on the night of the screening. The theater fills. The filmmakers and studio executives arrive and take their seats to observe, often in nail-biting suspense, how the audience will react. As they know only too well, the voices of moviegoers ring loud and clear at the box office.

More than a dozen specially trained staffers are lined up to work on the night of the preview, and time is reserved with the data processing unit. Coders and data processors work the graveyard shift out of our Los Angeles headquarters. Their day begins as we go to sleep, and they work throughout the night to tabulate the answers from the questionnaires so moviegoers' responses can be analyzed beginning at dawn the following day. A full report summarizing all key findings gleaned from the research is issued within twenty-four hours of the test preview. In Hollywood, there is no time to waste; answers to multimillion-dollar questions hinge on the results of these tests. Now as we enter the third decade of the twenty-first century, we are migrating away from paper and pen to digital surveys that allow for instantaneous tabulation of the data. But much of what we do still relies on human diligence and attention to detail.

Even the most perfectly planned screenings can be derailed with unforeseen problems that are beyond anyone's control. I once saw a rat scurry across the floor in front of my focus group, but I don't believe any of the participants noticed despite the fact that I was stomping my feet in a spasmodic fashion to keep it from coming back. I wasn't so lucky another time, when an entire family of mice invaded the theater just after we screened *The Hills Have Eyes*. It was disgusting, and the entire group of twenty participants was revolted by the sight. Somehow I was able to recover their attention and finish the line of questioning. Needless to say, I found the theater manager afterward and told him we would never use his venue again for any research (the theaters are compensated quite nicely for these events) if he didn't address his rodent problem pronto.

One of the worst experiences of my career occurred not that long ago when I conducted a screening of *Mission: Impossible—Rogue Nation*. The franchise is a jewel in the crown of Paramount Pictures and a source of pride for its very involved star and producer, Tom Cruise. Given the high profile of the *Mission: Impossible* films, they're typically tested out of town, far from Hollywood. This particular test, held in a northern New Jersey multiplex, was planned as a "blind recruit," which means prospective attendees were told only that the film they would see is an "upcoming action thriller from a major studio," rather than any specific description, title, or stars mentioned. The house held nearly four hundred seats, and we had three times as many confirmations, which is our typical goal because of no-shows, especially when people don't know what they're going to see.

All of the top brass at Paramount flew from Los Angeles on the corporate jet to attend the preview, and Tom Cruise traveled from London so he could see this current version with a test audience. I took a flight on the day of the screening, and when I'd landed in New Jersey several hours earlier, I'd had enough time to stop for a bite to eat before heading over to the theater. I had been in contact with our screening supervisor, the person who was managing the logistics at the theater, but it was only after I had finished my meal that we all realized something was terribly wrong. Typically, for a four-hundred-person house, we have at least 100 or 150 people lined up outside the theater about one hour before the start. A half hour later, we are virtually full. On this evening, when more than four hundred people should have been in line to see the movie, there were fewer than forty. And by the time I arrived at the venue, there were still only forty.

During panicked phone calls to piece together the problem, we soon uncovered that someone in my Los Angeles office inadvertently sent a mass email cancellation notice to the entire list of confirmed moviegoers. The only people to show up to the theater were those few who had not checked their emails. To my absolute horror, we had a virtually empty house.

When I arrived at the venue, it took every ounce of courage in my body to inform the Paramount executives and Tom Cruise of the mistake. At that point, before we had learned what the problem was, I took full ownership of it. And they couldn't have been more understanding. Perhaps I had a few years of credibility to lean upon, or maybe they could tell from my ashen face and shaking voice that I was teetering on the brink. But for whatever the reasons, their kindness came rushing at me when I needed it most. After I delivered the news, I took a deep breath, asked them to bear with us while we figured out what to do next, and flew into action.

As luck would have it, the theater was connected to a very large shopping mall, so I instructed every member of my staff to quickly canvas the area and asked that each one convince twenty people to come watch a free movie. Within the hour, we had gathered about two hundred people, enough to give us a beat on how the movie would play. And play it did. At the end of the night, the scores reflected a hugely positive response, despite the willy-nilly recruit of shoppers who just happened to be in a Paramus, New Jersey, mall on a Thursday night in May. Paramount and Tom Cruise were pleased.

I'm not sure when my heart stopped pounding or how we all held it together that night, but I'm very grateful to the motivated screening staff who pulled out all the stops and averted a total disaster. And I know I will never forget the graciousness of Tom Cruise, director Chris McQuarrie, producer David Ellison, and Paramount executives Marc Evans and Karen Hermelin.

Many of the experienced studio executives interviewed for this book had crazy screening mishaps to share (although maybe none quite so bad as an out-of-town screening with no audience). Rob Friedman, who oversaw Summit Entertainment during its enormously successful *Twilight* period, and then became co-chair of Lionsgate Motion Picture Group after it acquired Summit, recalled a catastrophic screening of a romantic drama in the early 1980s. Friedman was working for Warner Bros. at the time, and the screening was being held in New York. This was a long time ago, when the picture and sound were still on two separate tracks.

"We were in the middle of this movie," recalled Friedman, "and it's a very serious family scene and the audience was going with it. And all of a sudden, the dialogue comes out in Spanish."

The New York moviegoers didn't understand what was going on, but they didn't seem too bothered by it at first. The movie continued and everything went back to normal in English. But a few minutes later, the dialogue was again in Spanish. At that point, the young director stood up from where he was seated, visibly upset because a crucial dramatic scene in the film was being ruined. Friedman, who was standing in the back of the auditorium, saw the director wobble up the aisle, looking ill. "I think he stumbled," said Friedman. "Literally. I thought he was actually going to faint. And then he ran out of the theater."

The movie was shut down and all of the technical people were running around trying to figure out what was going on. As it turned out, the sound system was picking up a two-way transmission from a Spanish-speaking cab driver who was in the neighborhood. It took a half hour to troubleshoot the problem, and amazingly, the audience sat in their seats and waited for the film to restart. The movie actually tested pretty well, although it probably took the director a much longer time to recover from the ordeal.

On what promised to be a broiling hot August day in 1997, I received a message from my office, the National Research Group, where I was working as a focus group moderator. A project from 20th Century Fox had just come in, and I was being asked to attend a meeting later that afternoon with Tom Sherak, then chairman of Fox's domestic film group, who wanted to meet face-to-face to outline his request for the test preview.

Within a couple of hours, I was passing through the gate onto the

Fox lot and hoping that I wouldn't have to walk too far from where I was directed to park given the blazing afternoon sun and soaring temperatures. I left the comfort of my air-conditioned car, hoofed over to Building 88, where the executives are housed, and met up with a couple of my NRG colleagues who were also there to be briefed. Sherak greeted us as his assistant ushered us into the inner sanctum of his office, then got right down to business, relaying the specifics that we would need to arrange the recruited screening.

The movie that Sherak wanted to test, *Great Expectations*, was based on the classic Charles Dickens novel but set in modern day and starred two rising young actors named Ethan Hawke and Gwyneth Paltrow. Robert De Niro and Anne Bancroft also had roles in the film, and the supporting cast included Chris Cooper, Hank Azaria, and Josh Mostel. Fox had selected a Mexican-born director, Alfonso Cuarón, for the project, and although few knew of him at the time, he would make his mark on Hollywood with this project and other well-regarded films that followed, including *Y Tu Mamá También*, *Harry Potter and the Prisoner of Azkaban*, *Children of Men*, and his 2018 film, *Roma*, for which he won Oscars for Directing and Cinematography. (Along with Guillermo del Toro and Alejandro Gonzalez Iñárritu, Cuarón is sometimes referred to as one of the "Three Amigos," a trio of highly talented contemporary Mexican directors.)

It's rather unusual for someone in Sherak's position to initiate the request for a screening, let alone discuss details that are typically handled by a more junior executive. What I remember about that meeting is that Sherak was insistent from the outset that the preview be held in Minneapolis. Usually after a discussion of the goals for the screening, we (the researchers) offer a list of four or five suggestions for the theater location where the test might be held. Our input is based upon the desired audience demographics and where we have the best opportunity to find them. We can replicate nearly any socioeconomic or demographic group in the US within a one-hundred-mile radius of Los Angeles, so unless there is a specific reason for holding a screening in a different market— the filmmakers live somewhere else, the marketing department wants to get a firsthand account of how the movie will play in a certain part of the country, or there is the need to be very secretive (like with *Mission: Impossible*)—a majority of screening research is conducted in Southern California for purposes of cost and expediency.

The logistics of handling an out-of-town screening are complex. In addition to an advance team of recruiters who are sent ahead to secure attendees, a number of other research company personnel must travel. A supervisor, focus group moderator, and analyst accompany about a half dozen other staff (augmented by additional local temporary hires) who are needed on the night of the preview to coordinate entry into the theater, seating, the distribution and collection of surveys, and the selection of the focus group participants. Plane tickets, rental cars, and hotel rooms must be arranged, along with all the other previously mentioned materials that are necessary for conducting any screening.

On the studio side, executives must travel as well, and while the corporate jet can usually get them back to Los Angeles on the same night (and in luxurious style), the trip consumes the precious time of top-level decision makers. So the choice to hold a test screening at a distant location is never taken lightly.

When I boarded the plane (a commercial flight) on the morning of the *Great Expectations* preview, I was actually looking forward to three and a half hours of downtime. I brought along a stack of reading material and was hoping for a restful flight because, even with the time change, it was going to be a long day.

As I settled in, I couldn't help but feel that there was something a little strange about this entire project. Why was Fox screening this movie in the Midwest? I could not reconcile the expense and time that an out-of-town preview requires, especially for this film that promised to be artistic and well acted but certainly wouldn't be a guaranteed blockbuster. Something was odd about Sherak's specificity for that particular city, and while on the flight, I chatted with another person from NRG and we speculated about what might be going on. It wasn't until we arrived at the theater in Minneapolis that I knew for sure.

I walked into the auditorium and saw the director, and it was not Alfonso Cuarón. I was not in Minneapolis to test *Great Expectations*.

There was the famed James Cameron, orchestrating the placement of additional lights in the theater. Suddenly, it all made perfect sense. I knew it was going to be an extraordinary night.

"I wanted to re-create history," explained Tom Sherak a dozen years after the screening in Minneapolis. "I had read something about David O. Selznick first previewing *Gone with the Wind* under great secrecy to an audience that had come to see a different picture. It was the most talked about movie in history at that point and the audience was stunned. When they realized what they were about to see, the applause was deafening. That's what I wanted to do with *Titanic*."

The analogies to *Gone with the Wind* were completely justified. There was huge anticipation for *Titanic* both among the moviegoing public and within the Hollywood community itself. Much had been written and reported in the media about the elaborate sets, including several specially constructed scale models of the ship, Cameron's underwater expeditions to the actual wreckage off the coast of Nova Scotia, and the spectacular special effects created by Digital Domain and Industrial Light & Magic.

Costs had escalated well above the $200 million range, and Fox had made the calculated decision to bring on Paramount Pictures as a partner to offset its own risk in the picture. Although moviegoers were generally excited by all of the prerelease publicity, there were plenty of skeptics betting against the film. Many predicted an offscreen disaster to rival the sinking ship and speculated that heads would roll, deservedly. A perfectionist director, a runaway budget, and an ending that everyone already knows—how could it possibly succeed?

"I was never worried," said Sherak emphatically. "I knew if anybody was going to make a great movie about one of the most famous events in modern history, Jim Cameron was that person. He's an underwater guy. He understands the environment. He was going to get you on the *Titanic*." Years before Cameron pitched the idea of making a film about the 1912 ocean liner disaster to 20th Century Fox, Sherak and the director had developed a friendship. In 1989, Sherak had shepherded into the marketplace another deep-sea film of Cameron's, *The Abyss*. At that time,

Sherak held the top distribution job at Fox, and when the release date for *The Abyss* was moved into August, it fell smack into the middle of a long-planned family vacation to Hawaii. For years afterward, Sherak's wife and kids reminded him how he had canceled that trip.

Eight years later, almost to the day, Cameron announced that he was finished with *Titanic*. The executives at 20th Century Fox knew that it had to be screened, but given the amount of attention it had received and conjecture around the costly production, Sherak decided that the screening must be cloaked in secrecy. Reporters disguised as ordinary movie-goers sometimes attempt to gain access to test previews, especially in the cases of highly anticipated films, and as the chairman of the domestic film group, Sherak felt a strong responsibility to protect the movie. He didn't want the film to be compromised by reports of early test audience reactions. He decided to hold the screening far away from the West Coast and to keep his plans under wraps for as long as he possibly could.

"Don't forget, it was the middle of the summer," Sherak recalled. "It was very hot, and here you have a movie that takes place out in the North Atlantic. The ship hits an iceberg. You want people to feel like they're there. So my thinking process was to find a location that was far from Los Angeles, but also where it wouldn't be 110 degrees in August. And I thought—Minneapolis! It's a perfect Middle American town and probably cooler than anywhere else in the country in August. And that's where we went."

Sherak's scheme included telling us and his own Fox colleagues that the test preview was for *Great Expectations*, a film that had been finished at about the same time as *Titanic*. The anticipated audiences for *Titanic* and *Great Expectations* were similar enough that the researchers would not question recruit specifications (although as it turned out, *Titanic* drew huge audiences that cut across just about every demographic). So the advance team of recruiters who traveled to Minneapolis truly believed that the preview would be for *Great Expectations*, as did the moviegoers who showed up on the night of the screening.

Meanwhile, the Fox and Paramount executives knew that a first cut of *Titanic* was going to be screened, but they were told only the time and place of the flight, not the city or theater where the preview was being held. Sherak refused to disclose the location until after they had boarded the Fox corporate jet. "Everybody was furious that they didn't know where they were going. But I knew if I didn't tell anyone, there couldn't be any leaks," commented Sherak. "We went to Minneapolis," he continued with a chuckle, "and I'll never forget—when we got off the plane it was 102 degrees. All my plans to find a cool place for the screening went up in smoke! So, we turned up the AC in the auditorium and made it as cold as possible."

While the recruited moviegoers lined up outside the theater, Jim Cameron, precise in every detail, was busy inside setting up special lights so attendees would have plenty of good lighting when it came time to fill out their surveys. (This is highly unusual. Typically, the lights in the house come up after the movie is over and whatever lighting exists suffices.) When everything was set up and ready, Cameron joined the studio executives and waited in a secluded area while moviegoers were ushered into the theater and seated. The lights went down. The director and the executives from both studios entered the theater under cover of darkness and took their seats.

No announcement was made. The logo for Cameron's production company, Lightstorm, appeared on the screen, then the shadowy underwater image of the wreckage. At first, moviegoers thought they might be seeing a trailer for *Titanic*. They didn't comprehend that this was the opening scene of the much-awaited film. A few more seconds passed, and then with the realization of what they were in for, the audience burst into cheers.

"The movie lasted over three hours and hardly anyone moved," said Sherak. "I have great peripheral vision, and I think only one person got up to use the bathroom, and he was running out and running back. It was amazing."

When the film ended, moviegoers were sobbing. It was a totally immersive experience. They were on that sinking ship and in those freezing waters. It was a movie unlike anything they had seen before, and they loved it. Cameron would trim a few minutes from the chase scene where Billy Zane's character pursues Leonardo DiCaprio's, the only change based on the screening results, and a very minor one at that.

"We knew right away that we had a huge movie. We didn't know it would do $600 million. We never knew that. But we knew Jim had made a masterpiece," Sherak said. "You do the craziest things. Sometimes it's right and sometimes it's just crazy. Some of the craziest things end up being the most fun. Look, we're talking about it years later."

There are many things that stick in my mind about the *Titanic* screening, including James Cameron supervising the installation of those spotlights. In that moment, he was acting as a scientist might—ensuring the ideal conditions to conduct his experiment and derive unspoiled data.

Cameron wanted nothing to skew or change what the audience wrote on the questionnaires, and with good reason. The two inches of real estate on top of the survey card are the most fraught and precious in Hollywood. That's where the numbers are, the data that tell you whether you have a potential for a blockbuster at your fingertips or a flop.

This chapter is about the smallest, yet most critical numbers in all of Hollywood: "the numbers" in what the industry often calls "the top two boxes." It's also about how producers and studio heads understand and internalize those numbers; how they rewrite and reshoot, hire and fire, lose their shirts and their minds, all because of those few small digits. And all of it begins with a screening questionnaire.

It's deceptively simple, just a basic survey that asks a viewer to rate the film like they might rate a shampoo brand or a politician—"excellent, very good, good, fair, or poor."

Today, we are migrating away from paper surveys and using handheld devices to capture test audience feedback. The answers are immediately uploaded to a secure data collection site and the results are virtually instantaneous, circumventing hours of manual data entry that is needed to process the paper surveys. By the time the theater clears out, we have a dashboard of graphics on a tablet, summarizing the entire audience's response right there on the spot. We continue to make improvements to the line of questioning, but the overall ratings and recommendations—whether collected on paper or digitally—remain the most telling.

DATE – **MOVIE** – *Please take a moment to let us know how you feel about the movie you just saw.*

1. **What was your reaction to the movie overall?** (MARK ONE)	2. **Would you recommend this movie to your friends?** (MARK ONE)	3. **Considering what you knew about the movie before you came tonight, how did it compare to your expectations?** (MARK ONE)
Excellent..................................( )1 Very good................................( )2 Good..( )3 Fair..( )4 Poor...( )5	Yes, Definitely...........................( )1 Yes, Probably.............................( )2 No, Probably not.........................( )3 No, Definitely not........................( )4	Better than I expected....................................( )1 About what I expected....................................( )2 Not as good as I expected..............................( )3

4. How do you identify? (MARK ONE)

Male ....( )1
Female ....( )2
Another gender identity ....( )3

5. Please indicate your age and the month and year you were born: (WRITE-IN BELOW)

Age: _____ _____   Date of Birth: Month: _____   Year: _____ _____ _____ _____

6a. Which of the following statements do you agree with the most? (MARK ONE)

This is a movie that **needs** to be seen in a movie theater.................( )1
This is a movie that **does not need** to be seen in a movie theater ..( )2
This is a movie that does **not** need to be seen at all ....( )3

6b. If you said that this is a movie that needs to be seen in a movie theater, would you say it needs to be seen... (MARK ONE)

In a movie theater as **soon as it opens**...( )1
In a movie theater, but **NOT** necessarily on opening weekend ...( )2

6c. If you said this is a movie that does not need to be seen in a movie theater, would you most likely... (MARK ONE)

Pay to watch as soon as it's first available at home ....( )1
Watch when it's on a service I subscribe to........................( )2
Wait until whenever I happen to see it on TV ....( )3

7. In a sentence, how would you describe this movie to others? (PLEASE BE SPECIFIC)

_____
_____

8. If you did not rate the movie "EXCELLENT" or would not "DEFINITELY" recommend it, please tell us why not.

_____

9a. Please list which scenes or parts, if any, of the movie you liked the MOST. (PLEASE BE SPECIFIC)

1. _____   3. _____
2. _____   4. _____

9b. Please list which scenes or parts, if any, of the movie you liked the LEAST. (PLEASE BE SPECIFIC)

1. _____   3. _____
2. _____   4. _____

10. How would you rate each of the following? (MARK ONE FOR EACH)

	Excellent	Very Good	Good	Fair	Poor
Character 1 (played by Actor 1)	( )1	( )2	( )3	( )4	( )5
Character 2 (played by Actor 2)	( )1	( )2	( )3	( )4	( )5
Character 3 (played by Actor 3)	( )1	( )2	( )3	( )4	( )5
Character 4 (played by Actor 4)	( )1	( )2	( )3	( )4	( )5
Character 5 (played by Actor 5)	( )1	( )2	( )3	( )4	( )5
Character 6 (played by Actor 6)	( )1	( )2	( )3	( )4	( )5
The relationship between Character 1 and Character 2	( )1	( )2	( )3	( )4	( )5
The story	( )1	( )2	( )3	( )4	( )5
The drama	( )1	( )2	( )3	( )4	( )5
The suspense	( )1	( )2	( )3	( )4	( )5
The settings	( )1	( )2	( )3	( )4	( )5
The beginning	( )1	( )2	( )3	( )4	( )5
The ending	( )1	( )2	( )3	( )4	( )5
The music/soundtrack	( )1	( )2	( )3	( )4	( )5
The twists and turns	( )1	( )2	( )3	( )4	( )5

11. What are your feelings about the way that the movie BEGAN? (PLEASE BE SPECIFIC)

_____
_____

Please turn the card over and answer the questions on the back.

12. What are your feelings about the way that the movie **ENDED?** (PLEASE BE SPECIFIC)

_____
_____

13a. What are your thoughts about the pace of the movie in the following areas? (MARK ONE FOR EACH)

	Moved Just Right	Moved Too Fast	Moved Too Slow	Generally just right, but dragged in parts
Overall	( )1	( )2	( )3	( )4
Beginning	( )1	( )2	( )3	( )4
Middle	( )1	( )2	( )3	( )4
Ending	( )1	( )2	( )3	( )4

13b. If you felt the movie moved **too slowly** or dragged in parts, which specific scene(s) were too slow or dragged? (PLEASE BE SPECIFIC)

_____
_____

14. Which of the following words or phrases best describe this movie? (MARK ALL THAT APPLY)

Entertaining ....( )	Too melodramatic ......( )	Nothing new/been done before ....( )	Good/interesting story...........................( )
Different/original ....( )	Not scary enough......( )	Surprising/unexpected.........................( )	Didn't care about the characters............( )
Confusing ....( )	Intense ....( )	Too corny/cheesy at times....................( )	Held my interest from start to finish ......( )
Too predictable...........( )	Boring/dull ....( )	Good/interesting characters.................( )	Weak storyline.....................................( )
Satisfying ending ....( )	Dramatic ....( )	Good scares..( )	Needs a better ending...........................( )

15a. Was there anything in the movie that did not make sense or was confusing? (MARK ONE)   Yes......( )1   No......( )2

15b. If YES, which parts specifically? (PLEASE BE SPECIFIC)_____

_____

16. What were the PRIMARY reason(s) that you attended this screening tonight? (MARK ALL THAT APPLY)

Actor 1 ....( )	The cast overall ....( )	From the director of _Movie Title_...( )
Actor 2 ....( )	The story/concept ....( )	Came with someone who wanted to see it ....( )
Actor 3 ....( )	The genre/type of movie................( )	

17. Before today, what was your opinion of the following? (MARK ONE FOR EACH) (79-88)

	Very Much A Fan	Somewhat A Fan	Not A Fan/ Never Heard Of		Very Much A Fan	Somewhat A Fan	Not A Fan/ Never Heard
Actor 1 ....( )1		( )2	( )3	Director ....( )1		( )2	( )3
Actor 2 ....( )1		( )2	( )3	Genre 1 ....( )1		( )2	( )3
Actor 3 ....( )1		( )2	( )3	Genre 2 ....( )1		( )2	( )3

18. Does this movie remind you of any other films you have seen? If so, please list: _____

19. Please mark which of these you have seen and enjoyed in a theater. (MARK ALL THAT APPLY)

Recent Movie 1 ....( )	_Recent Movie 4_............( )	_Recent Movie 7_...........( )	_Recent Movie 10_ ....( )
Recent Movie 2 ....( )	_Recent Movie 5_............( )	_Recent Movie 8_...........( )	_Recent Movie 11_ ....( )
Recent Movie 3 ....( )	_Recent Movie 6_............( )	_Recent Movie 9_...........( )	_Recent Movie 12_ ....( )

20. Who would you say this movie is mostly for? (MARK ONE FOR GENDER AND ALL THAT APPLY FOR AGE)

Males........................( )1	Females ....( )2	All genders equally ....( )3	
Younger teens...13 to 14.................( )1	Audiences in their 20s ....( )4	Audiences in their 50s ....( )7	
Older teens.......15 to 17.................( )2	Audiences in their 30s ....( )5	Audiences in their 60s & older ....( )8	
Young adults.....18 to 19.................( )3	Audiences in their 40s ....( )6	All ages equally ....( )9	

21. Please indicate with which racial or ethnic categories you most identify. (MARK ONE)

African-American/Black ....( )1	Caucasian/White ....( )4
Asian or Pacific Islander........( )2	American Indian or Alaska Native ( )5
Hispanic/Latino ....( )3	Other: _____( )6

22. What is the last grade of school you completed? (MARK ONE)

Some high school or less .....( )1
Completed high school ....( )2
Some college......................( )3
Completed college or more .( )4

23. Now, having seen the movie and having had more time to think about it, which of the following best describes your **overall impression** of it? (PLEASE CIRCLE ONE BELOW)   👍 👎

24. How many times have you been to the movies at a theater during the past 3 months?   # of _____ TIMES

**THANK YOU. Please give the completed questionnaire to the people collecting them at the exits.**

Over the years, researchers and film industry veterans have learned that a key measure of playability for any commercial film is defined by the "excellent" and the "very good" scores that the film earns from test screening audiences. The more familiar way of talking about scores is to combine the top two boxes, which is the percentage of moviegoers who rated the film excellent plus the percentage of those who assessed it as very good. These are the only scores that really matter for big studio pictures because any evaluation below very good is considered to be mediocre at best. When filmmakers and studio executives talk about scores, they're almost certainly referring to the tally of excellent plus very good scores.

Adding the top two box scores has become standard industry practice, although it does not reflect my own personal philosophy. As my respected colleague the late Teri Korban Seide always said, "We live in a top-box world." I couldn't agree more. Teri was the quintessential media guru in the movie business during the 1980s and 1990s. She held top media posts at several big studios, as well as working at advertising agencies on movie accounts and at two different entertainment research companies toward the end of her too-short lifetime. Teri understood moviegoer behavior, the plethora of choices they have, and the demands on their time and pocketbooks. Her comment about a top-box world encapsulated the importance of achieving excellent scores, and I'll explain why.

Moviegoers who rate a film excellent are also those who are the strongest advocates for it. They're highly inclined to recommend the film to friends and relatives, creating the positive word of mouth that encourages people to see it in its second, third, and fourth weeks of release. Willingness to recommend a film is a key question asked on the surveys, and only the "definitely" answers are reported on the "topline," which is a recap of the scores distributed to the filmmakers and studio executives on the night of the test screening. Specifically, it represents the quickly tabulated answers from the first two questions on the survey, broken out by age and gender "quadrants": younger males, older males, younger females, older females. The age break is determined prior to each preview, based on discussions with the studio.

Virtually everyone who rates a film excellent will also encourage friends to see it. Yet according to decades of research that we in the industry have gathered, only about half of those who rate it very good, just one level below excellent, will also definitely recommend it to others. So the distinction between those two levels of assessment is very telling. As the following chart demonstrates, Movie A and Movie B earned the same top two box scores from 80 percent of their respective audiences, but the definite recommendations are strikingly different because the ratio of excellent to very good ratings for Movie B is much greater than for Movie A. Consequently, the definite recommendations for Movie B are solidly higher than for Movie A, suggesting that it will have much stronger positive word of mouth.

	MOVIE A	MOVIE B
"EXCELLENT" RATINGS	20%	60%
"VERY GOOD" RATINGS	60%	20%
COMBINED "TOP 2 BOXES"	80%	80%
"DEFINITE" RECOMMENDATIONS	50%	70%

All of those who rated Movie A excellent (20 percent) plus half of those who rated it very good (30 percent) will definitely recommend it to friends (50 percent). Comparatively, all of the larger percentage of Movie B's test audience who rated it excellent (60 percent) plus half of those who rated it very good (10 percent) will definitely recommend it to friends (70 percent). Same top two box scores, but very different word-of-mouth outcomes. This twenty-point difference in definitely recommend scores could translate into millions of dollars of box office.

I refer to the definite recommendations as the "money number" because it's a very strong indicator of the film's potential "legs," how intense the momentum will be once the film has opened. A great marketing effort can open a picture, but it's the positive word of mouth that will ultimately sustain it.

For the past several years, I've been on a personal crusade to disabuse people in the industry of their focusing too heavily on the top two box scores, based on the explicit impact of excellent ratings upon word-of-mouth momentum for any given picture. Even so, most industry insiders continue to quote top two box numbers. Old habits are hard to break.

A quick word about "blind recruits," which again refer to test screenings where prospective moviegoers are invited to preview a film but the title, the cast, and even the briefest description of the film is withheld. Typically, a blind recruit is done for security purposes, to minimize the risk of word getting out ahead of time, especially on high-profile movies that might attract reviewers (professional or amateur) who are anxious to get a first look. Blind recruits are also used to prevent an audience full of franchise fans or genre enthusiasts from showing up and giving a false positive if the studio wants a read on how the film might play to a broader cross section of moviegoers.

I recently conducted a test on a second installment to a highly successful superhero movie. The studio was very concerned that only fanboys would show up if the title was used. So we implemented a blind recruit where we tried to fill the audience with moviegoers who were not necessarily fanboys but also weren't rejecters of superhero movies. It was a tricky process, to say the least.

Blind recruits are always challenging because we are asking people to give up more than three hours of their precious leisure time without knowing what they will see. Those who do show up are taking a gamble that it will be a big tentpole or a sequel to some popular film. But many people who are offered tickets to a blindly recruited screening turn them down. By the way, I generally dislike blind recruits, not because they're difficult to accomplish but because there's no self-selection factored in. In a real-world environment, people decide if they want to see a movie or not based on whatever they happen to know about it, including the title and cast. This is an important piece of information, especially later on when the studio is developing its marketing campaign for the film.

To help with the recruiting process when they don't want to disclose the title, a studio will occasionally use a bait-and-switch strategy. They'll have us recruit an audience using one title and its stars, then surprise the audience with an entirely different picture once they're seated in the theater, like the aforementioned *Titanic* screening in Minneapolis. This can backfire, of course.

Jeff Hall, who held studio-side research positions at Warner Bros. and Paramount, recounted an experience from his early days working at NRG, the research company where we once worked together. It was 1995 and Disney came to NRG with a request to set up a screening of *Operation Dumbo Drop*.

"But it was really the first screening of *Toy Story*," recalled Hall.

By then, Disney had already launched the trailer for *Operation Dumbo Drop*, so there was awareness of that movie in the marketplace, and enthusiasm to see it. On the day of the screening, with a full audience seated in the theater, the announcement was made that everyone would actually be seeing *Toy Story*.

"There were groans and boos, and people were leaving because they had never heard of *Toy Story* and wanted to see *Operation Dumbo Drop*," Hall remembered. "You look back now and, oh my God, those people had a glimpse of history! And they were just so annoyed that they weren't seeing Ray Liotta and an elephant."

If there's a filmmaker who knows the importance of test screening scores, it's Dean Devlin. Devlin is a writer-producer who, along with his former writer-director partner, Roland Emmerich, is responsible for some of the biggest event films of all time. In other words, he's really good at blowing things up.

He also has a mind for details and the uncanny knack for remembering the scores from nearly all of his test screenings. He has experienced the best—and the worst—of what can happen when a film is screened for an audience.

When his 1996 blockbuster, *Independence Day*, was secretly previewed in Las Vegas, the studio arranged for a blind recruit because they wanted to prevent any press from gaining access to an early showing.

After the audience was seated and the first frames of the film began to play, the title rolled onto the screen and the audience went crazy. There had been huge anticipation for *Independence Day*, and this was a film that would not disappoint. Devlin and Emmerich stood in the back, and as they high-fived each other, the film broke! (As mentioned earlier, rough cuts of films prior to 2003⁄2004 were "unmarried prints," meaning the film and the sound were on two separate tracks requiring special double system equipment to project the movie. It was not entirely unusual to encounter technical glitches, such as the film breaking, during recruited screenings since they were unfinished, often coming to the theater straight from the editing room.) It took five or six minutes to repair the film and restart the movie, and during that time, the applause never stopped. "By the time we were back up and running, we knew we had lightning in a bottle," Devlin recalled.

On the heels of *Independence Day*, Devlin and Emmerich collaborated on another big sci-fi extravaganza, *Godzilla*. This time, success eluded them. The studio, Sony Pictures Entertainment, had slotted the release for the week before Memorial Day 1998. The marketing department, led by my dear friend Bob Levin, who is now president and COO of my company Screen Engine/ASI, had planned an elaborate advertising campaign to kick off what they anticipated to be their big summer hit. But complicated special effects were holding up the picture and postproduction was pacing behind. In an effort to deliver the film in time for the release date, Devlin made the calculated decision to forgo the testing process.

The studio had been very supportive of *Godzilla*, and even suggested moving the opening to July in order to give the filmmakers more time to finesse it. But knowing that it would cost Sony a substantial amount of money to move the advertising, Devlin was loath to accept the offer of additional time. "I wanted to deliver what I said I could deliver," he explained. "It was the best of intentions, but the worst of ideas."

The first time Devlin watched *Godzilla* with an audience was at an exhibitor screening. Sony had invited a group of influential theater owners to preview it at a private screening before its scheduled release date, and Devlin remembers their ice-cold reaction. "It might as well have been a test preview, because I knew exactly what the cards would have said. I knew exactly what the focus group would have said. I knew exactly what was wrong with the film and I knew how to fix it. But it was too late. So that's when I made a promise to myself that I would never, ever release a film again without testing it."

Devlin and Emmerich went on to make *The Patriot* in 2000, then *Eight Legged Freaks* two years later. In 2004, Devlin became involved with a film called *Cellular*. It's the story of a kidnapped woman (played by Kim Basinger) and a boy on the street who receives her frantic call for help on his cell phone when she surreptitiously repairs a broken phone and taps into a random line. The boy doesn't know her, and she needs to convince him that she is telling the truth and implores him to help her. Nearly the entire film is a phone conversation between these two strangers. Devlin produced the movie but didn't write the script, and for the first time in years, he took on a project without his directing and writing partner, Roland Emmerich.

"Now, we never got a good score," began Devlin. "I had a strong feeling that we were screwing up the movie at the end of the shoot. We shot the boy first. And then the last two weeks, we were scheduled to shoot Kim Basinger on her end of the phone call. The night before we went to shoot her part, the director told me that he had rewritten it."

Devlin was dumbfounded. He tried to reason with the director, pointing out that the boy's side of the phone conversation was already shot and the original script matched Basinger's lines to the boy's dialogue. The director assured him that the new script also matched, arguing that the original script was too unrealistic. The director felt that Basinger's character was too proactive in the original version, and that she should be more upset, crying, even hysterical at times. Circumventing Devlin, he had already convinced Basinger and the studio that the revised script would work better.

"I walked off the set," recalled Devlin, who went to the studio executive overseeing the film and said, "Look, I'm not angry with the director. I'm disappointed with the studio because you've cut my balls off and you haven't allowed me to protect you from what I think is going to be a disastrous situation."

When the executive disagreed, Devlin replied with the closest thing in the movie business to Babe Ruth calling his home run—he called his own film's test score.

"Here's what's going to happen [then]," he told the executive. "You're going to test this [movie] four months from now, and you're going to get a fifty-seven." Devlin went further with his prediction: "The audience is going to say that they don't believe the setup, that they don't like the ending, and that they hate Kim Basinger. And you're going to have a choice to either reshoot the movie or go straight to DVD, and I'm frightened that you're not at that point going to want to invest in this to fix it." The studio held firm, and Devlin ended the conversation feeling defeated.

Four months later, the film was finished, and the studio arranged for a test screening. "And I was wrong," continued Devlin with a hearty laugh.

It did not score a fifty-seven.

It scored a fifty-six.

To cap it off, the audience's comments were so similar to what Devlin had told the studio exec that the director had thought he'd rigged the results. They didn't like the opening. They hated the ending. They hated Kim Basinger.

In a postmortem meeting at the studio offices on the following day, Devlin was prepared. He presented a list of changes in writing that he would make to the picture. The studio president looked briefly at the list, then turned to the room and said, "Let's try it Dean's way. Go and reshoot."

To the director's credit, once he saw that the studio endorsed the changes that Devlin proposed, he embraced them and reshot the sequences. The film was recut and tested again in Pasadena. This time, the top two box scores were seventy-one, up fifteen points from the first screening, and willingness to definitely recommend the film jumped ten points. Moreover, moviegoers were much more positive about Kim Basinger's character; they liked that she was less despairing and more in control of the situation.

"So now we at least have a film that I know is not embarrassing. We have a picture that can be released. I feel very good about what's happened, and I go off to do my next picture," said Devlin.

On location in Mexico, Devlin received a phone call from the studio executive who told him that there was going to be another test screening of the film. But to Devlin's amazement, the executive admitted that the film had been cut yet again, and the latest version was the one slated for the upcoming test. Devlin began to argue but caught himself before the conversation turned ugly. "Well, it doesn't matter what I think," he relented. "It doesn't matter what you think. Test it, and if the test says it's better, go with God. But if it doesn't, we should go back to my cut." The executive assured Devlin that in the long run the studio would release the best cut of the picture, regardless of whose version it was.

"So they test it. It gets a fifty. It's six points lower than the first test. I fly back from Mexico and decide to finish my cut because I figure if I had it at a seventy-one, I've learned some things from those tests, maybe I can get it up into the high seventies, maybe even an eighty. I've had a lot of luck in the past," said Devlin. He was in the editing room when the director and some of the studio people arrived and asked him what he was doing. Devlin, believing that the studio was going to settle on the best-scoring cut of the film, explained that he was finishing his version. Once again, the studio executive delivered news that floored the producer: "We're going with the other cut," he announced. An incredulous Devlin asked why, given that the latest cut had scored twenty-one points lower than his version. The studio people and director responded, "You weren't in the room. It played better."

"At the end of the day, we ended up with a compromised cut that was half my cut, half the cut that scored a fifty. We never tested it. My guess is it would have been in the midsixties," continued Devlin. "If they had gone with my cut, it absolutely would have done better. It wouldn't have opened better, but people would have told their friends to go see it in greater numbers. We opened at $10 million. If you can get past ten, if you have a movie with any kind of legs, you can get to a decent number. We ended up grossing a little more than $30 million domestically on the movie, and I think we could have had a movie that made $55 million to $60 million. There's no way of proving it."

Devlin finished by drawing an analogy between *Cellular* and *The Silence of the Lambs* (1991), a much more successful film. "When the girl is in the pit, she's not crying and screaming. She's saying, 'Fuck you!' And the audience loved her. They were rooting for her because no matter what was going on or what this guy was doing, she kept calling him a sick fuck. She never submitted, which made us root for her. Once she's in the pit whining and crying, she's a victim and we stop caring."

Dean Devlin's experience points to the issues that filmmakers and studios experience when they aren't on the same page. It happens, perhaps more often than not. Which brings me to another observation about the business.

As movie researchers, we're serving many different constituencies who may come into a test screening with different perspectives on what is right and wrong with the movie, and then leave the screening with different interpretations of how it played. That's where I try to insert myself in the process—unifying everyone around a common goal.

Think about all the stakeholders—the head of the studio who greenlit the picture; the production executives who have managed the entire process from the studio side; the studio marketing people who will ultimately be responsible for getting butts in seats to see the picture; the director, producers, editors, and sometimes the actors. I try to be sensitive to each of their individual pressures and align them under a shared agenda. Everyone benefits when we are united about what needs to be done to turn out the best possible movie.

As a researcher, I can start with the indisputable facts, but as an adviser, I try to go the extra mile. I don't just drop off a report. I pick up the phone and call the studio and filmmakers the next day. And the day after that. I'm with them all the way through. I often guide the discussion and keep it on track so everyone is at least willing to try the changes and tweaks that the data suggest.

Once I've tested a film, I become a stakeholder, too.

4.

THE GIRL IN THE
BLACK COCKTAIL DRESS

Mike Tyson, the former heavyweight champion of the world, didn't have much respect for opponents who entered the ring with a plan to win. "Everybody has a plan," Tyson famously said, "until they get punched in the face."

In the years since he's put away his gloves, Iron Mike has made a few film cameos, including some memorable appearances in the *Hangover* movies. But without a doubt, his most important contribution to the film industry is that quote.

Nothing so perfectly sums up the experience of a bad screening night when you're a filmmaker. You have a plan, one that you've spent years executing. You've found your story, tweaked your script, convinced investors, scouted locations. You've filmed every night until 8 p.m., then gone back to your room to watch dailies, only to be back at it again before sunrise. You've dealt with difficult talent. You've managed actors honing their craft. You've begged the studio for more money, more support, more time. You've secluded yourself in a dark room for weeks on end to edit. You've lived off cold pizza and lukewarm coffee.

And when it's all done, and the movie is in the can, you've brought the cut to the screening with hopes that the test audience will rise with the end credits, hailing your masterpiece and your tireless work.

That's the plan, at least. That's the idea. But instead, when the credits roll and the audience gives you their feedback, the topline results you're handed don't greet you lightly. The paper weighs less than an ounce, but it hits you like a Tyson right hook. Years of work rejected. A plan failed. *How do you respond?*

It can be a terrible situation—not just for the filmmakers but for me on occasion. As the bearer of bad news, I've been threatened, cursed, greeted with stone-cold silence, and—in true Hollywood fashion—told, "*We'll never work with you or your company again!*"

There's a reason the saying "Don't shoot the messenger" is a cliché—because blaming the messenger is often the first thing people do.

But after the tantrums end and reality sets in, filmmakers have to dig deep and figure out how to take the numbers and the comments and use them to turn their film into one that the audience more widely embraces. It's enough to make even the strongest of filmmakers want to turn to the bottle, which is the subject of our next film.

The movie ended and as the music faded, the lights in the theater came up. There was no applause, and for several seconds, not even a murmur from those in the audience. The studio executives sat in stunned silence, and as the producer later recalled, it was as if someone had raided the theater and yelled, "Everybody put your hands up against the wall!" An uncomfortable stillness enveloped the place for only a moment, but to the producer, it seemed like an eternity.

The silence was interrupted by eager staffers from the research company who thumped down the aisles to hand out questionnaires. Audience members shuffled the surveys and hunkered down to answer questions that would reveal their opinions about the film. The group of studio honchos and filmmakers exited the theater to pace in the lobby and speculate about how moviegoers would evaluate the picture.

Twenty minutes later, after most of the audience had completed the surveys and filed out of the theater, the executives reentered and took seats in the back while Joe Farrell from the research company probed a small group of selected moviegoers assembled in the front rows for their feedback on the film. The group was a bit uncomfortable at first, shy about answering questions, but Farrell's practiced casual style soon put them at ease. Their comments, increasingly more animated, revealed that the film had started well for them. They liked the characters, especially the rising young male star of the picture, and they were invested in the story. One moviegoer described the first part of the film as a "fun ride." But then, in a melodramatic turn of events, the levity had come to a screeching halt and the movie ended with a thud.

The next morning, the answers from nearly four hundred surveys that had been processed overnight confirmed what the focus group of twenty foretold: moviegoers were enthusiastic about most of the film but just *hated* the ending.

The film was *Cocktail*, a romantic drama set against the singles bar scene in the late 1980s.

Although it never earned critical acclaim and might be perceived as dated and silly today, it became one of the biggest grossing movies of 1988. Its success hinged in large part on what the filmmakers learned the night of that first screening, and what they did next.

Tom Cruise was just coming off *Top Gun*, and there was a lot of excitement at the studio, Disney's Touchstone Pictures, about casting him in the lead, playing a sexy bartender from New York who seeks his fortune in Jamaica and finds much more. Robert Cort, the film's producer, remembered a conversation that he had with Cruise's then agent, Paula Wagner, in which Wagner revealed that both she and Cruise were unsure of the film's commercial appeal. But it was a fairly dramatic role for the rising star who felt it could potentially help get him recognized as a serious actor.

Cort, on the other hand, had confidence about the film's appeal from the earliest script stage. An experienced marketing executive, he had overseen some of the biggest successes of the 1970s and early 1980s while working at Twentieth Century–Fox and Columbia, including *The Deep*, *Close Encounters of the Third Kind*, *The China Syndrome*, and *Nine to Five*. Now on his own, he had produced the number-one movie of 1987, and one of the most popular comedies of all time, *Three Men and a Baby*.

"I'd always seen *Cocktail* as a commercial, kind of cautionary tale movie," recalled Cort. "But I think none of us had a very clear sense of what the movie really was." At its first screening in a large theater on the Disney lot, they got their answer. Most of the movie played very well, bolstered by its hot stars, memorable music, and snappy dialogue. "It's a very participative movie," said Cort, "and I think if you had stopped the projector two-thirds of the way through, people would have described it as a comedy and would have rated it extremely high."

In the third act of the film, a tragic turn of events occurs in which the main character's former boss and someone who had presented conflict for him (played by Bryan Brown) dies by suicide. Cruise's character discovers his body, and in that early version, the movie ends quickly thereafter. "And that's when all of the air went out of the room," recalled Cort of the first showing. "You knew it was over because when people were filling out the cards, there was silence, a sense of morbidity in the room." For Cort and the others closest to the film, the message was clear: they had a problem.

After the screening, Cort and his colleagues, along with Joe Farrell, hunkered down to discuss their next steps. They were mystified. Having never set out to make a party film, they had no idea why it was playing like a comedy in the front, and hence, setting up moviegoers for a crash landing at the back. No one had any sense of how to fix the film.

They read through the surveys and feared the worst, that the movie had a fatal flaw. It was late at night when the executives decided to go home. And as Farrell walked out of the room, he made the offhand comment, "I guess the audience just doesn't want to know that Tom Cruise can't have it all."

Cort froze, as if a lightbulb had turned on. "Even in the moment it was very clear to me that we had written a character and cast an actor who embodied all of the can-do spirit that an audience wanted," remembered Cort. He replied to the group, "Man, it's the movies. He *can* have it all. We have to rewrite the ending."

The next few days were spent strategizing about how to fix the film and interpreting the research in the context of Farrell's observation. The filmmakers realized that it was fine to keep the suicide in the film, but it had to be followed with something uplifting for the main character. They decided to give him a challenge to overcome, something to leave the audience feeling good about at the very end.

"Like most really good heroic actors, Tom works best when he has somebody to fight against. And if there was nobody to fight against once the Bryan Brown character was gone, that was a real downer for the audience," explained Cort.

So a new character was created, an opponent for Cruise's character. By this part of the film, the main character is in love with a girl, played by Elisabeth Shue. The filmmakers decided to introduce a wealthy father into the story as the opponent. He tries to prevent Cruise's character from marrying his daughter by buying him off. But Cruise's character fights for her, and in the end, he gets the girl and learns a lesson from the whole experience. Cort elaborated, "He not only showed his courage, he showed the girl he really was the guy for her. When she leaves with him, she's saying goodbye to her father, who is not at the final wedding scene. Then we created a place for them to go, the whole idea of Cocktails and Dreams, their bar. That wasn't in the original."

Armed with new ideas and a new character, Cort and the filmmakers knew what had to be done. Both studio executives, Jeffrey Katzenberg and Ricardo Mestres, were on board, and Tom Cruise, who was already in Cincinnati shooting *Rain Man*, agreed to fly back to Los Angeles on weekends to complete the reshoots for *Cocktail*. But yet another problem surfaced. As the new antagonist and new scenes were being conceived, the Writers Guild went on strike.

Cort called the screenwriter, Woody Gould, and begged him to finish the rewrites so the movie could be saved. Gould sympathized but refused. "I can't do it," he told Cort. "My father was a labor organizer."

Cort did what any desperate producer might do in the same situation. He sat down and wrote the twenty-five pages himself. To end the film, the group had decided that Tom Cruise's character would be at his bar, and in the final scene, he would get up and recite a poem, closing with a note of levity. Cort had written limericks before, using them in his youth to impress girlfriends. So he wrote the poem, too. The scene was shot, and the film was wrapped.

The new version of the film was screened, and this time, the results were extraordinary. Cort still felt there was something missing, and at the last moment, he turned to Ricardo Mestres and said, "I've got it. Twins!" They went back to make one final change. Elisabeth Shue's character announces she is carrying twins, Cocktails and Dreams opens for business, and the drinks are on the house. Once again, the film was previewed, and this time, the scores were stratospheric.

Cort continued, "So now we're going out with the movie and I'm not hearing any of the advance reviews. We're all high as a kite because we think we've got this big hit. But they [the studio executives] don't tell me about the reviews." Cort inquired about the lack of press and was informed that the media were not responding well to the movie at all. Some considered the very premise immoral, highlighting sex and drinking at a time when AIDS was on the rise.

On the day that the movie opened, the reviews were vicious. NPR called it a "Molotov cocktail," and Vincent Canby of the *New York Times* wrote a scathing review telling readers that if they were unlucky enough to go see it and were tempted to leave midway through, they should stay in their seats for a not-to-be-missed scene at the end. Cort, reading the review, had a flash of optimism, thinking, "Oh my God! He loved my poem!" But in the next sentence, Canby referred to the poem as one of the most excruciating moments in film. Cort was beside himself. His mother-in-law, who typically phoned from New York to congratulate him on the opening day of his movies, had not called. She, too, had seen the reviews.

Cort spent a miserable day at the office, and at about four thirty, he glanced out his window, where he had a view of the Crest Theater in Westwood. A five thirty showing of *Cocktail* was scheduled, and he noticed a girl standing there alone wearing a black cocktail dress. His heart filled with appreciation, and he was tempted to go downstairs and thank her because he figured she might be the only person to buy a ticket for the show. But he held back. By five, there were about forty young women lined up, all in cocktail dresses, and at five thirty, the show was sold out. The movie went on to have a successful opening and grossed more than $171 million worldwide, despite the bad press.

Cort summed it up by saying, "What the preview process did, ultimately, was enable us to find the movie and reconceive it. Everybody's memory of it is, 'Well, that was a lot of fun.'"

Not all big surprises happen on the night of the first test screening, as they did with *Cocktail*. Some are discovered much earlier, when the filmmakers or studio executives watch a first cut of a film. Despite all efforts to make a masterpiece, that first viewing can be surprising and sobering.

A man for whom I have tremendous respect, Andy Fogelson, spent decades in the movie business as head of marketing at Warner Bros. and Polygram. Andy is of the opinion that very few filmmakers think they have made the perfect movie. He relayed something to me that he once heard from a big director.

"Let me tell you how it works," the filmmaker said to Andy. "You go out and shoot your movie. Then you work with your editor to put it together. When the editing is finished, you sit there and watch it for the first time. And as you do, you're absolutely, positively certain that you will never work in this town again."

Once they get over the initial shock of seeing the first assembly, filmmakers recover and continue working to improve their movies throughout the editorial process. But, for the most part, they're working in isolation, without the benefit of objectivity. So even after they have spent months editing, they may still have the inkling that something doesn't work. Some simply can't identify the point in the film where it veers off track. Others know what doesn't work but can't figure out how to fix it. The preview process can be enlightening in these cases because very often, moviegoers are able to express on the surveys or in postscreening focus groups what bothers them about a film and their comments help filmmakers formulate the solutions.

Such was the case on a much-anticipated picture that I tested for New Line Cinema in the fall of 2004.

When producers Chris Bender and J. C. Spink first read a script about two strong-willed women fighting over the same man, they knew they wanted to make the movie. Inspired by the real-life experiences that first-time screenwriter Anya Kochoff had heard from her girlfriends, the story had nothing to do with romantic rivalries but rather with what happens when a woman becomes engaged to the man of her dreams only to find herself entangled with his mother, who is intent on sabotaging the relationship.

J. C. Spink, who tragically died in 2017 at age forty-five, told me that the title alone had sparked his interest, that those three hyphenated words, *Monster-in-Law*, perfectly encapsulated the concept.

The script hit home for his good friend and business partner, Chris Bender, who was then engaged to be married and planning his own real-life nuptials. When his well-intentioned mother, far from being a monster, rearranged the kitchen cupboards in the home that he and his fiancée were setting up without asking them first, he reflected on Kochoff's screenplay and how it borrowed from situations that every young couple encounters as they grow accustomed to each other's families.

The producers, both barely thirty years old, had received the script for *Monster-in-Law* while they were still shooting *American Wedding*, the third film in their highly successful *American Pie* series. So here they were, on the set of one wedding-themed film while reading the script for another. Bender wondered if his entire life was being taken over by weddings. Yet both he and Spink felt the script was extremely funny and widely relatable. The duo took the idea to New Line, where they had a first-look deal; the studio agreed with their assessment and green-lit the project.

The stars aligned for *Monster-in-Law*. Literally. Bob Shaye, who was then co-chairman and CEO, tapped Paula Weinstein, the heavy-hitter producer, to get involved. Weinstein had a long list of successful movies to her credit (*The Fabulous Baker Boys*, *Analyze This*, *Analyze That*, and *The Perfect Storm*) and just happened to be a close friend of Jane Fonda's. The Academy Award–winning actress had been absent from Hollywood during her marriage to Ted Turner, and Shaye hoped that Weinstein could convince her friend that *Monster-in-Law* was the ticket back home.

Meanwhile, Jennifer Lopez was interested in the role of the bride-to-be. Beyond her stature as a pop icon, Lopez had also proven herself a strong romantic comedy lead in *Maid in Manhattan* and *The Wedding*

Planner, and the producers liked the idea of putting an additional spin on the concept by casting a Latina to play the bride who feuds with her WASPy future mother-in-law.

By the end of 2003, Bender and Spink felt they had assembled a dream team. Robert Luketic, the young Australian director of the hit *Legally Blonde*, was lined up for the project. Fonda and Lopez were on board, and although there was some initial trepidation about how the two powerful actresses might share the limelight, each revealed herself as gracious, down-to-earth, and professional. Michael Vartan was cast as the young doctor who unwittingly delivers his fiancée into the claws of his overbearing and conniving mother. The talented Wanda Sykes was brought in to play what would become the scene-stealing, sharp-tongued assistant to Fonda's character.

Principal photography commenced in the Los Angeles area in April 2004, using distinctive landscapes and architecture for the story's backdrop. The first day Fonda appeared on set, Luketic, a bit nervous about working with the legendary actress, rushed to greet her. "Welcome back, Ms. Fonda," he said with genuine sincerity as the crew dropped what they were doing to break into spontaneous applause. Fonda's eyes welled up with tears.

Monster-in-Law would turn out to be a piece of comedy confection that critics mostly panned but audiences gobbled up. The film begins by setting up Lopez's character as a sweet and talented young woman who juggles various jobs to make ends meet, leading a busy life in a Southern California beach community. Enter the handsome young doctor (Vartan) who is immediately smitten by her and vice versa. The trouble begins when he brings her home to meet his mother (Fonda), a famous TV news personality recently put out to pasture by her network. Fragile but still self-important, the mother takes an instant dislike to the woman, whom she regards as undeserving of her son. When the young man proposes marriage, the mother does everything in her power to stop the wedding from taking place.

Once Lopez's character realizes what her future mother-in-law is doing, the gloves come off and the battle begins. What starts as small verbal snipes soon develops into an all-out war, culminating in a wedding-day brawl with both women tearing at each other's dresses. The bride calls off the wedding and leaves.

There's a time cut, and then as Lopez is getting into her car one rainy day, Fonda surprises her with a visit. The two sit in the car and talk. The mother is contrite, telling the girl that her son is unhappy and won't talk to her anymore. She apologizes to Lopez's character and then says, "Go get him." Lopez runs through the rain to the hospital where the doctor is working and the two reunite.

It seemed like a good way to end a romantic comedy, a poignant moment of vulnerability, followed by the couple's reconciliation. But it didn't work. And the filmmakers knew it.

Spink would later recall, "When I saw the rough cut of *Monster-in-Law*, I just remember the ending being so depressing. Jane Fonda's character is full of regret in that car scene. I remember thinking that anybody who is older and sees this is not going to like it."

Bender added, "Our able villain had become sad and pathetic."

Toby Emmerich, who was then production chief at New Line (and now the head of Warner Bros. Pictures Group) saw the early cut and was also nervous. "I knew there were things that still didn't work," he would later tell the *Los Angeles Times* entertainment columnist Patrick Goldstein.[1] "But I'd be lying if I said that I knew how to fix them." So the studio and the filmmakers decided to let moviegoers weigh in. They arranged for a test screening of the picture in the Los Angeles suburb of Westlake Village. The film played well enough until the fight scene on the wedding day, then the energy on-screen and in the audience just dissipated.

"What had been funny and lighthearted became overly dramatic, melodramatic, in fact," said Bender, who still cringed a bit as he recalled that ending. "And then Jennifer Lopez is running to the hospital and Michael Vartan sees her through the hospital windows and the two reconcile. It was just so cheesy."

Beyond the film's ending, which was an obvious weakness for the Westlake audience, there were a number of other valuable discoveries from that first test screening. The filmmakers learned that Fonda's character was not particularly likable. Conversely, scenes with Wanda Sykes were favorites. The audience just loved the sassy assistant.

Following the initial test, the producers and New Line execs agreed that the film needed more work, and the studio, which Bender recalled as being "one hundred percent behind the picture," agreed to spend an additional $5 million for reshoots.

Over the Christmas break, while the rest of Hollywood vacationed on beaches in Hawaii and the slopes of tony alpine villages, producers Bender and Weinstein, along with the writer, Kochoff, and New Line's production executive, Richard Brener, stayed in Los Angeles to come up with new ideas that would make the ending lighter and funnier.

Brener remembered seeing a slap fight between the characters of Sam and Diane on an old episode of *Cheers*, and when he suggested it might be more comedic than the knockdown, dress-ripping scuffle that was featured in the original version, the group agreed.

They also decided that the story should resolve on the wedding day. As Bender explained, "In a romantic comedy, the heartrending moment should be quick. You don't want that downbeat to go on for too long because it becomes difficult to bring the audience back up again, as we found when we first tested the film. So, in the rewrite, we stayed with the wedding at the end. Jane and Jennifer have the argument, but very quickly we bring it around again."

The biggest change to the ending was the introduction of a new character, the mother's own monster-in-law, played to perfection by the venerable stage actress Elaine Stritch. Stritch's character arrives as an unexpected guest at the wedding and bursts into the bedroom, interrupting the slap fight between Lopez and Fonda. Stritch lashes out at Fonda, who had been married to her son, and old wounds flare up as the two blame each other for his untimely death. The bride looks on in disbelief, recognizing the animosity that is being perpetuated through the generations of women who marry into the family.

Afterward, Lopez and Fonda are left alone in the room and the bride concedes. "That's going to be you and me in thirty years," she says. "You win . . . the wedding's off." Lopez goes off to find the groom and tell him that she's backing out. But Fonda stops her, of course. The women call a truce, Fonda promises to be a good mother-in-law, and Lopez invites her to be involved with any future grandchildren. The wedding plays out.

The filmmakers also found ways to sprinkle in more scenes with Wanda Sykes, ending the movie with Fonda and her assistant walking into the house after the happy couple leaves on their honeymoon. Sykes tells Fonda, who is wearing a dress that her daughter-in-law wanted her to wear, that she looks like "a giant peach cobbler."

After the holidays, Chris Bender showed the episode of *Cheers* to Jane Fonda to demonstrate the idea of a more humorous rewritten slap flight. The new scenes were shot, and the film was tested again.

This time, with Fonda's character shown suffering the scrutiny of her own monster-in-law, moviegoers were more sympathetic and forgiving of her behavior. The dramatic resolution worked, and it happened quickly, allowing the audience to see the beautiful wedding take place after all.

Stritch's appearance registered as one of their favorite parts of the entire film, proving well worth the cost and effort to add it. The scores shot up, an astounding twenty points higher than the original Westlake Village scores.

"That was a huge victory," said Bender. "As a producer, I know that when you go into the editing room and see the first assembly, you generally have a heart attack and throw up in your mouth. So I'm used to that. But what I've learned through my experiences with research screenings—and especially with comedies and horror films—is the impact that a great ending can have on the overall assessments. If the ending is at all in question, there's at least a ten-point opportunity to improve the scores."

Monster-in-Law opened on May 13, 2005, just a few days after Mother's Day, and took the number-one position in box office gross for the weekend. Bender, by that time married, got points with his new wife for making a "chick flick." Both his mother and his new mother-in-law thought the film was hilarious.

Continuing to make their mark on Hollywood, Chris Bender and J. C. Spink went on to produce *A History of Violence*, *Red Eye*, and the runaway summer hit of 2009, *The Hangover*.

I attracted a bit of press for my behind-the-scenes role in the film. The *Los Angeles Times* had caught wind of *Monster-in-Law*'s troubles at the original test screening in Westlake, and they decided to write a story about how I helped fix it. Generally, it's my job to stay out of the spotlight, but with studio chief Toby Emmerich's encouragement, I shared a *few* details with the newspaper.

In the article, *Times* columnist Patrick Goldstein ended up dubbing me the "doctor of audience-ology" and the "Dr. Phil of Hollywood," titles my colleagues have never let me live down—and that may well end up on my tombstone one day!

Test audience research can do more than save a flawed movie. It can turn a good one into a classic. I know this because I've seen it happen time and again.

During the same period that *Cocktail* was being reshaped by Robert Cort and his colleagues, one of the most legendary case studies in movie testing was unfolding across town at Paramount Pictures. This one, the 1987 thriller *Fatal Attraction*, would become an often-repeated story of how the testing process propelled a modern-day film to success. More than three decades after its release, industry insiders still describe it as a seminal moment in screening research history.

I was still earning my stripes in the market research business, and even though I was young and relatively green, I recognized that I was witnessing something extraordinary as *Fatal Attraction* took shape. Based upon early test results, Paramount invested heavily to make changes to an already good film, and the outcome was nothing short of astounding. What I couldn't have known at the time was that *Fatal Attraction* would become a phenomenon, tapping into the zeitgeist of our culture, landing its stars on the cover of *Time* magazine, and driving fear into the hearts (and loins) of married men everywhere.

Fatal Attraction had all of the ingredients that make for an exciting motion picture: provocative subject matter, a well-crafted script, and memorable characters played by actors of notable talent and popularity.

Sherry Lansing, who produced the film with Stanley Jaffe, had already established herself as a tour de force in the movie business, having worked her way into powerful positions at MGM and Columbia Pictures. In 1980, when Lansing was only thirty-five, Twentieth Century–Fox appointed her president of production, making her the first woman ever to hold a top motion picture studio position. She was not only brilliant but also beautiful and charismatic, qualities that served her well on the heels of the women's liberation movement. It was easy to accept this unwitting trailblazer, feminine and diplomatic to the core, and motivated more by her love of movies than by a quest for power in the studio hierarchy. Lansing stayed at Fox for just three years before joining her friend Stanley Jaffe to form an independent production company, Jaffe-Lansing Productions, in 1983.

Fatal Attraction was their first big collaboration as a team, and Lansing remembers loving the material from the outset. The story centers on a seemingly happily married man, played by Michael Douglas, who has a weekend fling with a woman while his wife and young daughter are out of town. The affair turns dangerous when the woman proves to be mentally unstable and obsessively clings to Douglas's character, despite his increasingly desperate attempts to end the relationship. Glenn Close delivers a chilling performance as Alex Forrest, the woman with whom he has the affair. Anne Archer plays the decent and sympathetic wife, suffering in the aftermath of the affair, which he eventually discloses to her.

The film touched a chord with moviegoers, who could empathize with the characters and envision the choices they themselves might make if faced with the same situation (and during the 1980s, a time of self-indulgence and sexual freedom, the premise hit home for many). The film is superbly written and directed, leveraging a very genuine connection to the characters and their emotions, and earning Academy Award nominations for the writer, James Dearden, and the director, Adrian Lyne, and a Best Picture nomination for the film itself. Both actresses also received Oscar nominations, Close for Best Actress and Archer for Best Supporting Actress, although the picture won in none of those categories.

For all of the accolades eventually bestowed upon *Fatal Attraction*, it had been a tough film to get underway. Michael Douglas, already a big star, was attached to the project early on, but Lansing and Jaffe had difficulty convincing any studio that the picture had commercial appeal. Furthermore, more than two dozen directors, including John Carpenter and Brian De Palma, passed on it before Adrian Lyne, who had directed *9½ Weeks* and *Flashdance*, agreed to become involved.

Aside from Douglas, who was one of the film's biggest champions, casting also became an issue. Debra Winger and Miranda Richardson each declined the part of Alex, and Barbara Hershey, whom the producers felt would be perfect for it, was unavailable. Glenn Close's agent pushed hard to get her the role, but Lyne resisted, feeling she was too wholesome, "the last person on Earth" who should play the part.[2] He relented only after she volunteered to come in for a reading to prove that she could play a convincing seductress. Lansing recalled that Close asked that Douglas be there to read with her, and when she entered the room, she was in a beautiful V-neck black dress. "She was brilliant!" exclaimed Lansing. "In less than ten minutes, we knew she had the part."

After turning it down once, and with plenty of pressure from Lansing and Jaffe, Paramount Pictures eventually agreed to underwrite and distribute *Fatal Attraction*. The pieces had all come together and the final product was worth the wait. When Lansing saw an early cut of the picture, she was thrilled. She remembered the studio executives at the time, Ned Tanen, the president of the Motion Picture Group, and Frank Mancuso, the chairman and CEO, were also very excited when they realized what they had. Word soon spread across the Paramount lot that *Fatal Attraction* was going to be a big hit.

With great anticipation, the film was previewed to a test audience in Seattle, because Lansing viewed the screening process much like a play that is taken out of town for its tryouts. The results were decidedly positive but not spectacular, as the studio and filmmakers had expected. Lansing recalled, "Everyone was a little puzzled. You could almost sense a certain defeat in the theater when you heard the applause at the end. The reaction was good but not great."

After the screening, the executives huddled together and determined that they had an aberrant audience, speculating that it was just the wrong crowd for this film. So a second test was scheduled in the San Francisco area, then two more in Los Angeles. Each time, the results were exactly the same. The audiences were riveted, but something deflated them at the end of the movie.

In the original version of the film, Alex (Glenn Close) takes her own life with great melodrama, slicing her throat in a reenactment of

Madame Butterfly, an opera she and her lover had discussed earlier in the film. Michael Douglas's character is blamed for her death and is last seen on the screen as police haul him away in handcuffs. His wife subsequently uncovers evidence that will exonerate him, and the movie closes with a tearful Anne Archer running off to prove his innocence.

The filmmakers believed that the ending offered good resolution to the story, and both punishment and redemption for the unfaithful husband who suffers immensely for his indiscretion. Yet in focus groups held after each of the research screenings, moviegoers consistently said that they didn't like the way the film ended. Lansing and the others wondered why they were not embracing it.

Reflecting upon the various test previews, Lansing and her colleagues realized that in each one they had heard applause when the wife stands up to Alex, telling her, "If you come near my family again, I'll kill you, you understand?" Clearly, the audiences wanted the family to hold together. But did they want more? Did they want to see the wife exact revenge upon the woman who was pursuing her husband? In an interview done years later, Michael Douglas commented, "No one could anticipate the anger for the character that Glenn portrayed so brilliantly."[3]

The filmmakers agonized over what to do next. The studio encouraged them to make changes to the ending based upon the screening research. Lansing remembered going through a soul-searching process, wondering if a new ending was in the film's best interest. "Were we selling out? Were we damaging the movie?" she recalled asking herself.

Glenn Close, who had prepared for the role of Alex by asking two psychiatrists to weigh in on the script to determine whether or not her behavior was realistic, felt certain that the suicide was very much in keeping with her character's mental disorder. She argued that it should stay in the film. But after weeks of discussion and debate, the stars, the director, and the producers agreed on one thing: they needed to try something different.

To move things along, Ned Tanen at Paramount offered a low-risk proposition. The studio would bankroll a reshoot of the ending, and if it didn't work when it was tested again, the filmmakers would not have to use it. For three weeks, the actors and production crew reunited to complete a physically and emotionally exhausting new sequence.

The revised ending, now considered a classic, involves a terrifying bathroom scene in which Alex tries to stab the wife as she is about to step into a bath. In a violent struggle, Michael Douglas's character fends off Alex and drowns her in the tub, or so the audience thinks, only to be surprised when she lunges from the water a few moments later wielding the knife against him. In a desperate act to defend her husband, Anne Archer's character shoots and kills the deranged woman. It's arguably one of the most gripping moments in film.

Meanwhile, *Fatal Attraction* was starting to get bad press. Word of the research screenings and the reshoot fueled rumors in the media around town that the movie had problems. So when the revised version was screened to a test audience several months later, Paramount held the preview in a theater on the lot in an attempt to keep it quiet. Gary Lucchesi, who was president of production at Paramount then (and is now partner/producer at Revelations Entertainment), remembered sitting next to Lansing at the screening in the Paramount Theater. As the new bathroom scene began to play out, she grabbed for his hand. "We held hands real tight out of fear," Lucchesi recalled. "We wanted it to work so badly."

The theater held nearly three hundred moviegoers, and Lansing sensed that every single one of them, including herself and Lucchesi, jumped in their seats when Alex leapt from the water after presumably being drowned. The audience went wild, filling the auditorium with their screams. "It was a visceral reaction to a truly intelligent, suspenseful film," said Lansing. The new ending was everything that she could have hoped for, and the test scores at that screening skyrocketed.

Moreover, in large numbers that distinctly improved over the previous screenings, moviegoers now indicated on their surveys that they would definitely recommend the film to friends. The film had staying power in theaters throughout the fall of 1987. "It was transformative," continued Lansing. "It opened to $7.6 million, but I knew from that moment during the screening, when everyone reacted the way they did, that we would have good word of mouth. Ultimately, it earned $320 million worldwide.

"I'm a staunch believer in taking your film out, not being afraid, and letting your audience see it," she said. "If we hadn't changed the ending,

Fatal Attraction would have opened to $7 million and we would have made $30 million. But we unlocked the key. It was a quantifiable change. It meant hundreds of millions of dollars in business. The process does not corrupt your art, it helps you get your message through."

The story behind *Fatal Attraction* makes for modern-day legend among market researchers and movie historians. It exemplifies the very best of what can occur through the testing process. Consistent feedback from moviegoers, great insight into what might be done to improve an already good product, filmmakers who are open-minded and willing to listen, consensus regarding the changes, and support from the studio all manifested into a spectacularly successful outcome.

As a result of her experience with *Fatal Attraction*, Sherry Lansing became a believer in the testing process. I had the opportunity to work with her on hundreds of screenings over the years. In the early 1990s, she followed her partner, Stanley Jaffe, to Paramount Pictures, where she reigned as chairman for more than a dozen years (although Jaffe's stint with the studio was shorter-lived). During her tenure, the studio released some of its most successful pictures ever: *Indecent Proposal*, *Forrest Gump*, *Braveheart*, *Mission: Impossible*, *The First Wives Club*, *What Women Want*, *The Talented Mr. Ripley*, and installments in the *Star Trek* series of movies. Soon after she retired from the studio in 2005, the big theater on the lot on which the new ending of *Fatal Attraction* was tested was renamed the Sherry Lansing Theatre in her honor.

Stories like those of *Fatal Attraction* and *Cocktail* and *Monster-in-Law* show how screenings can help filmmakers solve big problems, the fundamental flaws in their movies.

Indeed, the movie business is generally a business of big things. It has been since at least 1930, when the oil magnate Howard Hughes spent a sizable portion of his fortune to make one of the first action movies with sound. It was called *Hell's Angels*, and it was about World War I fighter pilots. The production was so large that 137 pilots were required for filming, which was about a quarter of the number of battle-ready pilots in the entire US military at the time.

Hughes made an army to make a movie, and ever since, Hollywood has been a place of big budgets, big screens, and big egos, too.

But what's also remarkable about screenings is that they don't simply reveal the big flaws, they can reveal the small ones, too. Test audiences have a keen eye for detail in films and are unforgiving if even the tiniest thing is amiss—a skip in the logic, or dialogue that seems out of character, or something about the scene perceived as too silly or over the top. We characterize these hiccups as taking the audience "out of the movie" for a beat because this type of problem reminds filmgoers that they're watching something that is make-believe. Instead of remaining immersed in the story, their minds wander to questions about what just happened on-screen, questioning its authenticity.

Filmmakers sometimes have alternate shots of the same scene that they can substitute, or they may be able to correct the problem in the editing room by cutting around it. Occasionally, actors will be asked to record new dialogue that addresses the problem, commonly known as "ADR" (automated dialogue replacement) or "looping." The most drastic solution is to get rid of the scene altogether, something that sparks lots of discussion, and often, heated arguments. I remind studio executives and filmmakers that they can always test a version without the scene to settle the debate. If the movie works better without it, there is validation that it was the right choice to delete it. If there is no improvement, they can always put it back into the movie.

Small flaws such as these tend to surface early in the testing process, either on the surveys or in focus group discussions, because test audiences feel a duty to report things that seem odd or out of context. And they can be almost scarily good at this, as Renny Harlin discovered.

Sylvester Stallone describes Harlin as the "last Viking." The two men worked together on the 1993 action thriller *Cliffhanger*, and Stallone's reference aptly portrays the director's fearless determination to do the impossible. Many of Harlin's pictures reflect a type of daredevil abandon.

"I want to take the audience on a ride. Grab them in the first scene and hold on to them for the next two hours," he explained.

Growing up in Finland, Harlin fell in love with movie making at an early age. He began making amateur movies with a video camera when he was just fourteen years old, influenced by the impresario of suspense and thrills, Alfred Hitchcock, and the action sequences in Sam Peckinpah's *The Wild Bunch*. As an adult, he had a fair degree of success in his country, first as a commercial director and then directing motion pictures. But the government underwrote all production and dictated the types of films that it would finance. Harlin jokes that he didn't want to spend his life making movies about divorce, alcoholism, and suicide, so when he got an opportunity to move to Los Angeles in the late 1980s, he jumped at the chance to get a foothold in Hollywood.

At first, Harlin worked on a string of low-budget horror fare. But in 1988, when he was hired by New Line Cinema to direct *A Nightmare on Elm Street 4*, he hit gold. The film grossed $49 million, a record for an independent film at that time, and 20th Century Fox took notice. The studio hired Harlin to direct *Die Hard 2*, catapulting him into the big league.

A few years later, with several large commercial successes and the critically acclaimed *Rambling Rose* to his credit (which he produced, and Martha Coolidge directed), Harlin was approached by Carolco Pictures to direct *Cliffhanger*. Carolco had already signed Sylvester Stallone to the lead, playing a mountain ranger who sets out to rescue a group of stranded climbers only to discover that they're actually looking for boxes of money that were lost in a botched heist.

Although the story is set in the Colorado Rockies, *Cliffhanger* was filmed in the Italian Alps. Harlin scouted dozens of alpine regions around the world and came to the conclusion that the Italian Dolomites would provide the most stunning backdrop. The overseas shoot was difficult, requiring the cast and crew to spend long hours in harsh outdoor conditions, including everything from blizzards to mudslides. Stallone was in great shape for the role, but well-known professional mountain climbers were brought in for the stunts.

One scene required a particularly difficult and dangerous stunt, a freestyle move called a "king's leap," in which the climber literally leaps from one sheer rock face to another. In the movie, Stallone's character is forced to make a running jump from one cliff to another after the bridge connecting them is destroyed. On location, the stunt double made the leap and landed safely on top of the opposing cliff, but the scene took days to film in bitter cold weather and not without peril to the climber and the crew.

It was just the type of scene that Harlin loved, one in which he expected the audience to hold its collective breath as the character leaps, and marvel at the feat when it's successfully accomplished. Moreover, the ranger played by Stallone was set up in the story as being an extreme mountain climber, and the actor himself had the physique that made it seem plausible.

When *Cliffhanger* was tested before an audience for the first time, it seemed to get off to a fantastic start. The opening of the film sets up Stallone's character as an experienced mountain ranger who embarks on what should have been a routine rescue of a couple that had become stranded at the top of a very high butte. Both the man and the woman are good friends of Stallone's character. The man, an expert climbing buddy, has injured his foot, so after making it to the top of the butte, Stallone anchors a line to a nearby mountaintop where a helicopter is able to land. The injured man is harnessed and zips easily across dizzying heights to safety. His girlfriend, a far less experienced climber, is terrified to make the crossing and has to be coaxed inch by inch across the span.

Midway out, the equipment fails. As her boyfriend and the rescue pilots scream encouragements, Stallone manages to shimmy across the line and grab her by the hand as the last thread to her harness unravels. He tries to hold on to her, but contrary to what most moviegoers might anticipate from a Rocky/Rambo-type heroic effort, her hand slips out of her glove and she plummets to her death. It's a jaw-dropping scene, completely unexpected, and the beginning of Harlin's thrill ride.

To this day, Harlin remembered the test audience's screams. After spending a year and a half of his life making the picture, he allowed himself a measure of confidence that it was working. When the preview was over and the audience filled out the surveys, the director predicted the scores to come back in the mid- to high eighties (meaning 80 percent of the audience rates it either excellent or very good).

Instead, they were in the sixties. He was devastated.

During the focus group, none of the participants could voice what they thought was wrong with the picture. Frustrated and depressed, Harlin went home with a set of the questionnaires and began reading through them. There were several comments about the scene where Stallone leaps from one mountain to the next, a stunt that some moviegoers felt was completely far-fetched. "I realized that they wanted Stallone's character to be real, but that stunt made him into a superhero," said Harlin. "In that scene, he lost credibility."

Although it was a very real accomplishment in the world of extreme mountain climbing, an audience of regular moviegoers just didn't believe it could be done. It was a classic example of an audience being taken "out of the movie" for a beat.

For the next screening, Harlin made just one change. He deleted the king's leap scene and substituted it with existing footage of Stallone and costar Janine Turner standing on the mountaintop after discovering the bridge is impassable. Over a long shot of the two stars against the snow-covered landscape, Stallone looped new dialogue describing a plan to backtrack to a place where he can cross over to the adjacent mountain, circumventing the destroyed bridge. "We cheated it," explained Harlin. "But it provided enough explanation for getting to the other side on foot."

"That was the only change," continued the director. "And the scores were ninety-two percent at the next screening. There were those who felt it was a spectacular stunt and argued against taking it out. But after seeing the huge jump in scores, we proved it was the right thing to do."

In the final cut, Stallone is never shown making the long trek that reroutes him to the other side of the bridge. The small bit of ADR seamlessly ties the scenes together and he gets to his destination without making the superhuman leap.

"It's in the special features on the DVD, if you want to see it," said Harlin, laughing.

Like Cliffhanger, the original cut of *Thelma & Louise* caused audience outrage over a short scene—this one, too, involving a cliff. The film chronicles two friends as their road trip turns into a run from the law.

Greg Foster, the longtime CEO of IMAX Entertainment and senior executive vice president of IMAX Corporation, was working at MGM/ UA in the early 1990s and remembered that there was a lot riding on the film. For starters, Ridley Scott was a first-rate director who had made what the studio believed could be a huge hit. The script from Callie Khouri was so impressive that the movie had been green-lit on the spot. Two widely esteemed actresses, Geena Davis and Susan Sarandon, were sizzling in their roles, and although the studio didn't know it then, the movie would launch Brad Pitt's career.

Perhaps most important, MGM/UA was in deep merger discussions with Pathé Entertainment, the production company responsible for *Thelma & Louise*. Pathé had a history of making primarily low-budget movies for the home entertainment market and owned theaters in the UK and Europe but wanted to become a bigger player in Hollywood. In an audacious financial maneuver, Pathé was working on a plan to acquire MGM/UA. The collaboration of the two companies to bring *Thelma & Louise* to market was an important step in a courtship process that had everyone watching.

Foster had recently been promoted to vice president of production at MGM/UA, but he had come up through the research department, and Alan Ladd Jr., the head of the studio, asked him to oversee the testing on *Thelma & Louise* because of the importance of the relationship. Foster remembered taking it to Arlington Heights, Illinois, a northwestern suburb of Chicago, for its first test preview. He was happy to be involved with the research, an opportunity to be with the big group of colleagues from the studio that he didn't often get to see in his new position.

"The film was played for the recruited audience and everyone seemed to love it," said Foster. "In that version, at the very end of the movie, there was a scene after the car goes off the cliff. For a split second, Geena Davis and Susan Sarandon are seen driving again along the road, as if they had made it. But that wasn't Ridley Scott's intention. He just wanted to show metaphorically that their spirits lived on."

"Well, the audience went apeshit."

Afterward, during the focus group, Foster listened as moviegoers expressed outrage at that scene. "It's baloney!" they said. "You're glorifying what they did." They felt the ending was inauthentic and didn't represent the spirit of the story. When the cards were counted, the scores were significantly lower than expected. Susan Sarandon's agent, the famed Sam Cohn, was standing by, looking worried.

Later that night, Foster found himself with the executives and filmmakers at the renowned Chicago steakhouse Gene and Georgetti, trying to choke down a depressing dinner. The film's editor, Thom Noble, made a keen observation. "Well, I don't need to read the cards," Foster remembered Noble saying. "The problem is so obvious. We have to take that little moment out."

The next day, the group flew to San Francisco to test the movie for a second time. Noble went into the projection booth, where there was a KEM (an old-fashioned film editing table that is no longer used, replaced by modern-day digital methods). Because the offending scene was right at the end of the movie and there were no ending credits on that early version, Noble just surgically removed it. Snip, it was gone. The car with the two women soars into the void over the Grand Canyon and the story ends. The screening happened, and the audience loved the movie.

"Giant success," recalled Foster. "It's often one little thing that makes the difference."

For a long time, I've been thinking about why this is, about what makes moviegoers such harsh judges of detail, and my favorite explanation is a scientific one.

There may be a biological reason why moviegoers home in on "off" moments in movies, why test audiences reacted so viscerally to the stunt in *Cliffhanger* and the extra scene in *Thelma & Louise*.

If you ask evolutionary biologists, some say that all of this is Darwinian, that after tens of thousands of years of sitting around nightly campfires, our hunter-gatherer ancestors evolved into expert tellers of stories. In the same way *Homo sapiens* came to walk upright and possess larger prefrontal cortexes, our species also came to recognize, on a biological level, the rhythms and tones, plotlines and characterizations, of narratives. Our hatred for plot holes could be a product of our DNA.

There's no universally accepted view on why we evolved this way. It could've been that when our ancestors told better stories, they were more able to relieve the stress from being chased by a saber-toothed tiger. Or maybe when they told better stories, their community felt more unified, which gave them an advantage when they went to war with the clan across the river.

Of course, all of this is just a hypothesis, and there are certainly more straightforward explanations than the millennia-long process of randomly mutating genes. Perhaps we're so critical of stories because we've seen so many of them. We are bombarded with so much content, fed so many plotlines, that our bar for what's acceptable sits somewhere in the stratosphere. Like master sommeliers, our palettes are finely honed. We demand films of good vintage. None of the cheap shit.

That's a reasonable explanation, too, and I'm sure there are more. Nevertheless, I prefer the whimsical one. I like to believe that we're born movie critics, that when we spot a flaw in a film, it's our DNA telling us so; that when we enter the movie theater, we're bringing thousands—maybe millions—of years of human evolution with us.

Sometimes it's the audience that protects a scene in a film, and actually defends it from those who would remove it or water it down.

Director Ken Kwapis recalled such a situation on *The Sisterhood of the Traveling Pants*, his 2005 film based on Ann Brashares's novel of the same title. The ensemble piece centers on four girlfriends who share a pair of well-worn jeans during the first summer they ever spend apart from each other. The jeans, purchased at a thrift shop, seem to possess a magical quality. Each girl benefits by wearing them for a week's time, then mails them to the next friend for her turn to make a wish come true.

In the film, America Ferrera plays Carmen, one of the friends who plans to spend the summer in South Carolina visiting her father, who has not been around for much of her life. Upon her arrival, Carmen is surprised to learn that her dad is living with a woman and her two children. He treats Carmen quite shabbily during the visit, spending little time with her and devoting all of his attention to his new family. Devastated, Carmen returns home early. Later in the story, she summons the courage to confront him in a tearful phone call.

During the shoot, in take after take, Ferrera was giving the emotional scene her all. At one point, the producers pulled Kwapis aside and told him that they thought the performance might be a bit too intense. They suggested he ask the actress to pull back a little. But Kwapis felt he was getting exactly what the scene required. He wanted the level of emotionality that Ferrera was delivering.

When the film was finished and tested, Kwapis recalled hearing some giggles from a group of moviegoers during Ferrera's phone call scene. "Fuck," he thought, "I was wrong." But his panic lasted for just a split second when he heard an even bigger reaction as others in the audience went, "Shhhhh!" The scene actually played exactly as the director had hoped, pulling at the heartstrings of most in the audience, as Carmen finally expresses the hurt she felt from years of her father's indifference toward her.

Kwapis doesn't remember the exact scores but recalls that *The Sisterhood of the Traveling Pants* tested very strongly. It spoke to young females coming of age, took in a respectable $42 million during its theatrical run, and spawned a sequel.

In 2011, I had the opportunity to work on a "swords and sandals" film called *Immortals*. The genre was red-hot following the success of *300* several years prior, and then *Clash of the Titans* in 2010 and *Thor* in 2011. These films were huge in scope and featured mythologically based stories, epic battle sequences, and grueling mano a mano death matches. A certain segment of moviegoers couldn't get enough, and all the aforementioned films earned big bucks at the box office and gave rise to successful sequels.

Enter Relativity Media, the mini-major studio that, up until that point in time, was mostly involved with mid-budget productions like *Limitless*, *Brothers*, *The Spy Next Door*, and *Dear John*. *Immortals* would be Relativity's first foray into the big leagues, a $100 million investment starring Henry Cavill as Theseus, a mere mortal who takes on King Hyperion (Mickey Rourke) to save ancient Greece and all of humanity. Freida Pinto portrays the virgin oracle Phaedra, and two versions of Zeus are played by Luke Evans and John Hurt.

I was involved with the research from beginning to end, and when we needed to pull out all the stops to make the film a more satisfying experience for its audience, the studio trusted me to implement a highly unusual insight-generating tactic.

Tucker Tooley, who was president of Relativity Media at the time and executive producer of *Immortals*, remembers when it was first tested in a small theater on the Fox lot. Director Tarsem Singh had created an artistically stunning film, shot in high-definition 3D. It was a glittery, shimmery visual feast, but it leaned away from its core male target audience. The results of the first preview were a wake-up call.

"Once you get past the initial emotional reaction, you need to talk yourself off the ledge," Tooley explained years later. "The muscular nature of *300* was the yardstick to measure any film in the genre, and we needed to get closer to that for the audience we were targeting. I remember calming myself down and talking to the other Relativity executives and Tarsem, and asking them to experiment by taking out everything the audience vehemently rejected to see what remained. That was task number one. Tarsem agreed and everyone regrouped, and we laid out a plan."

The first test was of an early cut of the film, and the studio still had plenty of time to finesse it before its November release. In addition to an aesthetic that wasn't gritty enough, there was some confusion about character motivations and an ending that many in the recruited audience felt was too ambiguous. Over the course of the next few months, other small test screenings were conducted in Los Angeles to guide editorial refinements.

In May 2011, a double screening of the film was held in a large New Jersey theater, seating several hundred moviegoers in two different auditoriums to watch slightly different versions. The responses at those showings were better than those at the small Los Angeles screenings, but in both cuts, the ending remained problematic.

At the center of the story, King Hyperion (Rourke) is on a quest to find an all-powerful weapon called the Bow of Epirus. He intends to use it to unleash the Titans, who have been imprisoned in Mount Tartarus after losing a battle against the gods. Hyperion then plans to use the legion of Titans to annihilate the gods and claim dominion over all mankind. As he makes his way across Greece in search of the weapon, he arrives in a village where Theseus (Cavill) and his mother are living. Theseus has been trained in the art of hand-to-hand combat, and when he stands up to Hyperion, the evil king grabs Theseus's mother, slashing her throat and killing her in front of her son. Hyperion then enslaves Theseus. Later, with the help of Phaedra (Pinto), Theseus escapes and leads an uprising against Hyperion.

The story concludes with armies from both sides, one led by Hyperion and the other by Theseus, clashing at Mount Tartarus. Hyperion eventually gets his hands on the Bow of Epirus, using its power to free the Titans and prompting Zeus and the other gods to descend from the heavens for a ferocious battle. Meanwhile, Theseus and Hyperion face off in a fight of their own, with Theseus being beaten to a pulp but managing to kill Hyperion before he himself dies. But moviegoers just weren't buying it.

After those New Jersey previews, the filmmakers and executives at Relativity knew they had to recraft the ending but felt they needed more specific input on what fixes to make. "Most of the time it's intuitive and the research backs you up," said Tooley. "But in this situation, we had to dig deeper." The director and the Parlapanides brothers, who had written the original script, hunkered down with another screenwriter, Christian Gudegast, who was brought in to help with rewrites. Together, the team workshopped possible outcomes to the story, concentrating their efforts on the showdown between Theseus and Hyperion and its aftermath.

"Meanwhile, Kevin came up with a truly inventive idea," said Tooley. "He knew that we needed insight into what it would take to deliver an ending that moviegoers would embrace and rally behind. We weren't going to get that level of input using tried-and-true movie testing methods. So, he proposed something altogether different."

Two small screenings were set up at Raleigh Studios in Hollywood, one with men between the ages of seventeen and twenty-four, and another with somewhat older men ages twenty-five to thirty-four. But unlike the typical test preview where the movie plays through to the end and respondents fill out surveys, these showings actually stopped the film at a crucial point in the story. Right before the big battle at Mount Tartarus, the screen went dark and the theater lights came up.

"Kevin then walked to the front of the screening room and asked the audience, 'What do you think will happen next?' He was uncovering their expectations for how the story would play out," Tooley explained. "Then he asked, 'What do you *want* to happen next?' This was where he drilled down into what they needed to feel emotionally. It turned into a very creative exercise.

"We weren't looking for numbers or ratings. Kevin approached it from two different realms, satisfying the brain and satisfying the heart. That's what made this whole process so valuable."

After some discussion, four possible outcomes that the writers had conceived were described, and the audiences weighed in on the pros and cons of each. "Here's where Kevin was looking for consensus," Tooley said. "He wanted to be able to distill what we were learning into action-able next steps for the production team." Finally, the rest of the film was shown, and further discussion ensued about changes that would make the ending more gratifying.

"What we learned from that exercise was that everything happened so quickly at the end, with Theseus taking over and leading an army against Hyperion. And he wasn't proactive in killing Hyperion," Tooley recalled. "There wasn't even much of a fight."

The Raleigh Studios research gave clear direction that Theseus must earn his status as leader of the rebel army, that his fight with Hyperion must be as thrilling as the battle taking place between the gods and the Titans, and that his death must feel heroic.

The filmmakers went to work on the changes. When *Immortals* was tested again a few months later before a large audience, there was ex-tended footage of Theseus rallying his followers to rise up against the vicious King Hyperion. "We had more shots of him walking back and forth, talking to the troops and motivating everyone," explained Tooley. "The fight between Theseus and Hyperion was reshot to make it far more exciting. Stunt coordinator Garrett Warren, who had a background in mixed martial arts, was tapped to create an ancient Greek version of that type of physical combat."

Moviegoers at Raleigh Studios had likened these opponents to boxers—Theseus the featherweight using speed and cunning, Hyperion the heavyweight who relies on brute force. These skills were highlighted in an MMA-style confrontation in which Theseus kills Hyperion before succumbing to his wounds, avenging his mother's death and sacrificing his own life to save humanity in the process. As both characters lie dying, Zeus destroys Mount Tartarus, burying the Titans and what's left of Hyperion's army underneath the rubble. Theseus's spirit ascends into the heavens (an additional visual effect that was not in the original cut), and he earns his place in history.

The audience at that final screening of the film was nothing short of enthusiastic. Positive scores for the film, intent to recommend it to others, and evaluations of the ending shot up. *Immortals* opened a few months later as the number-one movie of the weekend and went on to earn $227 million worldwide over its theatrical run.

"It was a multistage process, and, ultimately, we were very pleased with the results," Tooley recounted. "It was super profitable and a big statement for our company."

Stopping a movie and pulling the audience out of the story to discuss possible endings was a daring move, and I admit that I didn't know if it would work when I suggested it. But in the situation with *Immortals*, after months of traditional testing, I knew we had to think outside the box. We weren't asking moviegoers to rewrite the ending; we were asking them to express, at that moment in the film, what would make the final act both intellectually and emotionally satisfying.

On the Relativity side, I had a very willing team with whom to work—people who knew the stakes and entrusted me to guide them. That was a big responsibility. But they were ready to listen. There was a point at which they had done everything they could with the picture but still lost the audience in the third act. They needed to rethink the DNA to get to the next level, and I'm proud to have used audience feedback to make it a far more satisfying experience for moviegoers and, consequently, a hit for the studio.

5.

KNOW THY AUDIENCE

There are few individuals in Hollywood who are more educated than Shawn Levy. Today, Levy is a rock star director-producer known most recently for Netflix's hit series *Stranger Things*.

But growing up near Montreal, Levy was known as something of a boy genius.

He entered Yale at the age of sixteen and graduated within four years—with honors, no less. After working on several popular and groundbreaking TV shows in the late 1980s (*thirtysomething* and *Beverly Hills, 90210*), he was accepted to USC Film School, one of the most prestigious in the country. In a class of fifty, he was one of just two who have gone on to have big careers as mainstream feature film directors (the other is Jeffrey Nachmanoff, who directed *Traitor*).

Back in the mid-1990s, when all of his classmates were making thesis movies that were dark dramas, a genre that was in vogue at the time, Levy bucked the trend and settled on romantic comedy material about two thirteen-year-old kids who decide to break into the *Guinness Book of World Records* by being the youngest couple ever to get married.

"It's three acts in twenty-seven minutes," explained Levy of his student film. "And even though it looks like shit and sounds like shit, the story is extremely funny and warmhearted." On the night it was screened at the USC First Look Festival, Levy's *Broken Record* was one of seven to be shown. He remembered the night clearly. "Mine was fifth. Drama, drama, *Pulp Fiction* derivation, *Reservoir Dogs* knockoff."

Levy's film came on next, and for the first time in his life—but certainly not the last—he experienced the euphoria of knowing that the audience was "synergizing" with the film the way he had intended. It was a film student's dream. When the movie ended and the credits came up, the audience broke into thunderous applause that seemed to go on forever. For Shawn Levy, that was the night that would change everything.

"The next day," recalled Levy, "I got forty-seven phone calls from agencies and the studios. Literally. I remember the number, forty-seven, by one p.m., which is industry-standard lunchtime. It was unreal."

Broken Record launched not only his career but also the Shawn Levy brand. "I didn't set out to brand myself, and in fact I was mocked for making a soft, poignant comedy." But his little student film unwittingly positioned Levy in a category that he has grown to love: all-audience comedy with heart. "If anything, I find the branding hugely ripe with opportunity, and though in my younger years I chafed at it, I realize I know how to do this. And I own it proudly."

Although it caused a tidal wave reaction among the Hollywood scouts, the preview of Levy's student film was not a test screening; no questionnaires were handed out and there were no scores to quantify the audience's appreciation of what they had seen on the screen. But for Levy, that experience was an indelible lesson about what a filmmaker can learn from audiences about his or her film. "There is a dynamic in that room in the dark, a live, breathing thing, and you need to learn from it as much as from the cards and scores."

In the years after graduating from USC, though, Levy learned to love his brand. In fact, he became a hit-making machine in his category, directing movies like *Big Fat Liar*, *Just Married*, and then a remake of *Cheaper by the Dozen*, starring Steve Martin.

When these films were test screened, none of them ever saw a top-two-box score that wasn't stellar. In fact, the final screening of *Cheaper by the Dozen* scored a ninety-five—and a perfect one hundred with mothers in the audience.

Levy loved his experience screening these movies. "You'd sit there and the laughs wash over you like the greatest fucking bath, just wave after wave," he told me. "And then you get those numbers and it legitimizes . . . what you felt in the dark."

Unfortunately, bath time was about to end for Shawn Levy. He may have been one of the most educated men in Hollywood, but another chapter in his schooling was about to begin.

In 2005, Levy began work on a modern-day version of *The Pink Panther* for MGM. Blake Edwards had directed and cowritten the original film, released in 1963, which stars the incomparable Peter Sellers as Inspector Jacques Clouseau.

It's easy to forget now, but Clouseau was originally meant to be a bit part. The script centered around a jewel thief played by David Niven and two women who are in love with him, and Clouseau, the bumbling French detective, only appeared on-screen to provide some comic relief.

Sellers, however, stole the show in the original *Pink Panther*. The critics agreed that his comedic performance was one of the best of all time, and it inspired five more films before his death in 1980, plus a cartoon series, books, comics, and action figures all in the *Pink Panther* canon.

This was the legacy that Shawn Levy would now inherit. Fortunately, he had his own comedic genius in Steve Martin, who not only played Clouseau in the updated film but cowrote the new screenplay (with Len Blum) based upon Blake Edwards's original characters.

On the second day of production, Levy received a call from the legendary producer Walter Mirisch, who wanted to meet with him. Mirisch had produced the 1963 film and, learning of the new film, was anxious to speak with the young director. Levy went over to Mirisch's offices where he was regaled with stories about the earlier film. Mirisch, well into his eighties at the time, explained to Levy that Blake Edwards would screen cuts of the movie and learn, fine-tune it, then screen it again and learn again. Mirisch was imparting the lessons learned forty-plus years earlier. And Levy was listening.

At the end of production, Levy assembled *The Pink Panther* and MGM lined up an initial test screening in Sacramento. During postproduction, Levy had a nagging feeling that something wasn't quite jelling with the film. He wasn't certain that it was working on all levels, as he had been with his previous films. So he flew to Sacramento with an open mind, ready to listen to what moviegoers had to say, as Blake Edwards had done so many years before. What he heard was painful. For the first time in his charmed career, Shawn Levy got a taste of what many directors fear most—audience rejection.

"We knew it the first time a joke swung and missed that this wasn't going to be our night. And then those scores came in and I'd never seen anything below an eighty, to be honest with you, and these were well below that. There was just no denying, the audience was *not* with the movie. They didn't like it, and in particular, they didn't like the tone of that early version. I've never been sent a message as resounding as that."

The plane ride back with the studio executives on the MGM jet to Los Angeles was miserable. Compounding matters, MGM was struggling financially, and the hope that this film would help catapult it back onto firm ground was now all but gone. Levy felt the weight of the world on his shoulders. One thought kept replaying over and over in his head: How in the hell are we going to fix this film?

As is often the case when faced with huge challenges on movies, filmmakers rebound with a new sense of determination. The next day, still licking their wounds from the previous night, Levy and the production team resolved to do whatever it took. Armed with the research, they read through the cards and the research report, interpreting what was behind the subdued scores. What they discovered was that the humor, especially the tone of the comedy reflected in the Clouseau character, was at the center of the problem.

That early version of the movie was quite risqué. The script—especially Clouseau's dialogue—was rife with double entendres. But the film also relied on physical comedy, the type of humor that typically plays to family audiences. As an adult comedy, the physical humor was out of place. And as an all-family comedy, the adult humor was unacceptable.

It had an identity crisis, with Clouseau speaking out of both sides of his mustachioed mouth.

"You can't do an innuendo-laden sexy romp and also ask people to bring their kids," explained Levy. "People don't want to go to a *Pink Panther* movie and worry about what their kids might see or hear."

This was a valuable lesson that the director was learning: *When you try to make a movie for everyone, often it ends up being for no one.*

A decision needed to be made on which direction to take the film, and it didn't happen overnight. In fact, the team would work for the next six months to reconceive the comedic tone of the script and make changes. During the process, Sony acquired the cash-strapped MGM in a complicated $4.85 billion deal. A new influx of money, along with fresh perspective from Sony executives, helped Levy recraft and reshoot the film. He removed the sexual innuendo and doubled down on the physical comedy. *The Pink Panther* was to be a purely fun, family-friendly film.

"We cracked it," Levy told me, and he was right about that. The movie earned $20 million on its opening weekend, which was no small feat considering it premiered during the Winter Olympics, and blizzards kept much of the Eastern Seaboard home that weekend.

Despite this happy ending, Levy's experience with *The Pink Panther* is a cautionary tale for filmmakers: the first commandment of making a successful film is "know thy audience." Understand what you have before you go into production, and whether the film you plan to make appeals to an audience segment that will get behind it, buy tickets on opening weekend, and become advocates for it.

That's the moral of this story. It's the same lesson that they teach you when you write your first short story in freshman English, and it's just as true when you're making a hundred-million-dollar film.

Consider our story from the last chapter about *Cocktail.* It succeeded at the box office, but not because it "spoke" to everyone (it certainly didn't speak to the film critics). Instead, at its core, it appealed to a slice of the population: young women in cocktail dresses who wanted to believe that Tom Cruise "could have it all." They weren't a huge chunk of the moviegoing population, but they were enough to form a critical mass of evangelists who would tell their friends about *Cocktail* and drive positive word of mouth.

Today, filmmaking is often a game of these subgroups, what is known as "psychographics." Movie executives must know if they're speaking to the cocktail dresses. Or soccer moms. Or fanboys of graphic novels. They must know whether they're making a movie for families or a movie that speaks just to the adults in the room.

Whereas demographics refer to a specific gender and/or age ranges— for example, males aged eighteen to thirty-four—psychographics refers to these more thinly sliced, diced, and microtargeted audiences. It's the way in which people are categorized by their attitudes and behaviors, or other psychological criteria. And for more than three decades, it's been my job to help filmmakers find these audiences and to speak to them.

Five or six times a week, I pull into a crowded parking lot just outside a movie theater, take a few deep breaths, and say a silent prayer that we've filled the house with an audience that reflects the right demographics and psychographics for the film that we're testing. During the car ride, I've already been on the phone once or twice with the screening supervisor to see how things are going inside the auditorium.

I've seen reports from my field personnel, who have been working day and night, stationed outside movie theaters and in malls offering tickets to people who seem to fall into the right demographics. Email blasts have been sent to our own massive database, all in the hope of qualifying a few hundred of the right respondents to turn out for the screening.

The blurb about the film that is used to entice moviegoers to the screening has been painstakingly crafted and edited by the studio executives and me, or by Rachel Parness, my protégée who runs the research end of the business at my company, often with filmmakers and studio executives weighing in. It typically discloses the film's basic premise, the names of the actors who have major roles in it, and even the title. The filmmaker's credits may also be included, particularly if associations with other well-known hits can be leveraged. Getting prospective moviegoers to commit to a screening is particularly tough if there are no major stars involved in a film, or if the subject matter is limiting. Comedies and big action movies typically compel greater interest than dramatic fare or smaller, indie/arthouse-type pictures.

Regardless of how easy or difficult it may be to get enough prospects to show up for a screening, we aren't interested in soliciting just anyone to fill the seats. Test audiences are carefully selected and demographically balanced to mirror the moviegoing public for that particular film, based upon what the studio and we anticipate it to be—and we can be wrong (more on this below).

Cities and theater locations are scrupulously considered as well, as we attempt to find the perfect microcosm to test the film, one that reflects the real world in which the movie will eventually be distributed and marketed. This entails finding a theater that has the best representation of the *presumed* target audience. I sometimes think of the theater as a giant puzzle that needs to be assembled piece by piece in order to achieve the perfectly balanced audience for the test.

The process is tricky, a far cry from the way it was done during the golden age of Hollywood, when it took only an announcement on the marquee to bring moviegoers into a theater to see a work in progress. Back in the 1940s, customers would buy tickets for the main attraction and stay to see the second feature, a bonus screening of a new film that the studio had just completed. As touched on earlier, the marquee sign alone, posted on the morning of the preview, would be enough to fill the theater with moviegoers that night (although sometimes a newspaper announcement was also used). Patrons would attend and pay for the regularly scheduled show, typically newsreels and a movie, and stay on to see a second film for free, one that had been billed only as an "important major-studio preview tonight."

Surprise was welcomed; attendees had no prior idea of subject, stars, or even the genre. The audience may have come to see a musical but stayed on to see a preview of a new Western. The opportunity to be among the first to see the picture, and another ninety minutes of entertainment in the pretelevision era, was enough to keep them in their seats.

We now live in an era of hypertargeted marketing, when Google knows everything about you from your annual income to the last time you called your mother. So at first glance, it may seem fairly simple to find a group of specific individuals in your metro area who are willing to see a free movie on a given Tuesday night. But this is not the case.

To the contrary, recruiting a test audience is among the most challenging tasks in my business.

It's tough because it's a big ask when you require attendees to get into their cars (usually on a weeknight, after work or school), fight traffic, find parking, grab a bite to eat, and line up outside a theater by 6 or 6:30 p.m. for a 7 or 7:30 p.m. start time.

As I know only too well, any number of things can go wrong with the recruit. Bad weather, traffic jams, and big televised sporting events can keep people home, even if they confirmed their attendance earlier that same day. This can cause swings in any direction in the demographic composition of attendees, and it's always a delicate situation when groups who've waited in line for an hour are turned away because of their gender, age, or sometimes even ethnicity, religious affiliation, sexual orientation, or education level. (This data is typically collected using a "recruit screener," a short survey that captures personal information and helps us to qualify prospective attendees when we're seeking a specific audience composition beyond age and gender.) We may be looking for females under the age of twenty-five, but if most of them show up with their boyfriends, we have to weigh the impact of letting the couples in against the risk of losing the young females because we don't want the males.

Director and former actor Ron Howard knows what it feels like to have the wrong audience watching your film. The legendary filmmaker knows his way around the screening process and uses it as adeptly as anyone in Hollywood. Most of his films have been huge crowd-pleasers—*Splash*, *Cocoon*, *Parenthood*, *Backdraft*, *Apollo 13*, *A Beautiful Mind*, *The Da Vinci Code*, and *Hillbilly Elegy*, to name a few—but, perhaps surprising to some, Howard does not use research to make his pictures commercially appealing. He embraces the preview process because he wants to be the best storyteller he can possibly be.

"I find a story that I personally love and believe in," Howard explained. "It has something for the audience, but it needs to be exciting and meaningful for me. First and foremost, it has to challenge me, interest me, and stimulate me in some way. From that point forward, I go about with the idea that I respect the audience and that movies are a kind of communication. What the previews are great for, more than anything, is for understanding how the film is actually communicating—not how you *want* it to communicate, not how you *dreamed* it would communicate. What is it *actually* saying to most people and how are they responding to it?"

As a young filmmaker, Ron Howard never thought about the preview process. He vaguely knew, from his acting experience, that television pilots were tested through a company called ASI (the very company that I now own). A pioneer in the entertainment research field, ASI operated Preview House in Hollywood, a four-hundred-seat laboratory theater equipped with a handheld "dial system" that audiences would use to record their second-by-second reactions to TV shows and commercials.

From an early age, Howard knew that he wanted to make the transition from acting to directing. When he was in his early twenties, Roger Corman, the master of B movies, gave Howard his break. In exchange for Howard taking a leading role in one of Corman's movies, Corman agreed to finance Howard's first feature film as a director, a youthful comedy called *Grand Theft Auto*, which features hot pursuits and big car crashes. (The film is no relation to the popular interactive game of the same title.) It's the story of a rich girl who steals her father's Rolls-Royce and runs off with her boyfriend to Las Vegas, where the young couple plans to marry.

Howard wrote the script and stars as the boyfriend. Even in 1977, the $602,000 budget that Howard received to make the film didn't go far. But it was a huge amount of money for Corman, who watched over the production with an eagle eye.

"The dailies were black-and-white dupes; we weren't allowed any 'temp music' or sound effects," remembered Howard, who kept to the tight budget throughout filming. When the movie was finished, Corman tested the film before a recruited audience and gave Howard notes on how to improve it based upon moviegoers' feedback.

After paying for a couple of test screenings, Corman, ever the deal-maker, announced to Howard that he had worked out a relationship with ASI (Audience Studies Incorporated) to screen the film for free. He explained that on days when people were recruited for TV commercial testing, they became disappointed if they only saw a minute or two of advertisements. ASI was looking for entertainment content to intersperse with the commercials, and the company was willing to provide Corman with free "dial system" research on *Grand Theft Auto* in order to keep their respondents engaged for a longer period of time. "So I'd like to have a screening at ASI," Corman told Howard. (Developed by ASI, this type of research seats participants in a theater equipped with devices that have dials. As commercials or other content are shown, participants are asked to turn the dial in one direction if they enjoy what they're seeing, and in the opposite direction if they dislike or are uninterested in what they're seeing. Detailed graphs are then provided to the client who commissions the study. This methodology is used to this day, especially for TV pilot testing. In 2014, my company acquired ASI.)

Unlike typical recruited screenings, which are conducted during evening hours when moviegoers are done with work or school, the ASI test was scheduled midday, which was unsettling for the young film-maker. He had never imagined that his film would be tested in this way, so when they arrived at the theater, Howard was already a bundle of nerves. Things got worse when he discovered that ASI was testing Geritol commercials that day, ads for an "iron-poor blood" remedy marketed to seniors.

"We walked in and it was literally blue-haired old ladies. I was completely freaked out, and Roger said, 'An audience is an audience, Ron. I think you'll find that.'"

Howard sat in the theater as the women watched his movie, this bawdy teenage-runaway, car-crash comedy with a lot of physical humor such as kicks to the groin. The ladies watching the movie had their hands on the dials, turning them up and down to indicate what they liked and disliked. Two women seated in front of Howard were completely disgusted by what they saw. Observing their reactions, Howard slumped lower in his seat, absolutely mortified.

When the screening was over, ASI produced a timeline of the film, noting key lines of dialogue or bits of action over which audience reaction, gathered from the dial mechanisms, was graphed. It was a visual depiction of where the film got its big laughs, and where it flattened out. Amazingly, the "blue-haired old ladies" had laughed . . . a lot. They really seemed to like the film.

Corman looked at the charts and pointed to the dips. "Just get rid of all those low points," he instructed Howard, who still finds humor in Corman's words because it was impossible to get rid of *all* the dips. But after additional postproduction work to improve the film, and testing it again with a more appropriate audience, Howard noticed that the movie did get a lot better. "It was a real eye-opener for me."

By the mid-1980s, Howard had directed a string of big box-office hits and had also achieved status as an independent producer, becoming fiscally responsible for his production budgets. Thinking back to his early experience on *Grand Theft Auto*, he realized he ought to be screening all of his films. At first, he did it on his own dime. He made up his own questionnaires and used the feedback to help guide his postproduction decisions. His method improved his movies and ultimately saved time and money.

To this day, Howard conducts small "friends and neighbors" screenings in his home in Connecticut before he shows his movies to the studio, just to get a jump on how well they're landing. After, when the studio previews his films using the formal process, he finds that early reactions from his friends and neighbors are often predictive of what he learns from the larger screening.

"Years ago, I got final cut," he said, referring to the creative control he has over his own films. "It's so much more liberating for me, because I never have to fear that a runaway focus group or a set of bad numbers is going to push my movie in a direction that I don't want it to go thematically. That said, I don't want to be shocked on opening day. I'd rather understand the aspects of the story and the movie that are difficult for an audience. And then I get to make a decision."

Howard talked about the choices that filmmakers face once they see how their movie plays to an audience. He may opt to change a part of the film that does not communicate what he intended. But like so many successful directors, he also weighs his changes against his original vision for the film, the story he wants to tell. "I won't change it if it's not the movie I want to make. I'm going to live with the fact that something disrupts the experience for the audience or disappoints them in some way. They may wish it went in another direction. But I'm going to choose not to act on that."

Howard described the testing process as a triangulation of the movie with the storyteller and the audience. "I always say it's just like telling an anecdote at a party. It's too long and you sort of fumble the punch line. But you can see people like hearing the story, and you like telling the story. So, you say to yourself, 'I think I can tell it a little better.' And the next time, you do."

Today, the audience selection process for all test screenings—including Ron Howard's films—is thankfully much more sophisticated and analytical. But that doesn't mean it's free of problems. We once held a screening for a movie that was decidedly skewed toward an older audience. But to understand if it could play more broadly, the studio executives wanted to gauge how it might fare with younger moviegoers. In the recruit specifications for the preview, we were asked to meet an under-twenty-five quota.

We booked the screening in a complex that typically attracts an older crowd, and by the time I arrived at the screening, there was a long line outside the theater, mostly people in their forties and fifties. The auditorium was already getting full, and given the length of the line, we knew we had more moviegoers than we actually needed for this particular preview.

The supervisor was carefully trying to balance the audience according to the specifications provided by the studio, and he was short on the under-twenty-five male and female groups. Staff members from my company began to pull young people from the line and escort them into the auditorium, passing by older people who had waited longer to gain entry. When it became obvious that younger moviegoers were being selected ahead of the older ones, things turned ugly. Understandably, many older people were upset and became quite vocal about their feelings. A group of women in their fifties shouted, "We're going to sue for age discrimination!"

It's regular practice to hire security for screenings to help with crowd management and, even more important, to protect against piracy. At this particular preview, one of our security guards was an off-duty policeman who occasionally moonlights with us to earn a few extra bucks. He literally had to flash his badge to calm down the crowd as we attempted to explain why we were allowing the younger moviegoers into the theater ahead of the older folks. It was an explosive situation that could have gotten out of hand.

Sometimes, however, a "wrong" recruit can turn into a happy surprise.

On a November evening in 2005, Betty Thomas arrived at the theater in Woodland Hills, about ten miles outside Los Angeles, that has been a favorite research site because of the good cross-section of socioeconomic segments in the surrounding area. She was early and assessed the long line of moviegoers waiting to get into the screening of her film. An Emmy Award–winning actress, having played Officer Lucy Bates in ninety-seven episodes of *Hill Street Blues* during the mid- and late 1980s, Thomas had already established herself as a successful feature film director. Her first big studio picture had been *The Brady Bunch Movie* (1995), and she followed that in quick succession with the Howard Stern film *Private Parts* (1997), *Dr. Doolittle* (1998), *28 Days* (2000), and *I Spy* (2002).

On that particular night, 20th Century Fox was conducting the first test screening of her latest film, *John Tucker Must Die*. Sitting in the mall's food court just outside the theater entrance with her production team, Thomas was fuming.

John Tucker Must Die is about a group of high school girls who retaliate against the star basketball player when they discover that he is secretly dating three of the girls at the same time. Thomas had cast an ensemble of talented and beautiful young actresses, primarily from popular TV shows, and the hunky gardener from *Desperate Housewives*, Jesse Metcalf, in the title role. In her mind, she had "a great little feminist movie" and she was certain that the film would appeal to young females.

Looking at the line, there were way too many older moviegoers waiting to gain access into the screening, and she was worried that they would skew the scores in the wrong direction. She knew how important it was to have the film play well that night, as the results would determine how much support the studio would throw behind her picture, the breadth of distribution, and the amount of advertising that Fox would allocate to it.

Thomas was confident the story was solid and that the comedy worked. But she also knew that the under-twenty-five crowd, particularly girls, would drive good scores, and she was really upset that so many guys and older people were entering the theater. "I took one look at that line," she said, "and thought, 'Old people! How are we going to find out anything?'"

Thomas recalled finding the screening supervisor from my company and telling him that the wrong audience had been recruited. "I had spoken with the studio executive earlier in the day and he told me that they were going to throw in a few older moviegoers. He asked me what I wanted, and I told him: young girls. So don't let me show up and see eight rows of forty-two-year-old guys."

The theater actually contained a lower percentage of older males than Thomas may have perceived. The studio wanted to see how the film played across genders and had requested a certain number of males be recruited. But, on their own, guys had little interest in seeing the film, and the research company staff had been worried all day about being light in the male demos. Those who arrived at the screening came mostly with their girlfriends, or in groups of friends that included both genders. The supervisor, his forehead dotted with beads of perspiration, had attempted to explain the situation to Thomas.

His words did little to calm Thomas's nerves. "On your first preview, the studio makes decisions," exclaimed Thomas. "They take the scores and can use them against us."

Feeling a sense of doom, Thomas entered the theater as the audience settled down. The usual announcement was made, asking moviegoers to forgive any imperfections in the still-unfinished cut of the film. The lights went down. The audience seemed engaged in the characters, three high school rivals who realize they're all dating John Tucker and a fourth girl who helps them uncover the deceit. They took delight in the plot to seek revenge on him. Thomas had been correct: the comedy worked, and there were laughs in all the right spots. Furthermore, she could hear a group of guys seated behind her laughing pretty hard throughout much of the film. "I turned to my editor and said, 'Holy shit! The funny stuff cuts through!' It appealed to guys as well as girls."

The film ended sweetly, punctuated with a good message about being genuine and honest. When the lights came up, the audience was smiling and there was light chatter in the theater as the survey cards were distributed. The focus group following was upbeat, drawing analogies to other popular teen hits like *Freaky Friday* and *Mean Girls*. At the end of the night, when Thomas reviewed the audience's scores of her picture, she saw that teen males rated the film nearly as highly as the female teens, and their intent to recommend the picture to friends, while not as high as females, was well above average. Older moviegoers liked it as well. Whereas older males scored it just averagely, older females were quite enthusiastic. "No guy who ever went to that movie said, 'I just saw this great feminist movie,'" said Thomas. "But guys did like it, and that was a nice surprise."

If Betty Thomas only imagined how the wrong audience might skew the results of her screening, recruitment missteps actually do occur from time to time. Just ask Mark Canton, producer of *300* and *Immortals*, who has felt the very real sting of a wrong recruit.

Canton grew up on the studio side of the business, starting in the mailroom at Twentieth Century–Fox after graduating from UCLA. He went on to head up production at Warner Bros. for more than a decade. In 1991, he became chairman of Sony's Columbia/TriStar Pictures and during his tenure, he green-lit many of that studio's broadly appealing hits like *My Best Friend's Wedding*, *Men in Black*, and *Air Force One*. He has participated in his share of research screenings and refers to a first test preview as a seismic change in the life of a film. "Most directors, especially the good ones, never really want to release their movies,"

Canton observed. "They would rather just keep working on their films. The screening process and the market research is sort of that time when they're realizing the baby is coming out."

While at Warner Bros., Canton had attended the very first research screening of *Goodfellas* in Sherman Oaks, California, first not only for the film but for its director, Martin Scorsese. Scorsese had not tested any of his previous films, so there had been a lot of anticipation, and some trepidation, about this preview. The audience was assembled, and Scorsese entered the theater under the cover of darkness. The film started, and promptly broke. "Where do you go from there?" asked Canton. It was not a good way to launch a test, and the experience was in the back of Canton's mind when he and Scorsese met up at another screening a few years later.

Canton's first movie as head of Columbia Pictures was *The Age of Innocence*. Scorsese had painstakingly crafted a tribute to Edith Wharton's novel about unrequited love in nineteenth-century New York. The film stars Daniel Day-Lewis as the aristocratic Newland Archer, Winona Ryder as his prim and calculating high-society fiancée, and Michelle Pfeiffer as the divorced Ellen Olenska who steals his heart. Along with lavish backdrops and authentic costuming, the story was clearly geared to upscale, well-educated moviegoers who would appreciate the period settings and classic characters. Yet, for reasons no one could later explain, the theater chosen for the initial test screening was situated in a lower-middle-class area of New Jersey. "I knew when we walked into the mall and there was a bowling alley. I could tell immediately it was the wrong audience makeup," Canton recalled.

With only a few minutes until the film was scheduled to start, and Scorsese already entering through the back door of the theater, Canton steeled himself for what was about to unfold. The movie started. The audience squirmed and fidgeted, and a few sighs of boredom could be heard. Before long, a couple of moviegoers walked out. Then a few more followed. "When Daniel Day-Lewis knelt down on his knee to kiss Michelle Pfeiffer's shoe, fifty guys got up screaming and left," Canton remembered.

After the screening was over, Canton, Scorsese, and a few others squeezed into a tiny office in the back of the theater and talked. It was the wrong audience, but there were still things to be learned from that preview. "It allowed me to tell Marty straight-up what I thought some of the issues were," remembered Canton. Ultimately, Scorsese would make big changes to the film, and although it never played to a broad audience, *The Age of Innocence* was critically acclaimed, nominated for five Oscars, and won Best Costume Design. It earned a respectable $32 million domestically. But the wrong audience drove home a big point, as Canton readily admitted years later: "If you want people to come from all around the world to see a film, you have to deal with bowling guys from *The Sopranos*."

George Folsey Jr. is an accomplished editor and producer, with five decades of movies and TV shows to his credit. He has regaled me with many interesting stories about the test screenings of his films, including a disastrous preview of *Animal House*, the 1978 frat comedy starring the legendary John Belushi. The film was directed by John Landis and shot in Eugene, Oregon, for less than $3 million. It was groundbreaking for its era, establishing a new genre of "gross-out humor," and when it was finished, the studio tested it in Denver, where it played like gangbusters. The very next night, it was scheduled for a preview at a big booksellers' convention in Atlanta. Someone associated with the film—Folsey couldn't remember who—thought it would be a great public relations opportunity for *Animal House*. The year before, *Star Wars* had been shown at the very same convention and had been a huge hit. Belushi, already a big star on *Saturday Night Live*, had agreed to travel to Atlanta for the preview, where he would surprise the crowd with his appearance.

After the Denver test preview was over, Folsey and head mixer Bill Varney packed up the film and took a late-night flight to Atlanta, arriving at about 5:00 a.m. Tired but bolstered by the great audience reaction to the film in Denver, they made their way to the hotel to catch a few hours of sleep. Their good mood quickly dissipated when they arrived at the convention center later in the day. The sound system was terrible; the screen in the room was an odd size, and they spent hours struggling to get the picture to project correctly; and, to add insult to injury, the movie didn't get underway until 9:30 at night, and by then, the conventioneers were tired . . . and quite drunk. They weren't set up correctly either. The crowd of erudite literary types was totally unprepared for the raunchy comedy that they were about to see. And it bombed.

"Belushi comes up to me at the end of the screening and he's like, 'What the fuck? We've got to recut this movie. It played terribly!'" Several of Belushi's friends were there, and they had also been at the Denver screening. They calmed the actor down, telling him that the movie was great. "The audience was the problem," they told him. "Leave George alone."

But Folsey learned an important lesson from the experience. "If it's the wrong audience, they're going to hand your head to you."

Most movies play best to a crowd, as long as it's the right crowd, as George Folsey and others have learned the hard way. In general, movies are conceived and developed as collective entertainment experiences. It's for this reason that most major studios now conduct press screenings with recruited audiences that fill the house. This has become a nice part of my business—setting up press screenings, where journalists are invited to watch a film before its release date and critique it. Studios have wisely recognized that a film has a better shot of getting a good review if the critics see it in a packed auditorium where they can hear the audience laugh, scream, or sniffle.

Marshall Herskovitz spoke to me about this, recounting what happened on *Dangerous Beauty*. Herskovitz, who directed the tasty artisan period piece, screened it for production executives Arnon Milchan and Michael Nathanson, who at the time were at New Regency, the studio that had produced it. Herskovitz remembered that they hated the picture and were quite vocal about their feelings. When the film was over, Nathanson said, "I just don't get it. I don't get this film. I don't feel it."

Four days later, the same cut of *Dangerous Beauty* was tested in Santa Monica to a full theater of recruited moviegoers. "It played really well," recalled Herskovitz. "It needed the audience in the room. People got into the movie and applauded at the end."

After the test screening was over, Nathanson approached Herskovitz and graciously said, "That does it. That's the last time I watch a movie for the first time in a screening room with three other executives. I apologize to you. The movie played so beautifully tonight, I don't care what the scores are. I cannot believe the difference!"

The ease or difficulty of recruiting moviegoers to a screening is often a first indication of the triggers that inspire innate interest to see a movie. The concept, the genre, the movie qualifier list (mention of previous movies of a similar type), and the film's stars are typically used to entice people to a test preview. We keep track of how many invitations we offer for a screening versus the number of people who accept, confirm, and actually show up. This is called the "recruit ratio." A broad-based comedy with a big-name star or two might be a moderate recruit, translating to an eight-to-one recruit ratio. Anything less than an eight-to-one ratio is considered relatively easy. This typically occurs with a sequel or a film within a popular franchise.

More often, recruiting is much tougher. I have seen thirty-to-one recruit ratios, and in certain cases, we have to offer incentives to moviegoers (a free movie ticket to a film of their choice, to be used at a later date, or even a cash incentive) in order to get them to attend a test screening. We encounter such difficulties when the concept is limiting, the cast is unknown, or the director and producer have no associations with other well-enjoyed films.

It's my policy to share this information with my clients by issuing a "recruit report" on every movie that I screen. Before the research is conducted, usually the day before or the day of the scheduled preview, we will send over a brief summary of feedback we obtain from randomly selected prospective audience recruits. The report will include the projected recruit ratio, which sometimes varies by gender or age, and what seems to frequently appeal to moviegoers as they accept the invitation or turns them off if they decline. This feedback is helpful to my clients, because it's often the earliest, real-world indication of the groups most interested in the film's basic premise, its title, and its cast.

By and large, we generally get the recruitment right. It's like the overall film research process itself, a combination of art and science, and there are few better examples of how a screening requires both data and finesse than the test screening of a little film called *Good Will Hunting*.

The story of how Matt Damon and Ben Affleck turned a Harvard writing project into an Oscar-winning film—and established themselves as movie stars in the process—is well-known Hollywood lore. It's one of my favorite anecdotes in this book. But around the time I completed writing this chapter, it became impossible to tell it without acknowledging a new and disturbing development, because this story includes Harvey Weinstein.

Today, Weinstein is known to all. Scores of women in our industry have brought his decades of sexual assault and harassment to light, and those crimes—more than any film—will most likely define his legacy.

While writing this book, I struggled with how to include Weinstein, or whether to include him at all. In the end, I decided that his part in these stories should not be played down or papered over. Weinstein remains a part of movie history—and will always remain so. Therefore, Weinstein will appear a few times in these pages, including right now, during the discussion of Damon and Affleck's screenplay for *Good Will Hunting*.

Most spec scripts sit on shelves accumulating dust, but Damon and Affleck's story was a hot commodity in the late nineties. And the two unknown actors drove a hard bargain: if studios wanted the script, they'd have to cast Damon and Affleck in the movie, too.

It would be an understatement to say that studios are hesitant about pouring millions of dollars into a film headlined by unknown actors. Movie stars drive people to the theater, not two unknown kids from Boston. But Weinstein took a chance on Affleck and Damon's deal and left it up to his lead researcher to see if the two upstarts with Boston brogues could put asses in seats.

That researcher was a man named David Kaminow.

Kaminow, having spent years at Sony as president of Strategic Worldwide Marketing, oversaw the market research on big movies with major name talent attached, films like *Men in Black 3*, *The Amazing Spider-Man*,

21 Jump Street, The Girl with the Dragon Tattoo (2011), *The Social Network, Quantum of Solace, The Grudge, Casino Royale,* and *Bad Boyz II.* Hardly the kind associated with difficult screening recruitment. He went on to become president of marketing at United Artists Releasing, working on critically acclaimed films like *American Hustle, Detroit,* and *Phantom Thread.*

But Kaminow's earliest years in the business were spent crunching numbers in the research department of Miramax at that special moment when the Weinstein brothers owned the independent movie business. Working for the studio that released only art-house pictures, one that often acquired foreign-produced films with no recognizable stars, Kaminow quickly learned the challenges of filling an auditorium for a test. "If we had calculated recruit ratios at Miramax, which we didn't, they would have been about eighty-to-one. For some of those screenings, we just couldn't get anybody into the theater," he recalled.

Fresh out of college, Kaminow was hired as a three-day-a-week assistant at the New York–based studio. It paid so little that his salary didn't even cover the cost of his commute into and out of Manhattan from his parents' home on Long Island. He took on a second job at Banana Republic just to make ends meet. On his first day at Miramax, he arrived at the office to learn that there was going to be a test screening that evening. With no concept of what that meant, Kaminow was "thrown in the deep end," as he describes his experience with the preview process.

Arriving at the theater that night, he remembered taking it all in— the people waiting in line, the surveys, Harvey Weinstein smoking cigarettes, the huddle around the scores, and the discussion afterward. "I was thinking, 'What's going on here?' But it kind of had this electricity. It was so exciting," Kaminow recalled. The night ended around 11 p.m., and all of a sudden it occurred to the eager young employee that the trains had stopped running and he had no way to get home to Long Island. "That's when I was introduced to car service," he said. "I thought that was just about the most luxurious thing!" (The studio paid for it, of course.)

Luxury was not a word often associated with employment at Miramax, however. The company was scrappy and there was constant pressure to keep overhead down. The offices—in an old industrial space in

Tribeca, way before industrial buildings and Tribeca were cool—were a mess of ancient equipment and scattered papers. To save money, most of the research was done in-house rather than outsourcing it to a professional market research firm.

Kaminow soon took on all kinds of menial tasks, rifling through stacks of surveys, hand-tabulating scores, and standing in front of the city's theaters for hours to conduct exit polls. He can remember sitting on a curb outside Carnegie Hall Cinema, counting the results of an exit poll survey for *The House of the Spirits*, then racing to a phone booth to call Harvey Weinstein to give him an update. (These were in the days before cell phones were ubiquitous.) It was a tough way to earn a living, but Kaminow was soaking it all up and loving every minute of it.

His diligence paid off. Weinstein soon took note of Kaminow and gave him more responsibility. Kaminow's star was rising within the company at a good time.

In 1996, Miramax released *The English Patient*, which won nine Academy Awards, including Best Picture, and earned nearly $80 million. The following year, the studio's slate included a film directed by Gus Van Sant, who had worked on a number of critically acclaimed films—*My Own Private Idaho*, *Even Cowgirls Get the Blues*, and *To Die For*, among others—none of which had done big box office. This one, *Good Will Hunting*, was the script that Matt Damon and Ben Affleck penned about a janitor who has a gift for mathematics and must wrestle with his troubled past to achieve his dreams. The two then newcomers star in the picture along with the late Robin Williams, who plays the role of the therapist who helps the young genius face his fears.

The executives at Miramax, including Kaminow, watched the movie when it was finished and they all loved it. But without an audience to confirm their own perceptions, they didn't know for sure how it would play. So Kaminow arranged for a test screening in Mountainside, New Jersey.

The recruit was very difficult. Damon and Affleck were totally unknown, and Miramax was resting on Robin Williams to pull moviegoers in. Williams was a big-name star, of course, but moviegoers were used to seeing him in comedic roles. The concept of him playing a shrink in a sensitive drama about a mathematical genius was not widely appealing, to say the least. "We were sweating it out, but we somehow managed to fill the theater . . . and it was a big house," said Kaminow.

Within the first ten minutes of showing the film to an audience, the Miramax executives knew that *Good Will Hunting* was going to be something extraordinary. The New Jersey moviegoers were clinging to every word, applauding, laughing, and crying. When the movie ended, the audience was ecstatic. The surveys were passed out, and Kaminow could hardly wait to get them back and start counting. The scores were unbelievably high.

"They were ridiculous! We had never seen anything like it at Miramax. You were there at the moment when an audience discovers something. It was truly a magical night." No one could have predicted, however, that this little film would catapult Damon and Affleck to stardom, and that their script would win the 1997 Oscar for Best Original Screenplay.

Most of Miramax's films were platformed, released into just a few theaters so positive word of mouth could build before they were distributed more widely. This is still a typical strategy for releasing independent or art-house films to save on marketing and distribution costs, and to allow them to "find" their audiences.

So it's not surprising that when *Good Will Hunting* was released in December 1997, it opened on just eight screens in New York and Los Angeles. Given the difficulty the studio experienced when they tried to recruit moviegoers to the test screening, they knew that word of mouth was needed to carry the picture.

On opening day, someone at the studio had the idea to rent a van and drive around New York City to see if they had managed to fill the theaters, and to get a sense of how audiences were reacting to the film. Matt Damon, Ben Affleck, and Minnie Driver were in New York at the time, so they were invited to ride along. Kaminow, along with the actors and some of the production executives, crammed into the van and off they went, theater to theater. "Every single one was packed," he remembered. "People were literally sitting in the aisles. It was so exciting!"

When the night was winding down, the group was feeling pretty terrific and decided to go for dinner at a place on the West Side called Café Luxembourg. When they arrived without a reservation, they were told they would have to wait a few minutes for a table, which they did. Standing in the front of the restaurant, they glanced into the main room, and one of them exclaimed, "Oh my God! Would you look at all those stars?" There, sitting across the room having dinner together, were Diane Sawyer, Mike Nichols, Goldie Hawn, Kurt Russell, David Mamet, Steve Martin, and Rebecca Pidgeon.

Without missing a beat, Matt Damon turned to his group and said, "You know what? One day people are going to look over at a table and say, 'Oh my God! It's Matt Damon and Ben Affleck!'"

One of the great paradoxes of moviemaking is this: it's not just that films aimed at everyone often end up for no one. The opposite is also true. When you make a movie that speaks to *someone*, sometimes it speaks to *everyone*. Consider the film *The Devil Wears Prada*. If there was ever a film targeted to a specific demographic, it was one set at a fashion magazine with the word "Prada" in the title.

Nevertheless, the studio was shocked and delighted when they first tested the comedy starring Anne Hathaway and Meryl Streep. Jim Gianopulos, then co-chair and CEO of Fox Filmed Entertainment, now the CEO of Paramount Pictures, shared his experience about the screening night, where I, too, happened to be present.

"You may remember it played across the board," he told me. "We realized that the movie is not about the fashion industry or the fashion anything. It's about entering the workforce. It's about aspirations. Those are universal themes. *Prada* never would have done the numbers it did if not for the males." (According to Meryl Streep, as mentioned in her 2010 Barnard College commencement speech, when men tell her which of her characters they enjoy most, it's almost always Miranda Priestly, the imperious fashion editor who many assume was inspired by Anna Wintour.)

Similarly, Russell Schwartz, who was president of marketing at New Line Cinema during the early and mid-2000s, recalled *Wedding Crashers*. "The research turned our heads," Schwartz noted. "Remember, this was always conceived as a young male comedy, guys crashing weddings to get laid. All of our initial [marketing] efforts went toward that demographic. We had a bunch of production executives, as well as the director and producers, singing the same tune and drinking from the same shot glasses."

At the initial test screenings of *Wedding Crashers*, the results—while strong across all demographics—pointed to women, both young and old, who loved and identified with the film.

From that point on, the studio realized the movie played strongly across all four quadrants and created advertising materials that addressed a broad swath of moviegoers. When the film opened, there was validation.

"The overall audience for the theatrical life of the film ended up being fifty-five percent female, forty-five percent male," continued Schwartz. "Production executives don't always know what they have."

In my line of work, sometimes we stumble into a happy accident. This was one of those times. When a movie is expertly crafted, the broader population tends to respond—no matter the genre.

We tend to think of America as a country of tribes—of NASCAR dads and soccer moms, of white collars and blue collars, ROTC cadets and hipster kids. And in many ways, I think we are that country. But not so much when the lights go down and the curtain parts. A well-crafted, entertaining movie can speak to everyone. In the darkness of the theater, people of all types and beliefs will suspend their differences for a couple of hours and just get swept away.

6.

FROM STRAIGHT-TO-DVD
TO FIVE F*CKING SEQUELS

J ason Blum has the strangest vehicle in Hollywood. He rides around in what looks to be a plumber's van from the outside but is totally tricked out as a fully functioning office on the inside, replete with computer, printer, and a monitor for watching movies.

I've known Jason for nearly two decades and have worked on research for most, if not all, of the movies he has produced. On any given evening outside a theater where we are screening a Blumhouse film, a line of limo drivers stands around their Chevy Suburbans and Lincoln Navigators, waiting to drive the big studio executives home. Jason's van is always parked a short distance away, and inside, his assistant answers emails and manages his schedule. After the preview is over, Jason sprints to the van and off they go, never missing a beat.

Few people in the movie industry have a better nose for sniffing out content and turning a nice profit on it than Jason Blum. Since opening his own company, Blumhouse Productions, in 2000, he has carved out a niche for himself as the preeminent producer of horror films, including the *Paranormal Activity*, *Insidious*, *Sinister*, *The Purge*, and *Ouija* franchises. He is among the best people in Hollywood at finding that next great indie hit—and getting to it before the competition even has time to put their car in drive.

There's an adage in Hollywood that nobody knows anything. The late William Goldman, the brilliant screenwriter behind *Butch Cassidy and the Sundance Kid*, *All the President's Men*, *Marathon Man*, and *The Princess Bride*, coined the phrase in his 1993 book, *Adventures in the Screen Trade*, and it's repeated often and with conviction to this day. Jason Blum quotes those very words when telling the story of how he came to produce the most profitable film of all time.

Blum was not yet thirty years old and working at Miramax, Harvey Weinstein's shop that dug up indie hits like they were San Francisco gold in 1849. Blum led their acquisitions operation and was the chief gold miner. It was his responsibility to find the next year's Oscar contender or breakout smash.

It was in the late 1990s when he first saw a "found footage" picture (a movie made to resemble home video) called *The Blair Witch Project*. It was being shopped around, and Blum, along with other Miramax executives, passed on it. So did everyone else in the industry. The film was screened at Sundance in January 1999 to a lukewarm response. Miramax passed again, opting instead to buy *Happy, Texas*, one of the most well received entries that year.

Meanwhile, Artisan Entertainment, a little-known distributor at the time, walked away from Sundance with *The Blair Witch Project*, for which it paid just over $1 million. Released in July 1999 and marketed principally via the Internet using faked police reports and news interviews, the little homemade horror film ended up taking in $140 million in the US and nearly $250 million worldwide. *Happy, Texas*—the darling of Sundance, and the film Miramax had acquired for $10 million—would earn just under $2 million when it was released in October of that year.

"Harvey [Weinstein] never let us forget it," said Blum. "It's one thing to hear over and over that nobody knows anything, but until you see it up close, it doesn't really sink in. All the buzz was about *Happy, Texas*, and there were nine other movies that distributors spent more money on at Sundance, none of which you've ever heard of."

The experience was a good one for Blum, because if he hadn't witnessed what happened with *The Blair Witch Project*, he never would have acted on another film that ultimately sent his career skyrocketing. "Cut to about eight years later," explained Blum, "and I got a DVD of *Paranormal Activity* as a directing sample."

In the movie, a young couple living in the suburbs of San Diego is terrorized by increasingly aggressive paranormal occurrences in their house, often in the middle of the night. Like *The Blair Witch Project*, the movie is filmed in the found-footage style and opens with scenes of the couple's everyday life, captured with their home video camera.

As strange, unexplained incidences continue to happen, the couple sets up the video camera on a tripod in their bedroom so they can record any ghostly activity while they sleep. The video time code is shown at the bottom of the screen, advancing in fast motion when the couple is sleeping peacefully but slowing to regular speed when the ghost is about to manifest. "I didn't think it would be a phenomenon," recalled Blum, "but I definitely thought there was some theatrical business in that movie."

By now, Blum had established Blumhouse Productions and signed a three-year "first look" deal with Paramount Pictures. He had offices on the Paramount lot and the muscle of the studio behind him. So he picked up the phone and called CAA, the agency representing *Paranormal Activity* filmmaker Oren Peli. Blum explained his interest in the little film and was told that it was too late. CAA had shopped it around, no one was interested in releasing it theatrically, and Anchor Bay had already purchased the rights for $150,000 to take it straight to DVD. Blum asked if the deal was inked and learned that the papers had not yet been signed.

Seizing the moment, Blum convinced CAA to hold off and set up a meeting with the director, a video game programmer from San Diego who had made the film on his own dime. Meeting with Oren Peli a few days later, Blum told him all about *The Blair Witch Project* and how the company that had seen its potential had turned that film into a gold mine.

"Luckily," explained Blum, "Oren was thirty-seven years old and had a job. He wasn't a destitute filmmaker. While $150,000 from Anchor Bay was a lot of money, it wouldn't change his life."

Plus, Blum offered a generous deal. He wouldn't take a percentage until after Peli had made at least what he would have gotten from the DVD deal that CAA had negotiated. The first-time filmmaker had little to lose and the possibility of a lot to gain. He agreed to let Blum come on as a producer of *Paranormal Activity* and try to get theatrical distribution and more money than the Anchor Bay deal.

Jason Blum swung into action. "The first thing I did," he recalled, "was show it to horror writers and directors. We held a screening at CAA, and I showed it to people in the horror community, and they liked it a lot. That gave me confidence." Next, Blum showed the film to two experienced entertainment journalists whose opinions he valued: John Horn, who was then writing for the *Los Angeles Times*, and Anne Thompson, who was with *Variety*. "Both thought it was really cool, and that gave me even more confidence."

When Sundance rejected the film because it had already been shown at the Hollywood Horror Film Festival, Blum submitted it to Slamdance, a festival that showcases emerging talent. And because the film had been shopped around by CAA, Blum and Peli recut it. Blum explained, "Oren had made a great movie, but it allowed me to call up all the distributors who already had a DVD of it and tell them that I have a new cut and they should come see it at Slamdance."

Just before Slamdance, John Horn wrote a glowing piece about *Paranormal Activity* for the *Los Angeles Times*, and Anne Thompson did the same in *Variety*. Blum sent copies of the articles to all his contacts, inviting every mover and shaker in Hollywood to Slamdance to see the film. But there was little interest. "I couldn't get a major decision-maker to sit in an audience with the film," Blum recounted. "Not even Harvey, who I had worked with for five years," he said, referring to Weinstein, who had pounded his own people for passing on *The Blair Witch Project*.

Blum called in favors. Begged. But it did no good. A few midlevel executives showed up at Slamdance, but once again, no one picked up the picture.

Meanwhile, the ever-tenacious Blum was also working his connections at Paramount, where Blumhouse Productions was housed. But he could not muster interest from anyone at the studio, and after several attempts, his phone calls to appeal for reconsideration were not even returned.

At the time, Paramount owned DreamWorks, and Blum had established a nice relationship with two of the executives from that company, Adam Goodman and Ashley Brucks. He gave them a DVD of *Paranormal Activity*, which they watched. Goodman and Brucks were not interested in the film as it stood, but they came back with an offer of $250,000 for the remake rights. In other words, they wanted to buy the movie so they could completely reshoot it.

"You and I know that remaking this movie is ridiculous," Jason told Peli, but it was their only option.

Plus, Jason had an idea.

He wanted to make the reshooting of *Paranormal Activity* subject to a test screening of the movie. "And the DreamWorks decision makers will have to attend that test screening. Real research in a real theater with real horror fans. Right?" Blum knew that the audience's response to the film was the best sales tool he had.

"It was the greatest idea I ever had in my career," said Blum. "I had seen how it played with horror enthusiasts when I screened it at CAA and Slamdance. I knew it would give the executives confidence."

At the screening, the film played just as Blum anticipated. It was a great night all around. Stacey Snider, then co-chairman/CEO of Dream-Works, attended, and she described how she envisioned the TV campaign to support the film's release. Along with Adam Goodman and Ashley Brucks, Snider was another top executive who would champion the film.

Two days later, Steven Spielberg, one of the founders of Dream-Works, watched a DVD of the film at his home. He liked it. A lot. And he quickly responded with ideas to make it even better, including several alternate endings that might be even scarier. The studio honchos met and agreed to invest money in a reshoot of the ending. All three of Spielberg's ideas were covered in that reshoot, including the ending that was eventually used in the film. The sound was also remixed to help ratchet up the scare quotient.

A second research screening was conducted to test the revised version with the new ending and sound design, and the scores shot up.

Realizing that the film worked, plans for the rewrite and reshoot were abandoned, and DreamWorks announced an October 2008 release. Jason Blum and Oren Peli were over the moon.

Then, as the release date neared, a strange quiet descended over the project. Phone calls to Blum stopped. In September, he found out why. DreamWorks and Paramount announced they were severing their relationship, and the fate of *Paranormal Activity* was up in the air. The parents were getting a divorce, and no one wanted the kid.

The film's advocates headed off in separate directions. DreamWorks formed a new alliance with Disney, and as much faith as Stacey Snider and Steven Spielberg had in the film, *Paranormal Activity* would be too odd a choice to release under the new circumstances. It wasn't going to happen at Disney.

Adam Goodman and Ashley Brucks moved into the Paramount organization, taking the US distribution rights for the film with them. Goodman became co-president. But internally, an ongoing debate about *Paranormal Activity*'s potential persisted. Although Goodman believed in the film, there were others in the senior ranks who argued strongly against its release. Once again, the movie was in limbo, and Jason Blum feared that for all intents and purposes, it was dead domestically.

Winter stretched into spring. "I'm producing other movies by now," recounted Blum. "But imagine Oren. He's just sitting there, watching his dream being crushed."

Finally, word came down that the studio was going to schedule another test screening, this time for Paramount Film Group president John Lesher. Lesher was a no-show at the preview, but all the other Paramount top brass attended. What they experienced was something they could not have foreseen by watching a DVD of the film in their offices. In a darkened theater filled with horror enthusiasts, *Paranormal Activity* played even better.

At the Paramount screening, just like every other time the film was previewed to a crowd, the time code triggered a Pavlovian response from the audience. As the seconds at the bottom of the screen ticked off, first in fast motion but then slowing to real time, the tension in the theater became palpable. There were audible murmurs, nervous laughter, shifting in seats. When the ghost's presence became evident, there was a collective jump. Later in the story, as the demon drags the sleeping woman from the bed, the screams from the audience were deafening.

It was a textbook case of how test screening research can inform big decisions and a turning point in the film's destiny. Based on that preview, everyone at the studio became excited, and the Paramount machine was put into high gear behind it. "They woke up and saw that they might actually make money on it," said Blum.

Paramount Pictures released *Paranormal Activity* in twelve theaters on September 25, 2009. It performed so well that more theaters were added in each consecutive week. By Halloween, the studio had expanded distribution to more than 2,400 screens, with full marketing and publicity support behind it.

The little homemade horror film that initially cost just $15,000 to make would go on to gross nearly $108 million domestically and take in another $85 million in the international market. It spawned a franchise that has generated nearly $900 million in worldwide business to date and made Oren Peli a very rich man.

Paranormal Activity catapulted Jason Blum's career, and he is now one of the most influential producers in Hollywood. In addition to his very lucrative horror franchises, he has produced *The Gift*, *The Boy Next Door*, *Split*, *Truth or Dare*, *Halloween* (2018), *The Invisible Man*, and the critically acclaimed films *Whiplash*, *Get Out*, and *BlacKkKlansman*.

"Until you screen it in front of strangers and feel what it feels like to be in that theater with those strangers, you have no perspective on your movie," said Blum, a nod to William Goldman's axiom that nobody knows anything.

"I knew it would work theatrically," he admitted, "but I didn't think that there would be five fucking sequels."

This is what I remember from the first screening of *Paranormal Activity* in March 2008—I was not looking forward to seeing it. As I drove to Glendale, I was bracing myself for a long night of work. It's not that I dislike scary movies. I like good ones very much. I just didn't want to watch yet another found-footage movie with a shaky camera that makes everyone in the theater nauseated. Paramount had just released *Cloverfield*, which was filmed in this way, too, and I thought I was in for a knockoff.

I was wrong. Very wrong.

Later that night, after seeing *Paranormal Activity*, my attitude drastically changed. After the audience had cleared out, I approached the studio executives with the topline scores, thinking, "Holy shit! This is one scary movie."

Stacey Snider, then the CEO of DreamWorks, had to be escorted to her car afterward—she was too creeped out to be in the parking lot alone. Then there was Christine Birch, the head of marketing for Dreamworks at the time, who had to sleep in a hotel room that night. She didn't want to be alone in her house.

Without question, it was terrific horror genre filmmaking.

I would be remiss in sharing Jason's Blum's story of *Paranormal Activity* without crediting Paramount Pictures for its stellar marketing and distribution strategy. The studio platformed the film, releasing it in just a few theaters to let word of mouth spark demand in a broader swath of the country. Based on many findings from the research process, expansion was carefully calculated, leveraging a social media component to build anticipation. And rather than cutting traditional horror movie TV spots that feature suspenseful scenes from the movie, the studio filmed real audience reactions at the earliest showings and used those clips in its TV advertising. It may not seem unique now, but it was cutting-edge at the time. The well-planned viral campaign turned what could have existed as a great little cult movie into a full-fledged blockbuster.

At the outset of this book, I mentioned that the award-winning director Ang Lee once quipped that "Picasso never audience-tested his paintings," and Ang is not alone in leveling that criticism. By far, the biggest argument against movie screenings is that somehow audiences don't know—*can't know*—what a good movie is.

With all due respect to Ang, who happens to be one of my five favorite living directors, and everyone else who shares this belief, that's a load of crap. My experience in fact is exactly the opposite. Not only do audiences know what a good movie is—sometimes, they know better than the filmmakers themselves and the executives charged with shepherding the films to the screen.

Paranormal Activity is just one example. There are so many moments in Hollywood history when audiences have saved a movie from the scrap heap—or, just as important, prevented the studios from changing an innovative film because they thought it wasn't marketable enough.

Indeed, one of the most powerful lessons I've learned from more than thirty years in film screening is this: most of the time audiences can sniff out a commercial movie better than the people who work in the business.

The producers Chuck Roven and Alex Gartner shared a story about the time they partnered with Warner Bros. to adapt the old TV show *Get Smart* into a film. The movie features Steve Carell as the bumbling secret agent Maxwell Smart, and it was daring in that it presented an uncharted combination of big action sequences akin to those in *The Bourne Identity* and shticky humor reminiscent of the original Mel Brooks–Buck Henry television show.

The studio wanted to make sure the movie worked, so they tested it four times in several different locations. And each time, the audience agreed. "It wasn't a fluke," Roven said. "The great thing about *Get Smart* is that every screening was a great screening."

The movie was only changed in minor ways from the original before it was shipped to theaters, where it would earn more than $230 million worldwide. "*Get Smart*," as Gartner said, "was more a process of validation than of change."

If there's a takeaway from this chapter, it's this: movie research is just as important for validating that a movie works as it is for identifying any issues that spark any changes to it.

Donald De Line, the top-tier Hollywood producer behind films such as *Ready Player One*, *Fool's Gold*, and *Body of Lies*, learned this firsthand back in 2003. He recalled a disconcerting phone call with Sherry Lansing, who, sixteen years after the release of *Fatal Attraction*, was ensconced at Paramount Pictures, running the studio with Jonathan Dolgen.

De Line, who currently has a production deal at Warner Bros., had been a studio executive for many years, beginning his career at Disney and eventually serving as president of Touchstone, where he oversaw *Pretty Woman*, *What About Bob?*, and *Father of the Bride*, among other big hits. Now operating under his own banner, De Line Pictures (based at Paramount at the time), he was in the throes of postproduction on *The Italian Job*. The movie is a complex heist picture, and the production team was rushing to assemble the pieces so they could make an end-of-May release date. Now down to the wire, De Line and his director, F. Gary Gray, felt the movie was still missing something, an elaborate chase scene that would help it compete with the other big action movies slated for the summer.

De Line had phoned Lansing to ask if Paramount would put up an additional $6 million to shoot another action sequence. Lansing pushed back. She said, "Let's see what the editor's cut looks like, and if I agree that you need it, I'll give you the money. If not, we'll test it and see what an audience thinks."

De Line felt a chill go down his spine. "If we test it and find out it doesn't work, we won't have time to shoot the additional footage and still make the summer release date," he replied.

Lansing's voice softened. "Honey, we're not making a release date. We're making a movie. Don't worry about the date; we can release it later."

De Line respected Lansing's point of view. Having been on the studio side for eight years, he would have said the very same thing had the tables been turned. But at that particular moment, and in his role as producer of the film, he could not help but feel disappointed. "You do whatever you can to protect your movie and I truly did think we needed the additional footage. It had been such a complicated process. We knew we had a good film, but we thought it was incomplete."

De Line went back to the cutting room and said, "Okay, guys, we're not going to get to do our additional shooting. We're going to put the movie together to the best of our abilities right now and we're showing it to Sherry. She wants to see it in ten days."

The team—including Chris Rouse, a particularly talented editor who would go on to win awards for his work on *United 93* and *The Bourne Ultimatum*—jammed round the clock to finish a cut of the film. When they delivered it to Lansing, it had cards in places where they thought they needed additional sequences. They watched it together in a screening room on the lot, and when the lights came up, Lansing turned to the group and announced, "It's fantastic. You don't need anything." She instructed them to remove the cards, told them where to piece the film together, and as she turned to leave the theater, she said, "Let's go screen it."

On one hand, De Line and his team were excited by Lansing's genuine enthusiasm for the film. But they also knew it faced its biggest challenge yet, a test before a real, live, moviegoing audience. Without a big action sequence in the third act, they still had serious doubt that the film was ready.

"We didn't have the wave," said De Line, referring to *The Perfect Storm*, a big-hit film of 2000 that starred Mark Wahlberg, who was also one of the leading actors in *The Italian Job*. "This is a very 'handmade' movie," he explained. "We did it on purpose that way, harkening back to the seventies. It wasn't CG [computer generated]. It didn't have visual effects. Our biggest stunts were all practical. We didn't have these things because that's not the movie we made. It's a heist film. Nonetheless, the studio wanted to compete on that level.

"The marketing department had been telling us they were having trouble cutting competitive advertising materials because everything else that summer had giant 'set pieces,'" De Line continued. "This is where things get confused and people get confused." His reference is to the spectacular chase, fight, or action sequences that distinguish most tent-pole films. Those set pieces are often teased in the trailers and television spots to entice moviegoers to see big-production summer and holiday movies.

On the day of the screening, De Line's team was subdued and nervous. They knew that if the movie didn't do well at its test, it was going to be pulled from the summer release schedule, and pushing the release date of a film typically sends a signal to the world that there is a problem with it, a stigma that the filmmakers dreaded. Early in the day, De Line drove to Pasadena, where the movie would be previewed, to do a sound check. It was a beautiful day; the sun was out and warming the morning air. But to De Line and his people, it felt dark and dreary. "We were expecting the worst."

Later that evening, in his car on the way back to Pasadena for the preview, De Line received a call on his cell phone from the famed Hollywood agent Ari Emanuel, who represented Mark Wahlberg. Emanuel was nervous. He, too, had spoken with the studio honchos and learned that the May 30 release hinged on the film's performance that night. De Line's worst fears took shape in his mind. This was going to be a public humiliation.

By the time he got to the theater, the audience was seated and the studio executives were arriving one by one. Everyone had come out to see how the film would do at its first preview. De Line nervously greeted Lansing and Dolgen. An executive from the research company announced that the film was about to start, and De Line took his seat. He reflected on the three years of work he had invested in the film, and braced himself for the screening. "If it doesn't work, you go through months of mourning. You then have to go through selling the movie and putting on your game face, all the while knowing you have a sick child. And you can't show that to the world because it's your obligation as a professional to push that baby out the door and love it."

And then something wonderful happened. He realized he was listening to an audience falling in love with a movie. It was entertaining them. They were having fun with it. It was exciting and engaging, and everything that a summer film should be. While he had been focusing on what he thought it was missing, he forgot about everything that it had. It took a few hundred ordinary moviegoers to put things back into perspective for De Line. When the lights came up and the moviegoers filled out the surveys, their evaluations of *The Italian Job* were terrific. "We literally walked out of the auditorium, got the numbers, and Sherry said, 'Lock it.' We never screened it again. We never tested it again. We finished the movie and released it."

Just as planned, on May 30, 2003.

One of the best and most meaningful examples of an audience rising up to protect an important film happened to Dick Zanuck—the producer we met during the *Jaws* story. Zanuck readily admitted to me that he tried to finesse the recruit when *Driving Miss Daisy* was first tested. He told the story with a twinkle in his eye, a principled man admitting to something mischievous, not unlike a straight-A student owning up to once ditching class. But the strategy was serious business at the time, and Zanuck talked about it to illustrate the lengths to which he and his partners went to protect their picture.

In the decade following *Jaws*, Zanuck and his partner, David Brown, were busy building an impressive roster of successes with films like *Cocoon* and *The Verdict*. Along with Zanuck's wife, Lili Fini Zanuck (whom he had married in 1978), they acquired the rights to *Driving Miss Daisy* from the playwright Alfred Uhry, who intended to launch it as a Broadway play. The story touched the producers, and they felt the writing was brilliant.

Originally, the Zanucks and Brown took the film concept to MGM/UA, but when Alan Ladd Jr. left the company in 1988, any chance of a deal fell through. The producers then shopped the project to every other major studio in Hollywood, but not a single one was interested in making a period picture about an elderly Jewish woman and her African American chauffeur. At a time when *Batman*, *Indiana Jones*, and *Die Hard* reigned at the box office, no one thought *Miss Daisy* would stand a chance.

After three pitch meetings at Warner Bros., the producers offered to slash their production budget to $7.5 million, a paltry sum that was a fraction of what the typical movie cost in the late 1980s. As Zanuck explained, "They finally relented. We shamed them into making the movie, eventually asking Warner Bros. for just $5 million. We put up the completion bond, which I'd never done before and will never do again. And the studio wouldn't insure Jessica Tandy, who had heart problems and was nearly eighty years old at the time. So we took that on, too. It was a big risk, and we were on the line ourselves personally."

The Zanucks, who by this time had split off from David Brown to form the Zanuck Company, found the balance of the funding they needed to make the film through international distribution deals and proceeded to shoot the picture on a shoestring, cutting corners wherever possible and bringing it in on budget to avoid what could have been their own financial ruin. When it was finished, Zanuck phoned the head of Warner Bros. at the time, Bob Daly. "We're ready to show you the picture, Bob."

Daly responded by telling Zanuck that he would gather the studio executives and arrange a time to screen it on the lot. "I'm not going to do that," replied Zanuck. "I want you to see it in front of an audience."

Daly bristled, telling Zanuck that when the studio sees a film for the first time, they want to look at it in the privacy of a screening room, not with the general public in a regular theater. But because he knew it would play much better with an audience, Zanuck persisted. "Bob," he said, "this is how we're going to do it. Give us the courtesy." Daly finally agreed.

Zanuck then called the research company that most studios used and said, "Look, we need to pick a theater in a Jewish neighborhood. I want a lot of older people, and some older African Americans, too." After he hung up, he thought about what he had just done. Wouldn't the Warner Bros. executives walk into the theater, take one look at the audience, and realize that he had stacked the deck? So Zanuck went a step further, and on the day of the screening, he told the studio people that he always hates when the executives march in after the audience is seated. He said, "I'm going to run a short prior to the film, and while it's playing, come in and take your seats in a less obvious way." So when the studio people got to the theater, they entered under cover of darkness as the short was playing, and all they saw were the silhouettes of seated moviegoers.

After the short, *Driving Miss Daisy* was previewed to uproarious reactions. Zanuck remembered moviegoers laughing, crying, and applauding. At the end, some rose to their feet and actually cheered. The studio executives were dumbstruck. They were so ecstatic with what they saw, both on the screen and within the crowd, that they seemed to excuse the preponderance of gray hair that emerged from the seats as the theater emptied.

Afterward, there was pandemonium in the lobby as the studio execs congregated to talk about the gem of a film they had just watched. Basking in the glow, Zanuck recalled the head of Warner Bros. distribution, Barry Reardon, approaching the group. Reardon took a piece of paper from his pocket and said, "I had no idea. I thought this was going to be something for *Masterpiece Theater*. Here's my distribution plan." He then proceeded to rip the paper to shreds, signaling that he would rethink the way he would distribute the movie for a much broader audience. Bob Daly, who was standing nearby, concurred. "This is a commercial picture," he exclaimed.

Zanuck's ploy had worked, and the Warner Bros. executives knew they had something special. The studio released the picture just before Christmas 1989 to qualify for that year's awards. It built momentum for months, commanding the number-one box office position for four weeks, then held within the top-five highest grossing films for another six weeks. Studio executives all over Hollywood kicked themselves for passing on the project. *Driving Miss Daisy* grossed more than $100 million domestically, nearly $150 million worldwide, and pulled in another $50 million in VHS and DVD rentals.

In addition to the film's winning the Academy Award for Best Picture of 1989, Jessica Tandy—whom the Zanucks had paid to insure— won for Best Actress in a Leading Role. (It was the first Oscar for the actress, who had begun her career in the 1930s.) The writer, Alfred Uhry, who won a Pulitzer for the stage version of *Driving Miss Daisy* in 1987, also received the 1989 Oscar for Best Adapted Screenplay. A fourth Oscar was awarded for Best Makeup. (Morgan Freeman and Dan Aykroyd both received nominations for their roles in the picture.)

Yet, despite all the accolades on Oscar night, the best epitaph for *Driving Miss Daisy* might have been penned months before by the film critic Roger Ebert. "After so many movies in which shallow and violent people deny their humanity and ours," he wrote, "what a lesson to see a film that looks into the heart."

Dick Zanuck died in 2012 and went to his grave still a little apologetic for what he did that day. "Even all these years later, I would hate for those studio executives to think I was trying to pull a fast one," he had told me. "But I wanted Warner Bros. to be one hundred percent behind the picture, and I did what I thought needed to be done to ensure that."

If he were still here today, and feeling bad about his underhandedness, I'd remind him what Ebert wrote.

And I'd say: "You know, Dick, no matter what you did, it wasn't you who convinced the studio of *Driving Miss Daisy*'s heart. It was the moviegoers. They've done it before, and they'll do it again."

In these stories that have been shared with me by some of Hollywood's biggest luminaries, I'm struck by the range of emotions that the screening process evokes. I expected to hear about feelings of angst and fear, frustration and disappointment, or joy and relief when things go well. But so much more happens within the psyches of filmmakers and studio executives when they take their films out for what is essentially a trial run with a real-world audience.

Mike Medavoy is a tough, experienced studio executive and producer with a long list of modern classics to his credit—*Platoon*, *The Terminator*, *The Silence of the Lambs*, and *Sleepless in Seattle* among them. Yet he was brought to tears when *Philadelphia* was screened.

"I knew it was going to be one of the last movies I did at TriStar," he explained. "And I was also choked up by the fact that I'd done something that I really felt proud about." The 1993 film, which was directed by Jonathan Demme and stars Tom Hanks and Denzel Washington, was revolutionary for its era, tackling prejudice against victims of the HIV/AIDS epidemic during a time when they were feared and ostracized. On the night it was screened to a test audience of perhaps three hundred moviegoers, Medavoy recognized the power of its message and how it might influence audiences around the world. The movie earned critical success, and Academy Awards for Hanks for Best Actor in a Leading Role and for Bruce Springsteen's "Streets of Philadelphia" for Best Original Song.

Another memorable and emotion-filled story was shared by Steve Carr, who is probably best known as the director of *Daddy Day Care* and *Paul Blart: Mall Cop*, broad comedies that had wide appeal and hit blockbuster status. But some of his most indelible and cherished memories are around the test screening of his very first film, a stoner comedy called *Next Friday*.

From the time he was a child, Carr knew he wanted to be an artist. Raised by a single mother who lovingly supported his dream, he became an accomplished painter. He's not only extremely talented but also very determined. After attending the School of Visual Arts in Manhattan on a full scholarship, he partnered with an equally talented graffiti artist, Cey Adams, and the two became, essentially, the in-house design studio for Def Jam Records. They were responsible for all of the album cover art during the label's heyday.

Carr eventually approached Def Jam's founder, Russell Simmons, about directing a music video. Carr knew virtually nothing about directing or filming, but his artistry and tenacity were enough to convince Simmons to give him a chance. While filming his first video, the crew asked him a question that he couldn't answer. Lacking experience and unaware of how to handle the situation, Carr excused himself to use the bathroom. Alone, he tried to calm his nerves and hoped that the answer would miraculously come to him. It did not. But by the time he returned to the set, the crew had figured out what to do on their own. The question never came up again.

Before long, Carr had the process down and was working with major rap and hip-hop artists like Jay-Z, Lauren Hill, Moby, Redman, Nelly, and Public Enemy. When he moved from New York to Los Angeles, where a majority of the music videos were shot, a friend put him in touch with Mike De Luca, who was then president of production at New Line Cinema (now chairman of Metro-Goldwyn-Mayer Motion Pictures Group). New Line had an Ice Cube film in development, a sequel to the comedy hit *Friday*, called *Next Friday*. De Luca was looking for a director who could handle the project, and the young music video director wanted the job—badly.

De Luca and Carr hit it off, and a meeting was set up with Ice Cube's producing partner, which also went well. The next step was to pass muster with the star himself. So New Line arranged for Carr to fly to Arizona, where Ice Cube was shooting *Three Kings*. Carr, who by now was a big, award-winning music video director, was more than a little surprised when he boarded the commercial flight and discovered that New Line had booked him a seat in coach. Scrunched into the very last row on the plane in a seat that didn't even recline, Carr was thinking, "What am I doing? I could be making a Mary J. Blige video right now."

But he hit it off with Ice Cube and ended up getting the job. "It was a small movie. I think it cost $6 million to make. But I had the best time," recalled Carr of his theatrical directing debut.

When the film was finished, it was screened in New York and Los Angeles, and the studio recorded the audience laughter during the previews, which is done quite often to see where the jokes land or miss. (It's also often done on horror films to gauge the scares.) After the tests were completed, New Line gave Carr a copy of the film with the audience laugh track.

"I still have the VHS," Carr admitted as he recounted his first experience with test audience previews. "Later on, as years went by, if I was in a bad mood or upset by something, I would put it on and just hear the people laughing. And I loved it. The best way I can describe it—and I don't know that I can articulate it—there's a warmth, I mean a physical warmth that I feel."

On the night that *Next Friday* opened, Carr, the producers, the studio executives, and a few friends hired a limousine and went around to theaters to see how the movie was playing. In Westwood, an area with several large movie houses near the UCLA campus, one of the theater managers came up to the group and told them that he couldn't keep his ushers out of the auditorium. They kept running in to see bits of the hilarious new comedy.

Carr and his group walked into the theater and took their seats in the darkness, listening to the audience's laughter. Years later, he recalled, "It was one of the most wonderful things that has ever happened to me in my whole life."

7.

SCORES SETTLE SCORES

The craziest thing about the 2017 Academy Awards was how predictable they were . . . until the last five minutes.

All of the favorites won in their respective categories that evening: Casey Affleck won the Oscar for his work in *Manchester by the Sea*; Viola Davis won for her powerful performance alongside Denzel Washington in *Fences*; Damien Chazelle won Best Director for the musical *La La Land*.

La La Land, of course, was the favorite to win Best Picture that evening. The film was set in Los Angeles and ornamented with beautiful song and dance numbers. It's a picture about the magic of Hollywood, a tribute to the movie business, and there's nothing the movie business loves more than some self-congratulation. So at the end of the evening when Faye Dunaway and Warren Beatty announced that it had won Best Picture, no one was surprised.

In fact, I was so sure that *La La Land* would win that my husband and I had already started making our way out of the theater and downstairs to our car. I didn't see what happened next: a flurry of hushed and frantic conversations on stage, followed by one man—who was not well-known to casual moviegoers—stepping up to the microphone and taking control.

It fell to Jordan Horowitz, the producer of *La La Land*, to tell the room and the one billion people watching around the world that his film hadn't actually won. "*Moonlight*, you guys won," he said. Then he added, "This isn't a joke."

Most people never have their dream ripped away from their grasp in such a fashion, and I would venture that Horowitz and his colleagues are the only ones who've had it happen on live TV in front of one-seventh of the world's population. Had it been me, I'm not sure how I would have reacted. I certainly wouldn't have been as Zen about it as Jordan.

Months later, I asked him about being the victim of one of the worst gaffes in television history, and he began by saying, "You know, Kevin, the nice thing about it was how it brought out the human side of Hollywood."

The chain of events leading up to Faye Dunaway and Warren Beatty announcing the wrong winner may have involved a representative of PricewaterhouseCoopers handing the wrong envelope to the stage manager because he was too busy snapping a photo of Emma Stone to post on Facebook. But at this point, who cares?

Hearing Horowitz talk about it months later, I was struck by the fact that the most important outcome of the error was how it refocused attention—at least within the film industry—on the filmmakers themselves. During awards season, movies become like horses in a horse race. They're seen less as art than as vehicles to win some shiny gold trophy. Everyone becomes a prognosticator, a pundit, an oddsmaker. But when Oscars night 2017 went sideways, the movie business was jolted out of that mindset. People suddenly had sympathy for anyone associated with the gaffe—the women and men responsible for *La La Land* who left the stage empty-handed, and for those who rightfully won for *Moonlight*, who were robbed of their moment of glory.

For my money, the most important story about *La La Land* was not what happened during the last five minutes of the Academy Awards but rather what happened during the first twelve minutes of its first test screening. Because the story of *La La Land* is one of the more important examples of the power of test research. And I was lucky enough to be along for the ride.

Let's flash back to about a year before the 2017 Oscars. Production on *La La Land* had just wrapped, and Horowitz and the studio, Summit Entertainment, called my firm to set up a test preview.

La La Land was one of those rare pictures that came out of postproduction almost fully polished. The final scene, a beautiful dance number between Emma Stone and Ryan Gosling, left few dry eyes in the theater.

There was one hitch with the film, however. *La La Land* was a musical, but for the first twelve minutes of the original cut, no one sang, and no one danced. The film had an overture, introducing Ryan Gosling's character fiddling with a tape in his car, and then Emma Stone's character rehearsing an audition. The first musical number, "Someone in the Crowd," occurred after that setup, when her roommates try to convince Emma Stone's character to join them for a night out. The girls break into song and dance. It was the first signal that *La La Land* wasn't a standard romantic comedy, and the audience, understandably, was like, "What the hell?"

"People just didn't know what the movie was," Horowitz said of the first test screening.

Marc Platt, who produced the movie with Horowitz, explained. "The rules of the film hadn't been set up at the beginning. [The test audience] didn't reject the film. But they weren't prepared for the singing. Twelve minutes into it, all of a sudden, characters started singing and they didn't know why."

Eventually, the moviegoers at that first test picked up on what was happening. "Oh, this is a musical," they realized, but for the first act, they were distracted. "People were focused on their confusion instead of being focused on the picture," remembered Horowitz. "So after that screening we went back and we thought about how we could open the picture."

Interestingly, they already had what would become their solution in the can, so to speak. They had filmed an incredibly ambitious musical sequence, "Another Day of Sun," on a portion of a real Los Angeles freeway where they had staged a traffic jam. That scene, which the filmmakers referred to as "Traffic," had not been included in the first version of the film.

"We loved the number and we were so proud of how hard it was to shoot it," explained Platt. "It was done on a freeway during a heat wave, and we had only a set number of hours to shoot it. But we felt stylistically that it was different from the rest of the film. It was not main characters singing. It was not narrative like the rest of the songs. It wasn't furthering the story."

"We all thought the number was great," Platt elaborated, "but we just weren't sure that stylistically it was part of the film. It was more of a thematic expression." So by the time the first test screening rolled around, "Another Day of Sun" had been cut altogether.

"But then the screening happened, and ultimately, that's when we figured out that we needed to just open with 'Traffic' straight up," recalled Horowitz.

Marc Platt explained, "Through the previewing process, we learned that the strongest way to start the film was to have 'Another Day of Sun' be the overture, then the title, then have the movie begin. Then you meet the Ryan Gosling character and the Emma Stone character and you're off to the races. Once we got into the story, the audience was on very firm ground."

Horowitz added, "The test screening helped us understand how to integrate the traffic sequence and how to better set the tone for the picture. We didn't really change that much else about the movie."

They didn't need to.

The new version of *La La Land* opened with the sensational musical overture, panning across the 130-foot-high express ramp as the actors, stuck in gridlocked traffic, emerge from their cars and begin to dance. They leap onto the hoods and pirouette on the concrete median. A band appears in the back of a truck, and dancers appear as if they're stretching back to the horizon. The music swells, the title comes up, and then the camera pans down and introduces us to the lead: Ryan Gosling.

La La Land's reviews singled out the traffic sequence as a "bravura" scene, its "boldest musical number." It set the tone of the film perfectly, signaling for audiences that they were about to watch an "ode to the city of Los Angeles, a world of endless possibility, constant beauty—and repetitive disappointment."[1]

We tend to think of film as a visual medium, and it is, but it's also the medium of composers like John Williams and Hans Zimmer and, in the case of 1964's *A Hard Day's Night*, the Beatles.

A movie's score, its music, is often an afterthought for most casual filmgoers, but it can—and often does—affect how we remember a film. "Music can *change* an image," Horowitz told me after his experience with *La La Land*, and I agreed.

For example, when I think about *Driving Miss Daisy*, I can't help but also think of the movie's theme. I think of songs like "Mrs. Robinson" in *The Graduate*, or "Over the Rainbow" in *The Wizard of Oz*, or "As Time Goes By" in *Casablanca*, or "Streets of Philadelphia" in *Philadelphia*. When Springsteen sang those lyrics—"I was bruised and battered, I couldn't tell what I felt"—it seemed to capture the entire spirit of the film and of the 1980s AIDS crisis.

Sometimes a song or score is so perfect for a film (like in *Cinema Paradiso*, which happens to be one of my favorite movies and scores of all time) that it becomes a character. It remains the thing that is most iconic about the movie.

The 1990 romantic comedy *Pretty Woman* is a fantastic example of this. In fact, the film wasn't originally titled *Pretty Woman*. The movie, which features Julia Roberts as an escort with a heart of gold, was first called *3,000*, because that was the fee Richard Gere's character negotiates for her services. It wasn't just a sexual agreement but one where she would accompany him for a few days while he's in Los Angeles to attend several business and social functions. Jeffrey Katzenberg, who was then running the studio with Michael Eisner, clearly saw the film as a Cinderella story and suggested calling it *Princess of the Boulevard*. That may have been the final title had one Disney executive, president of worldwide marketing Bob Levin, not come up with another idea. Looking through a list of *Billboard* all-time top hits, he came across the old Roy Orbison song from 1964 and a lightbulb went off. Levin ran his idea by the director, Garry Marshall, who agreed that "Oh, Pretty Woman" captured the vibe of the movie. Marshall wondered where to place the song within the film itself. "The Rodeo Drive shopping sequence, of course!" exclaimed Levin. And it worked perfectly. The only hurdle to overcome was Roy Orbison's widow, who didn't want the anthem that defined her husband's career to be used in a movie about a hooker. The studio persuaded her to attend a screening of the film, and immediately afterward she gave her approval.

When the film was tested for a recruited audience, the crowd went wild. Once the movie was over, Katzenberg assembled his studio executives and, as Levin recalled, instructed them not to breathe a word about the stellar test results. He recognized that Julia Roberts was going to be a huge star and wanted to cut a multipicture deal with her management before anyone knew just how good she was in the picture. (At that point, her career was only starting to take off—*Steel Magnolias* would be released a few months before *Pretty Woman*, but it had not yet opened.) Of course, by the next day, all of Hollywood knew how well *Pretty Woman* had tested. There are no secrets in Hollywood, right?

Bob Levin, as mentioned earlier, is now the president and COO of my company, and when he looks back on *Pretty Woman*, it's always with a gleam in his eye. "Mothers took their young daughters to see that picture," he told me. "It was, after all, a classic Cinderella story, and it was easy to forget that it was about a prostitute!"

If only selecting music for one's film were as easy as browsing through *Billboard*, or in today's world, through Spotify. The *Pretty Woman* story is a rarity. Usually, it must be done far more carefully, with an ear toward what sound will be truthful and in keeping with the spirit of the film. Sometimes studios misfire when choosing a song or scoring their pictures. (I should point out there is often a difference between a song like "Pretty Woman" and a movie's score. The latter tends to be what you might think of as a soundtrack, which can be anything from ABBA to just the instrumentals that are included as atmospheric music under a scene.)

When studios have a weak movie, for example, one where the audience doesn't emotionally invest in the characters, they'll often try to force some sense of emotion through the score. You've probably seen something like this before. A couple appears on-screen. They have little chemistry. The actors might be miscast. But when the climax of the film arrives—when the male lead returns back from war, for example—and takes the female lead in his arms, the music swells, and the two characters kiss amid a grand symphony of strings.

This kind of manipulation rarely works. Audiences know that love is not four violins and a brass quartet. They're smart enough to realize— even if it's subconsciously—that the song is trying to do what the script and the on-screen chemistry can't. With music, the filmmaker is sometimes trying to put lipstick on a pig. Moviegoers generally react poorly to this.

When done right, however, the score can be accretive to a moviegoer's experience; it can add something to the film that wasn't there before. The opening number of *La La Land* signaled to the audience that they were about to see a musical. And not just any musical but one so full of love and nostalgia for Hollywood that it was set on a Los Angeles freeway.

La La Land proved that music—and sometimes only music—can set the right tone for a film. But it certainly was not the only movie to do this.

"*Moonstruck is a great anecdote* for how the simplest things can make the biggest differences," reflected Greg Foster (who shared the *Thelma & Louise* story earlier). Foster recounted his early years in the movie business when, freshly graduated from Georgetown, he joined MGM/UA and became involved in setting up test previews for the pictures the studio made.

Foster first saw *Moonstruck* when a director's cut was shown to the studio executives, and he remembered thinking that it was absolutely spectacular. The venerable Norman Jewison brought the film to life from a script written by John Patrick Shanley, a playwright who had grown up in the Bronx and used his firsthand observations of the Italian American families who lived in his neighborhood as fodder for the fictional characters he created in the story. Shanley would go on to have a prolific career, penning the stage play *Doubt* (for which he won a Pulitzer for Drama and a Tony Award for Best Play) and the screenplay for the 2008 movie version, which earned Oscar nominations for Meryl Streep, Amy Adams, Philip Seymour Hoffman, Viola Davis, and for the writer himself. Norman Jewison was sixty years old when *Moonstruck* was being completed and a well-established name in Hollywood, having directed *In the Heat of the Night*, *The Thomas Crown Affair* (1968), *Fiddler on the Roof*, . . . *And Justice for All*, *A Soldier's Story*, and *Agnes of God*, plus another dozen movies.

MGM/UA had high hopes for *Moonstruck*, and Foster recalled, "You could tell there was a twinkle in the eye of that movie. There was something sparkly and cozy and warm about the film. We couldn't wait to preview it to a recruited audience. John Goldwyn, who was the production executive, was elated when we first watched it."

The studio decided to schedule screenings on the East Coast because they wanted to first test it with audiences that would understand and relate to the film's characters. So Foster was told to set up two previews, one in New York City and another on the following night in the suburbs of New Jersey. The first test took place at the Sutton Theater, and Foster remembered, "It was a great crowd, more female than male and with more older moviegoers than younger ones. We expected the results would be through the roof."

With the audience settled, the lights went down and the movie began. On the screen, a full moon looms large, a smattering of clouds moving across its silvery face before clearing to reveal the New York skyline on a crystal clear night. Dramatic opera music plays underneath the opening credits as the camera pans to a night shot of the Brooklyn Bridge, lights twinkling over the inky East River. The scene shifts to the Metropolitan Opera House illuminated in the predawn hours, a lone worker installing a poster for *La Bohème* in its case on the plaza. The darkness gives way to morning and another view of the Brooklyn Bridge, this time in daylight, before the camera sweeps down into the streets of a Brooklyn neighborhood as pedestrians hurry to their jobs on an early winter morning.

Cher, playing a thirty-seven-year old bookkeeper named Loretta Castorini, walks with purpose to her appointment at a funeral home. She wears sensible clothing and shoes. Her hair, curly and streaked with gray, is loosely pulled back from her face in an old-fashioned style. Moments later, she is seen in the proprietor's office sitting at his desk and trying to make sense of the receipts in front of her. "She's doing her thing on a calculator, and you can immediately feel who this woman is," said Foster.

"So much happens in the first half hour that's absolutely hysterical and crazy as we get to know Cher's character, her family, and the situation with her fiancé and his brother," continued Foster. "But at that first showing, we noticed that the audience was not laughing to the extent that we expected. And for the rest of the film, there was a hesitant tone in the theater; the audience was cautious in their response. After the preview, we did the focus group, we counted the cards, and the results were disappointing based on expectations."

Foster continued, "Afterward, we went out to dinner, which we thought would be a celebration, and it was anything but that. We were all sitting around the table, thinking, talking, perplexed, depressed. As the father of three children, I find that it's like watching them play Little League. You're sitting there and the pitch is thrown, and if he hits the ball, it's all good. But if he strikes out, it's devastation not only for him but for you as the parent. That first screening felt as if our kid had struck out.

"This was during Laddie's reign," said Foster, referring to Alan Ladd Jr., then chairman/CEO of MGM/UA. Known throughout the industry by his nickname, "Laddie" was often described as a wise and benevolent leader by those who were fortunate enough to work with him. Foster adored him and considered him a mentor for years to follow, even after they both left the studio.

"And Laddie said to me, 'Greg, you've got to read some of these cards.' I had brought the stack of surveys along to dinner. Laddie has great intuition, and he could see that people were very uncomfortable and there was this undercurrent of tension in the theater. So I started reading the cards, and what became very apparent was that moviegoers hadn't gotten the humor. Lou Lombardo, the editor on the film, was there with us. He was the perfect editor for *Moonstruck*, a real pro with a roster of films that included *The Wild Bunch* and *McCabe & Mrs. Miller*, which is a movie my dad produced," said Foster. (His father, the late David Foster, produced films for more than four decades, beginning in the 1970s.)

Lombardo was the first of the group to voice what they would learn that night from the surveys. "They don't know it's funny," Foster remembered Lombardo saying. "We've got to show them it's okay to laugh."

It wasn't so odd that moviegoers were hesitant to laugh. The year was 1987, well before *My Big Fat Greek Wedding*, *Barbershop*, and other modern-day films that borrow humor from cultural idiosyncrasies. Until then, depiction of Italian American characters in movies was mostly of Mafioso or poor immigrant families. *Moonstruck* was one of the first to portray middle-class American characters of Italian descent, albeit with Brooklyn accents and some peculiar tendencies. Additionally, the sweeping and dramatic music underneath the film seemed to be sending signals that these characters were rather glum.

"Opera is a big part of *Moonstruck*," explained Foster. "It's a key character in the film, and operatic music and tonality is evident throughout the story. But Lou felt that it was the operatic music at the beginning that was setting the wrong tone from the outset. He had an idea, and with Norman Jewison's blessing, he went right to work."

As mentioned earlier, films in those days were tested on two separate tracks, one for audio and a separate one for the picture. So by 1:00 a.m. on that same night, Lombardo was swapping out Puccini for something he was certain would signal comedy: Dean Martin's "That's Amore." The song, which first hit the music charts in 1953, was often associated with Italian American family celebrations, and there was something familiar and comfortable about it even three decades later. It was iconic, upbeat if not downright silly, and a perfect choice to open a romantic comedy that centers on this Brooklyn Heights family.

The next night at the screening in New Jersey, the same images of the moon over the New York skyline appeared on the screen, but this time with Martin crooning, "When the moon hits your eye like a big pizza pie, that's amore." The audience was hooked.

"Nothing else changed," said Foster. "That simple change in the music was the only thing that was different from the New York preview.

But it was huge. The song reinforced that the characters were funny, and it gave moviegoers permission to laugh. The scores on the second night were through the fucking roof!

"That movie was a turtle, not a rabbit," he continued. "It opened in very limited release and built in an Academy sort of way, based on good press and word of mouth. It was always a terrific movie, but Lou Lombardo's change clearly helped it achieve success."

Moonstruck opened in just seven theaters on December 18, 1987, but as Foster correctly recalled, on the heels of six Academy Award nominations including Best Picture, it gained momentum and eventually landed in nearly 1,200 theaters. Cher won the Best Actress Oscar for her portrayal of Loretta Castorini, the late Olympia Dukakis won Best Supporting Actress for her role as Loretta's mother, and John Patrick Shanley won for Best Original Screenplay.

Foster reflected, "When you watch that movie and you hear that song, you want to put your arm around the person who is watching it with you."

Donald Petrie shared a strikingly similar story. Petrie, who has directed crowd-pleasing comedies like *Miss Congeniality* and *How to Lose a Guy in 10 Days,* talked about one of his earlier films, *Grumpy Old Men.* The 1993 picture reunited the incomparable Jack Lemmon and Walter Matthau, who twenty-five years earlier had hit the comedy mother lode when they starred together in *The Odd Couple.* Petrie's film, *Grumpy Old Men,* was the perfect vehicle for resurrecting the comedic pairing, this time in a story about the lifelong animosity between two Wabasha, Minnesota, neighbors that only intensifies when they compete for the affection of the sexy, somewhat younger woman (played by Ann-Margret) who moves into a house across the street.

The first test of the movie is Petrie's favorite screening story. "I was horrified!" the director recounted. "This was a comedy, and we didn't get a laugh for forty-five minutes. And here's why. You have to be very careful in the opening moments of the movie to *tell* the audience what they're seeing. It's a huge lesson I learned from that screening."

The film was shot according to what Petrie describes as a wonderful script by Mark Steven Johnson, which originally opened outside a church with the daughter of Lemmon's character (Daryl Hannah) and the son of Matthau's character (Kevin Pollak). Both look solemn and are bracing themselves for what seems to be a funeral. Their dialogue indicates that neither are ready for what they're about to face. After the opening scene, everything that follows is a flashback.

The story transitions to an IRS agent who is trying to serve a notice to Lemmon's character early one morning. Lemmon sneaks out of his house to avoid the agent, and runs into Matthau who greets him with, "Good morning, dickhead."

Lemmon responds, "Hello, moron," completing the first joke in the film.

Dead silence from the audience.

Three-quarters of the way through the film, Lemmon's character has a heart attack, dispelling any doubt that the opening sequence was his funeral. But . . . surprise! It actually turned out to be a wedding. "It was a big 'Gotcha!'" continued Petrie. "Only we had convinced the audience so well that it was a funeral they thought they were there to see a drama. Not only didn't they laugh, they thought they *shouldn't* laugh."

Petrie knew immediately that the opening set the wrong tone entirely. "It was so obvious. It hit me in the head like a ton of bricks," he recalled. So after the first screening, he went back to work. Luckily, he had second-unit footage of the Minnesota setting that he was able to put to good use, crafting an alternate beginning.

At the second test screening, opening credits were presented over shots of the wintery upper midwestern locales. Leafless trees against gray clouded skies, frozen landscapes, a plow clearing the streets of the small town on the morning after a big snowstorm. And in perfect contrast, Ella Fitzgerald's classic rendition of "Heat Wave" plays underneath. "We're having a heat wave, a tropical heat wave, the temperature's rising, it isn't surprising, she certainly can cancan." It was enough to bring smiles to the faces in the audience, even before the story began.

This time, at "Good morning, dickhead" and "Hello, moron," there were big laughs. At the end of the movie, the strong test scores proved that

Grumpy Old Men played as the resoundingly satisfying comedy that Petrie had intended. The juxtaposition of the music cue signaled comedy, and the audience knew from the get-go what they were about to see. Problem solved.

With the possible exception of *La La Land*, we've only spoken about songs that work as mood music. They add to the atmosphere. They're the vocals and rhythms that appear underneath the other stuff that's happening in the movie. They assist the plot. But they're not the plot.

Sometimes songs are part of the plot, however. This happens in musicals—in fact, it's the very definition of a musical. But on occasion, the plot and the song don't serve each other. They're at odds.

On the first movie he ever produced, Craig Zadan had a big disagreement with the director, Herbert Ross. Ross was already one of Hollywood's most successful directors, with classics like *Play It Again, Sam* and *The Goodbye Girl* under his belt. Against someone with such a formidable track record, Zadan, who was then a thirty-four-year-old first-time producer, didn't stand a chance. The argument was over a final dance scene in the 1984 film *Footloose*, in which Kevin Bacon teaches a puritanical small town the joys of rock and roll.

Both Ross and Zadan agreed on what the finale of *Footloose* should be, that Kevin Bacon and his friends would overcome the town's conservative forces, take over one of the local barns, and throw a giant dance. Ross just disagreed that they should actually show it on-screen.

He told Zadan that if you make a movie about a family wanting a house, the moment of victory is when the family approaches the front door and puts the key into the lock. "You don't need to show them walking through the kitchen, the living room, and the bedroom to make the point," he insisted. "The audience will feel good."

Zadan disagreed, even appealing to the executives at Paramount, the studio bankrolling *Footloose*. "When you have a whole movie about fighting for a dance, the payoff is having the dance," Zadan contended. But in the end, the studio sided with Ross. The dance scene never made it into the script, and production commenced. Zadan remembered feeling angry during the entire shoot, telling anyone who would listen, "You have no idea how you're screwing up this movie. It's not going to work."

The moment of truth occurred at the first test screening. From the opening credits, with the dancing feet and the iconic title song, the audience went crazy. The film played like a blockbuster, and Zadan remembered that the audience loved the music, the well-choreographed moments of stolen dance moves among rebellious teenagers, and the unfolding romance between the two main characters.

Then, in the last five minutes, something changed, and the movie collapsed. That's when the test audience realized that they weren't going to see the dance, that it was going to be yadda-yaddaed over. Ninety minutes of buildup, of hoping, of foreshadowing, had concluded without the payoff, and the air went out of the room.

The moviegoers' disappointment was reflected in the test scores, and only then did Ross admit that maybe they needed the dance scene to complete the picture. Zadan and Ross went to the Paramount executives to make their case for adding the scene.

The studio balked at first, not wanting to spend the money on the additional shoot. The movie had been filmed in Provo, Utah, and now with everything wrapped, the cast and crew had scattered and the sets had been disassembled. "It was a nightmare," recalled Zadan, who couldn't help himself from thinking it would have been so much easier had they shot the dance scene in the first place.

Eventually the studio relented and gave approval to re-create the barn set from Provo on a soundstage on the Paramount lot. The cast was called back to rehearsals and the scene was finally shot. "If you look carefully," Zadan pointed out, "you'll see that Chris Penn has really long hair that's glued down and doesn't match his look in earlier scenes. He would have had a haircut, but he was already shooting something else, so he had this huge amount of hair that had to be plastered down. None of the actors really looked like they did in the rest of the movie, but I don't think anyone really noticed."

The scene was shot and, with the new ending that culminated with the big dance, the movie was retested. Zadan was anxious as he walked into the preview. He had fought hard for the scene, getting Paramount's hard-nosed executives to cough up the money for the reshoot and calling the actors back from other jobs. He'd also spent weeks scouring Los Angeles dance clubs to find talent. (Along with professional dancers, the filmmakers had used some amazing street dancers that he had found, featuring their unique moves within the sequence.)

Zadan knew they had captured something special on film, but it was only when the test audience confirmed that it was everything they wanted to see was he able to breathe easier. The scene sent the scores through the roof.

For the rest of his producing career, Craig Zadan regarded *Footloose* as his most important screening experience ever. It taught him the importance of a film's score—how one musical number could completely change the audience's perception of the movie.

Years later, Zadan would remember this lesson during the production of another musical, *Chicago*.

Zadan was now partnered with Neil Meron in what would become a decades-old relationship grounded in the passion that the two shared for musicals. During the 1990s, Zadan/Meron Productions built a reputation for bringing stage hits to television, hoping to encourage wide audiences of viewers to appreciate what only the privileged few are able to see on Broadway. The team cast big-name stars in its small-screen versions of well-known musicals. *Gypsy*—with Bette Midler, Cynthia Gibb, Ed Asner, and Tony Shalhoub—aired in 1993. In 1997, the pop singer Brandy starred in Zadan/Meron's television version of *Cinderella*, along with Whitney Houston, Whoopi Goldberg, and Jason Alexander.

It was on that project that the producers first worked with a talented choreographer named Rob Marshall. They were so impressed with him that a year later, they offered Marshall his first opportunity to direct. The project was a television production of *Annie*. In 2001, Marshall returned the favor by bringing in Zadan and Meron as the producers of his first feature film, the big-screen interpretation of the perennial stage hit *Chicago*.

The project to finally bring the jazz-inspired musical to the silver screen was housed under the roof of Harvey Weinstein's studio, Miramax. "We had a lot at stake," Zadan remembered. "There hadn't been a successful movie musical in a long time."

Zadan was right. Musicals aimed at adult audiences hadn't fared well at the box office or among film critics during the '90s. Disney's animated musicals for families—*The Lion King, Beauty and the Beast*, and so on—had owned the decade, while Madonna's *Evita*, which had premiered in 1996, was probably the most recent adult musical to achieve decent box-office success. But even it had mixed reviews. (I personally think *Evita* was the best movie of that year.)

Zadan and Meron thought they could break this streak with *Chicago*, and by the time the lights came up on the first test screening, they were surer than ever. Initially the film was seen by a suburban New Jersey test audience in early 2002, and the scores were outstanding.

The movie played extraordinarily well to that first test audience, and as the producers sat in the theater, they slowly allowed themselves to accept the confidence that was welling up inside of them. The executives from the studio, Miramax, were thrilled with the scores.

Harvey Weinstein, however, needed to test the film again, this time with one new addition.

In the original script, there is a scene where Velma (played by Catherine Zeta-Jones) and Matron Mama Morton (played by Queen Latifah) sing a duet called "Class." Producer Martin Richards had fallen in love with the song, a funny commentary on the lack of manners and proper protocol in Prohibition-era society. Weinstein, Zadan, Meron, and director Rob Marshall thought the song was out of context with the rest of the movie, the only musical number that didn't take place in Roxy's imagination. Furthermore, the lyrics have a different tonality from the other songs in the film and include some vulgar language. At one point, it had been removed from the script altogether.

But Richards had insisted upon shooting the scene, so it was covered during principal photography. Afterward, in editing, the filmmakers were convinced it didn't belong in the picture and left it out. Now, following the first screening, Richards pressured Weinstein to test a version of the film with "Class" included.

The irony of the situation wasn't lost on Zadan, who knew only too well from his *Footloose* experience how a single musical number could impact moviegoers' perceptions of the overall movie. But this time, he was arguing on the other side—against including it. Unlike *Footloose*, however, the footage already existed, so there was little risk in adding it, as long as the film could be retested.

As Zadan recalled, at the second preview, "'Class' stopped the movie dead. When you're at that point in the movie, it's all about getting to Roxy's trial. The movie is on a path, and it has its engine going. It's moving, building speed and momentum to get you to the verdict. Then the trial stops midway and the story cuts to this scene between Catherine and Queen Latifah. 'Class' is funny, but it's a one-joke number, the tempo is slow, and the song lasts for nearly three minutes. It interrupts the flow, which had been moving like lightning. And then the trial never recovers."

"And what's interesting," added Meron, "is that in the research results from that second screening with 'Class' in the film, Catherine's and Queen Latifah's character scores went down. Not only did the song hurt the movie, people liked the two characters less for singing it."

Richards looked at the numbers from the preview and didn't argue. The filmmakers removed the scene, and *Chicago* went on to win six Academy Awards, including Best Picture, and became one of the top grossing films in Miramax's history.

That's the power of music at the movies.

A sad footnote to this story: Hollywood was shocked when Craig Zadan's prolific life was cut short in August 2018 due to complications following shoulder surgery. He was sixty-nine years old. After *Chicago*, he and Meron produced *Hairspray*, *The Bucket List*, three Academy Award telecasts, and his final project, *Jesus Christ Superstar Live in Concert*, starring John Legend, Sara Bareilles, and Alice Cooper.

8.

WHEN BAD THINGS HAPPEN
TO GOOD MOVIES

Like most of the country, I went into Election Day 2016 confident that Hillary Clinton would win. I ended the evening shocked and saddened that she hadn't. If I recall correctly, my precise reaction was *Oh dear God!*

I had believed that Donald Trump would lose on November 8—*I'd been convinced of it*—but not because I'm a member of the out-of-touch Hollywood elite. (The Hollywood elite, you should know, are more in touch than we get credit for. After all, most of us came from somewhere else. I'm still that kid from Jersey who grew up a stone's throw away from Exit 9 off the turnpike.)

I had believed that Trump would lose not because of some misplaced sense that everyone must find him detestable. I thought he'd lose because that's what most of the data indicated. On Election night, the pollsters had placed the likelihood of a Clinton victory somewhere between 75 percent and absolute, bet-your-life-on-it certainty. Hillary had a steady five-point advantage in the polls leading up to the voting, and "The Upshot," the *New York Times's* election forecasting model, predicted that Trump had only a 15 percent chance of an upset. Of course, 15 percent turned out to be enough.

The numbers were wrong.

This happens in film research, too. Most of the time the scores and the focus group feedback do what they're supposed to do. They're predictive of how a movie will play with audiences in the real world. But every once in a while, a movie's score is about as predictive as a Magic 8-Ball. The numbers don't tell the whole story. A well-rated movie ends up doing poorly, or a poorly rated movie eventually does well. "Cannot predict now," as the 8-Ball says.

I would say that for every hundred movies I screen, this happens maybe one or two times. It's an incredibly rare thing that a movie's scores aren't at least directionally correlative, but when it does occur, I don't see the film research process as a failure. Far from it. Instead, I see it as an opportunity to examine the many other factors that contribute to a film's success or demise.

Great test scores don't guarantee great box office. Many in Hollywood wish it were true because they could then test a path to success. Unfortunately, high-scoring films can be box office duds, not because the research was inaccurate or misleading but for any number of other reasons. That's what this chapter is about—the limits of data. It's about what the numbers *can't* tell you, about the many other decisions, beyond moviegoers' opinions, that determine a film's fate.

Sometimes, for example, a good film fails because of bad timing. Lynda Obst, a successful writer/producer whom I adore, knows something about this. Lynda and I experienced this during the screening process of the 1996 romantic comedy *One Fine Day*. It starred Michelle Pfeiffer and George Clooney and had tested at 99 percent in the top two boxes when it was screened. In fact, the studio was so encouraged by the test audience results that they moved up the release date. This proved to be a bad move.

Rather than waiting until February as originally planned, the studio premiered Obst's film five days before Christmas, and it landed among a murderers' row of crowd-pleasing films. *One Fine Day* was released a week after *Jerry Maguire* and a week before Nora Ephron's *Michael*. It also went head-to-head on its opening weekend with the first *Scream* movie.

For years, Obst blamed *One Fine Day*'s release date for its disappointing opening, and in 2003 she got the closest thing there is to vindication. That year, Obst produced a film in the same vein. It was called

How to Lose a Guy in 10 Days, and it, too, was a romantic comedy. The movie also featured a Clooney-Pfeiffer-caliber couple in Kate Hudson and Matthew McConaughey. More important, *How to Lose a Guy in 10 Days* earned almost identical test scores to *One Fine Day*'s.

The only major difference between the two films, it seemed, was the release date. *How to Lose a Guy in 10 Days* premiered a week before Valentine's Day and had virtually no competition for the rom-com audience it attracted. As a result, the film opened roughly four times stronger than *One Fine Day*, at nearly $24 million.

It's not just timing, though. It's marketing. Even a good movie can have no target audience. Moviegoers may like a film when they see it, but that means jack shit if they won't show up to the theater in the first place.

Today, people hardly remember films like *Cesar Chavez* or *Eddie the Eagle*. But both scored off the charts when they were tested. Nevertheless, both also crashed and burned at the box office. *Eddie the Eagle* was a soft idea, probably something you could easily consume on a streaming service, but there was not a great need to see it in a theater. *Cesar Chavez* was almost too medicinal, a worthy story but documentary-ish. No amount of advertising could convince audiences that these movies were worth paying to see.

The 2006 film *Infamous* is another example. The movie was based on the life of Truman Capote, and when people saw it, they loved it. It scored superbly. But when the movie premiered, very few showed up. There was an obvious reason: astonishingly, another film based on the very same historical plot, *Capote*, had premiered the year before to great fanfare, winning an Academy Award for the actor in the title role. No one cared to see the same story again, no matter how well told, and certainly not without the buzz of an Oscar-winning performance from Philip Seymour Hoffman.

On the other end of the spectrum, it's rare that a low-testing film becomes a big box office hit, although it's not entirely impossible. Examples include *The War of the Roses* in 1989 and, more recently, *Black Swan*. Movies with dark themes or sad endings, and those that are difficult to place in a particular genre, are prone to subdued test scores. Yet they can gain momentum at the box office with praise from the critics and strong word of mouth. But those are the exceptions, not the rule.

Experienced filmmakers will often point out the lack of straight-line correlation between test results and box-office performance. Faced with weak preview scores, a director or two has been known to bring up previous films that didn't test well but ultimately achieved financial success. Their memories don't always serve them well. Very few low-testing films have defied the odds.

After one particular screening I conducted of an R-rated comedy that achieved very average scores (translation: a C grade), the film's famous director tried to assuage the concerns of the studio executives, who were obviously disappointed with the results. The director pointed out that one of his previous films, which had taken in hundreds of millions of dollars, had not scored any higher when it had been tested. I began to challenge him because I recalled his earlier hit film and knew it had scored better. But he became defensive, and I didn't want the conversation to become even more awkward for him, so I backed off. The next morning, I called the studio with the accurate scores from the screenings of the hit film and they were, in fact, far better than the director recalled.

At best, test scores are only the beginning of the story. Movies are then released into the world and another measure of success—how much money they earn—plays out in the next chapter. Eventually, the way a film lives on in our hearts and minds is the ultimate test. Audiences shape the way it's perceived over time, and that's something research can never predict. People talk about movies, quote lines from them, mimic behaviors of the characters. Some are just a momentary blip on the radar, while others work their way into popular culture, earning a lasting place in history.

Few filmmakers are as astute about this phenomenon as Cameron Crowe, who enjoys discussing the way audiences shape perceptions of a film over time. A former journalist and accomplished author, Crowe has several books to his credit, and has written screenplays for most of the films he directed, including *Say Anything*, *Jerry Maguire*, and *Almost Famous*.

Visiting my office to share his test preview stories, Crowe spoke of Billy Wilder, the famed director whom he interviewed extensively for his 1999 book *Conversations with Wilder*. He and Wilder shared a special friendship, finding common ground in their experiences as writers and directors.

Crowe brought up an often-told story (Ron Howard also mentioned it) about a research screening of the 1939 film *Ninotchka*, which Wilder cowrote (with Charles Brackett) and Ernst Lubitsch directed. As legend has it, the filmmakers were in a celebratory mood after an extremely successful test showing in Long Beach, California. Riding in the back of the limousine with drinks going, Lubitch flipped through the stack of surveys from the preview and exclaimed, "Oh my God! This is the greatest comment I've ever had for one of my movies: 'Great picture. Funniest film I ever saw. I laughed so hard, I peed in my girlfriend's hand.'"

When Crowe heard the story and finished laughing, he thought, "Wow. Test previews have been a part of the process for a very long time."

Like many filmmakers and studio heads of his era, Billy Wilder was a little dismissive of screening scores. He once told Crowe, "I don't have to look at the actual numbers. I know sitting there when my ass itches and the audience is restless. I don't need cards to tell me that."

That may be true. Those of us who make our living in the film industry develop a heightened sense of the room. We know when an audience is "with" a picture, and when they become fidgety. But what Wilder couldn't have known was that *Ninotchka*, with its hard-to-pronounce title, would be a film that we would still be discussing eighty-plus years later.

Cameron Crowe is very perceptive of the screening process, and his opinions reflect a depth of understanding that few directors can articulate.

"Screenings are sort of a snapshot of how people feel at a point in time," he commented. "But what happens over time? There is a communal experience that happens over the life of a movie that may not turn up in the test scores. The movie gains a luster . . . or not. It hits culture in a way and really changes. That's what happened with *Jerry Maguire*."

Crowe dedicated years of his life to *Jerry Maguire*; the screenplay alone took him three years to write. After the film was finished, it was taken to San Diego for its first test preview. In the theater, Crowe didn't have a good feeling about the response and recalled thinking, "It's over. We did our best . . . and it doesn't work." It wasn't clear that his film had knocked the audience out.

But, in fact, it had. The surveys were collected and counted, and as Crowe was standing off to the side in the theater lobby, he watched the elated reactions of the Tri-Star executives and those around the executives who were seeing the scores for the first time. And then the vibe started coming toward him.

"There was a red, cushiony feel to the lobby, so it felt very dramatic," he recalled. "I'll always remember it because, personally, *Jerry Maguire* was the point in time when I truly felt that I was a director. This would be a lifetime job."

As with every film that undergoes the process, the scores from that first test audience were only the beginning of its success. There was a special momentum behind the film once it was released. The audience was meeting Renée Zellweger, a mostly unknown actress whom Crowe had fought to cast, for the first time. (Zellweger had been in a few smaller films before *Jerry Maguire* but was not yet a star.) There were many other popular actresses at the time who wanted the part, but the director prevailed, and his instincts turned out to be spot-on. Audiences fell in love with her.

"They also loved Cuba," recalled Crowe. Cuba Gooding Jr. turned in the Oscar-winning Best Supporting Actor performance in that 1996 film, and would become famous for his character's line "Show me the money."

"That was the thing people were quoting," said Crowe. "Cuba was like the hit single. Unexpected.

"But over time now, Tom Cruise gets all the love. In that character, Jerry Maguire, there was a sense of discovery about the biggest star in the world. You knew him from *Mission: Impossible*, *Top Gun*, *Rain Man*, and *Born on the Fourth of July*. But this was character comedy, a romantic comedy, and he was coming out of that box in which everyone had him. He was showing his stuff, and it delighted moviegoers. It was a glimpse of when actor, part, movie, and audience lock in. You just got that sense that this is when it all works, when magic happens.

"The entire film is fun," Crowe continued. "But people have come to realize that the movie doesn't work if you don't have that dude at the center, giving you everything. And that wasn't obvious at the time [of the screening]. He was welcomed into our hearts in a different way. To this day, people still come up to Tom and talk to him about that."

The film did, in fact, earn a place in people's hearts and minds. Not only did "Show me the money" become a pop culture phrase but so did "You had me at hello."

Crowe brought up an even more dramatic example of how one of his earliest films evolved in the hearts and minds of the public over time.

As a young twenty-two-year-old writer, he went back to high school for a full year to write a novel based on student life in a typical Southern California beach town. *Fast Times at Ridgemont High* was published in September 1981, and the film adaptation would follow a year later. Crowe wrote the screenplay, Amy Heckerling directed the movie, and Universal produced and distributed it. Crowe was on the set every day of shooting and attended all of the previews.

"The screenings only captured what happened on a particular night, which was a very mixed bag of outrage and laughter," recalled Crowe. "Audiences loved the surfer, Jeff Spicoli (played by Sean Penn), but they were also outraged. Roger Ebert would eventually write a review saying, 'How could they do this to Jennifer Jason Leigh? How could they put such a fresh and cheerful person into such a scuz-pit of a movie?' He was just giving a snapshot of what some people were thinking of the movie at the time." (Interestingly, years later, Ebert would recant what he initially wrote about *Fast Times at Ridgemont High*. The film eventually landed on AFI's "100 Years . . . 100 Laughs" list of the funniest American films of all time.)

"Of course, now it's almost tame," continued Crowe. "Still, when we put it out, Phoebe Cates is teaching you how to give a blow job, and all that stuff was just shocking! We did two screenings of *Fast Times*, and it did not do well."

"I remember Irving Azoff [a Universal Studios executive at the time, and producer of the movie] asking if we wanted to go around in a car on opening night and look at the theaters. Everyone declined. No one wanted to see how the movie was playing. They hated it. They cut the number of theaters at the last moment because they had such a lack of confidence in it," recalled Crowe.

On opening weekend, Crowe left town. He knew the movie was dead on arrival and didn't want to stick around and wallow in grief. So he and a buddy hopped into the car and drove to Arizona, where another friend was getting married. On their way, Crowe's friend turned to him and said, "Let's check out what's happening with *Fast Times*." They stopped in Tempe, just outside Phoenix. A big surprise was waiting for them.

Outside the theater, Crowe saw a crowd of kids lined up to see his picture. And as he looked down the line, he noticed that many were wearing checkerboard Vans in tribute to Sean Penn's character.

"They had already seen the film and they were waiting to get in to see it a *second* time," said Crowe. "That's the X factor. It's what the audience brings to it. They see it. They have an experience with it. It's the wild mercury of creativity meeting the audience."

Hearts and minds.

The studio was never able to catch up to the demand to see the film. They had already given up the theaters, a move they later regretted. But Cameron Crowe's picture would go on to become a huge hit . . . on video. The research could never have predicted the place that *Fast Times at Ridgemont High* would earn in the hearts and minds of a generation.

Not a chance.

The work I do can tell you what an audience is thinking at a specific moment in time, but film research is not well suited to predict where those preferences are heading, or where the culture will be on the day the film lands in theaters. Sometimes a perfect movie is made by the perfect director at the perfect time in our lives, and we cannot anticipate when that will be.

Even if a director or screenwriter has an idea that taps into the culture, there's no guarantee the culture will be the same when the movie reaches the screen. Culture is fleeting. It's quick. It's gone tomorrow. It can change even in the months between a test screening and the night of the wide release.

The original *Power Rangers* film is an A-plus example. A spin-off of a Japanese television series about a group of teenage superheroes, the Power Rangers franchise was at the peak of its cultural power around 1994, which is when 20th Century Fox green-lit a full-length feature. By the time it reached theaters, though, interest in the series had waned significantly, and the movie opened in fourth place to mediocre reviews.

Then there are movies like *The War of the Roses*, the 1989 dark comedy in which Michael Douglas and Kathleen Turner portray two sides of an outrageous divorce battle. Throughout the movie, Turner's character ratchets up the hostility to her husband, trying to force his hand into signing the divorce papers. In one scene, she tricks Douglas into thinking that she's turned the family dog into pâté. The test audience didn't get the humor. Divorce was no laughing matter.

Nor, apparently, were jokes about dead dogs.

The film was screened over and over again. Tom Sherak, who was head of marketing at 20th Century Fox at the time, estimates it was tested eleven times, and it never achieved strong results.

"I'll never forget," said Sherak years later. "I was sitting on the steps outside the theater with Jim [Brooks, producer] and Danny [DeVito, director] and whoever else was at the studio at the time. People were coming up to me and asking if I had anything to do with the movie. I said, 'Well, uh, I work for Fox.' And they told me they thought the movie was horrible and they would never recommend it. There was such a dislike for what was happening on-screen."

Months later, 20th Century Fox released *The War of the Roses*. They expected the response to be the same as at the test screenings—outright rejection. Instead, the press got behind the film as a witty, cautionary tale about modern divorce. Mainstream audiences were curious to see the two big box-office stars from *Romancing the Stone* slug it out on-screen, and when they showed up for the movie, they loved it.

It was as if, in the months between the test screening and the premiere, *The War of the Roses* had become an entirely different film. I think what was different, though, was something about the wider culture, something that the test audiences could not pick up. Perhaps it was that the conservative norms of the Reagan years were softening. Perhaps critics influenced audiences to like the film. Perhaps people were ready to laugh at what was once taboo.

The War of the Roses went on to become one of the highest grossing and most critically acclaimed comedies of that year.

As a film researcher, I grasp these limits of movie testing in theory. But sometimes even I overlook the possibility that a movie might just be the right film at the right time. To wit: I could have never predicted that in 2002, the world's biggest comedy would be about a big Greek family starring an unknown actress, Nia Vardalos. The best-known member of the cast would be the third-most-famous member of the boy band *NSYNC, Joey Fatone.

My Big Fat Greek Wedding scored well during its test screening, but not "blockbuster" well, and I remember lamenting to the studio executive, "Too bad the film doesn't have any major stars. Otherwise, this could do $15 to $20 million domestically."

My Big Fat Greek Wedding went on to earn more than $350 million worldwide at the box office. It was, at that point, the highest grossing romantic comedy of all time.

There's no other way to put it: some films just capture lightning in a bottle, and data can't account for that. Nor can it anticipate how well a movie will age with repeat viewings.

Most films age like bricks. They're the same when you watch them on Monday as when you watch them on Friday. Perhaps some of the surprise is gone with a second viewing, but rarely do you come away with a different appreciation of the film.

Every once in a while, though, a film ages like a bottle of 1982 Château Lafite. A second viewing reveals new depths, more flavors. A third, still more. Films take on lives of their own, as did *Fast Times at Ridgemont High*, which became a cult classic. So it's true that data can't predict a film's success or failure. But in the end, screening research is still one of the most effective tools we have for honing it into the best that it can be.

The dog pâté joke stayed in *War of the Roses*, but before we move on, I'd like to offer a little aside about killing dogs in movies. It's a cardinal sin. Adam McKay discovered that early in his career. McKay is a producer, writer, director, and comedian who had a long-term partnership with Will Ferrell. Together, they collaborated on a number of big comedies, including the first full-length feature film that McKay directed, *Anchorman: The Legend of Ron Burgundy*.

The year was 2004, and it was the first time that McKay had ever tested a film with National Research Group. (I had worked at NRG for many years but had already left the company to start the entertainment research division at OTX, so I was not at the first *Anchorman* screening.) The studio, DreamWorks, set up a screening at a large theater in Westwood, and McKay recalled that in addition to the big recruited audience, the whole studio had turned out for it. He was nervous as hell.

But the movie killed, getting laughs all the way through. Afterward, Jeffrey Katzenberg, one of the cofounders of DreamWorks, came up to McKay and patted him on the back, telling the young writer/director that it was the funniest movie he had ever seen.

Then the scores came back, and they were not good. Everyone was puzzled, because the audience had laughed so hard. But Terry Press, who was then head of marketing at DreamWorks, approached McKay.

"She didn't mince words," recalled McKay. "She said, 'Hey idiot, you killed the dog!' And we had. In the first cut, we killed Baxter, and he didn't come back. We love dogs. Ferrell has dogs. I have dogs. Our reasoning was it's so cartoonish. It's a silly comedy. Who cares? But it turns out that four hundred people in Westwood cared a lot."

Press, who earlier in her career worked on another dog movie called *Turner and Hooch*, lamented how that movie would have earned a lot more money at the box office if the dog hadn't died at the end. "People will watch any kind of movie in which a human gets killed, but killing a dog is a big no-no," she stated. (To be clear, it's perfectly fine, although usually sad, when a dog dies of natural causes in a movie. It's the killing part that is a red flag.)

With the support of DreamWorks, the filmmakers went back and did reshoots, bringing the dog, Baxter, back in a really silly, fun way. The film was retested, this time at a big theater in Orange County, California, which typically represents a microcosm of America. The scores went up by twenty-six points. (By the way, that second test was conducted by OTX and I was there to witness the results, and the ecstatic relief of everyone involved in the production.)

"*Anchorman* was my first movie," reflects McKay. "I was a geek. But I learned a lot from it."

Yeah . . . don't kill the dog!

9.

IT'S LIKE SEEING YOUR LOVER
NAKED FOR THE FIRST TIME

Not all directors embrace screening research, and some, like Clint Eastwood, Quentin Tarantino, Woody Allen, and others who have final-cut status, don't typically screen their pictures at all—at least not in the traditional research sense. I try to understand the logic behind this and have debated with many an apprehensive filmmaker who is hesitant to test his or her movie.

I think there is always a gnawing fear that the studio might use the research to force changes that will make a film more commercial but perhaps less artistic. What I try to impress upon directors is that there is always something to be learned from the research and they have options. Ultimately, they can decide what they want to change—or not—based on an informed understanding of what moviegoers take away from their picture.

Filmmakers fall along a continuum. On one end are those who want to make crowd-pleasing movies. They're inclined to test their films multiple times and implement changes along the way until the scores reflect the wide audience appreciation that they want to achieve.

A respected colleague of mine, who has for decades produced big, broadly appealing movies like *Jumanji: Welcome to the Jungle* and the original *Jumanji*, as well as *Runaway Bride*, *The Texas Chainsaw Massacre*, *Bill and Ted's Excellent Adventure*, and *The Hand That Rocks the Cradle*, came into the business with that sensibility. It was in his genes. He is the great-great-grandson of Marshall Field, founder of the famed Chicago-based department stores, which operated under the mantra "Give the lady what she wants."

"My feeling is, give the audience what they want," Ted Field explained to me. "I don't think test screenings ever lie to you. It's the height of arrogance for either a filmmaker or a studio producer to say the audience is wrong and we're right. I think the audience is always right."

Field, by the way, is one of the most financially prolific producers in the industry.

On the other end of the continuum are the "auteurs," those who make movies based entirely on their personal creative vision, and they really don't give a damn what others think. Over the years, I've discovered that most filmmakers are somewhere in the middle, open to making changes that will improve playability as long as those changes don't compromise their original vision.

Ed Zwick, for example, told me that he would never preview a film of his too many times, or make too many changes based on test results, because he would lose his feeling of authorship over the material. "It may be shit, but it's my shit," the writer/director/producer said to me. "I think I come from a school that cares a little bit less to please," he reflected. "What I have found is that the movies I've done that have scored best at research screenings are those that have in them elements that are the most comforting or reassuring to an audience, but not necessarily the most dramatically interesting or the most sophisticated."

On my way out of his office after a meeting one afternoon, I looked around and saw no Academy Award, even though I knew Zwick had won one. When I inquired, he said the Oscar he had received for producing *Shakespeare in Love* was "around here somewhere" and proceeded to dig into the back of a cabinet until he located it. He pulled the statue out, blew dust from it, and set it on his desk so I could look at it. I laughed at his casual regard for Hollywood's highest accolade, and wondered if it were mine, would I store it in the back of a credenza? (I think not.)

Zwick's work tends to tackle serious subject matter, issues of morality and honor that often incorporate military code and conduct. Most, but not all, of his films have been commercially successful, while some appealed to more limited, cerebral audiences, earning much smaller grosses. Zwick tests all his films—*Glory*, *Courage Under Fire*, *The Siege*, *The Last Samurai*, and *Blood Diamond* among them—at least once or twice. He cautions against trying to fashion a movie based on the test scores, but readily admits that there is always something to be learned from the experience of showing a film to a recruited audience, as he did when we screened *Legends of the Fall*.

Ed Zwick's 1994 film is the saga of a retired army colonel and his three sons, set primarily in the remote and expansive Montana of the early twentieth century. The material, based on a novella by Jim Harrison, is epic in proportion and spans decades. *Legends of the Fall* deals with complex family bonds, jealousy, love, guilt, and tragedy. Zwick spent years of his life getting the project underway, assembling a stellar cast, including Brad Pitt, Anthony Hopkins, Aidan Quinn, Julia Ormond, and Henry Thomas. The movie was meticulously filmed on location in the Canadian Rocky Mountains and would earn an Oscar for cinematographer John Toll.

After the film was finished, Zwick showed it to a group of thirty or so friends and colleagues upon whom he relies for the truth, and made some changes based on their feedback. When the movie was next screened to a recruited audience of several hundred people, Zwick was feeling very confident. He knew he had captured something special, and he had already addressed all of the issues that had come up in his "friends and family" screening. He was certain that the picture was in good shape.

A lot happens early in the movie, and Zwick felt he had "moved the narrative along at a good metabolic rate." Yet the screening audience was ahead of the story. Moviegoers could anticipate the romance that would develop between the characters played by Pitt and Ormond, and just wanted them to get on with it. They figured out too much too quickly, and Zwick could sense that the test audience was losing interest, becoming fidgety.

Before the movie was half over, his editor, Steven Rosenblum leaned over and whispered into Zwick's ear, "We're fucked." They knew, just by sitting with an audience of *regular* moviegoers—as opposed to a circle of confidants—that parts of the film were much too obvious. It was a painful realization for Zwick, because he knew in that moment that he was not yet finished with the film.

"When you've been working on a movie for so long—and that includes the writing process, production, postproduction, dubbing, scoring, all of that—you begin to look at nuance and refinement. You increasingly narrow your view of it. You tweak the sound, take two frames off that cut, work on the color composition, and inevitably, you forget the experience of seeing that movie for the first time," commented Zwick. "What happened in that screening of *Legends* made me suddenly realize that the audience wasn't thinking about nuance. They were figuring out how one character related to another, that the pretty girl was going to end up with the good-looking guy."

Zwick went back to work on the film. He didn't cut a lot from it, but he kept certain things from the audience for a longer period. "It was more about a rate in which things happened," he explained, "not giving it all away." A couple of weeks later, it was screened again, and although Zwick downplays the importance of the scores, when pressed, he admits that they went up dramatically.

"In any love affair in life, there is only one moment when you see your lover naked for the first time. And it's a significant moment that, however passionate your relationship remains, is never again replicated. That is the way it is for an audience when they see a movie for the first time," said Zwick. "The test screening is your moment as a filmmaker to let go of your film. You give it to an audience, and it's no longer yours. As you watch them watch it, you're reminded of how *you* felt when you first wrote those words or first read that script."

Something that I always try to encourage doing is filmmaker screenings where a very early cut of a movie is shown to a small audience of maybe fifty or a hundred people who offer their feedback before the studio sees it. These early, small, controlled previews allow the director and producers a more private forum to gauge playability, away from what might be the harsher gaze of the company footing the bills for production and distribution. Given the small size of these controlled audiences, the emphasis is more on qualitative findings as opposed to the scores.

Experienced directors like Ed Zwick and Ron Howard know all about these small screenings, and some even write the cost of a couple of them into their contracts and budgets. Director Martha Coolidge learned this years ago when Gary Lucchesi, who was then the president of production at Paramount, gave her some wise advice. "Don't ever screen a film for us that you have not already screened for other people, by yourself."

Coolidge took the advice to heart. When she directed a film called *The Prince and Me*, she convinced Paramount to let her have a small private showing. The studio set it up in a little theater on the lot that barely held thirty people. There were surveys handed out, but no report afterward. The movie played well, and there was a lawn mower racing sequence that was a standout favorite for the small audience that attended that early preview. Later, when Coolidge first showed the film privately to the studio executives, she got notes back that the movie was good, but a little too long. They wanted her to cut the lawn mower racing scene. She told them, "I'll think about it. But I really don't think we should take it out just yet." And she didn't.

Coolidge stalled until the first formal test screening. "I just wanted to see what the cards would say. And, of course, the audience's reaction was huge for the whole lawn mower sequence and identical to the earlier small screening. It was never discussed again. But had I cut it out, we never would have known how popular it was."

An all-too-common criticism that I hear from test audiences is that a movie is predictable. I try to drill down into what that means, exactly. Sometimes it refers to material that seems familiar—characters, situations, or outcomes that are too similar to those presented in other movies. Sometimes predictability can be related to pacing. The story may unfold too slowly, allowing the audience time to figure out (or guess) what comes next, before it actually happens. Movies that end in a predictable way are often penalized, even if the outcome to the story is satisfying.

Audiences love to be outsmarted. Give moviegoers a big surprise or twist and they will often reward a film with accolades, and strong test scores, especially if the revelation comes at the end. I've actually seen flawed films test quite well because they're able to redeem themselves with big shockers at the end. Moviegoers will often forgive transgressions such as confusing details or slow pacing once they're walloped with a surprise they didn't see coming.

Movies that are well crafted all the way through and then punch it up with an unexpected reveal are in a special class. *Get Out*, *The Sixth Sense*, *The Crying Game*, and classics such as *Chinatown* and *Psycho* are examples of films that incorporate powerful twists or surprises, which audiences loved. Interestingly, moviegoers tend to keep the secret. The experience of being surprised is considered so much fun that most moviegoers will keep it under wraps so as not to ruin it for others.

In the mid-1990s, I had the opportunity to conduct research on a film that blew me away, not just because of the acting performances—especially from an actor I had never seen before—but because of the powerful ending that surprised me and everyone else in the audience. For those who have not seen *Primal Fear*, spoiler alert! Watch it now before you read on. It still holds up as a terrific movie—and I don't want to be the one to ruin the surprise.

In 1995, all of Hollywood and much of the country was riveted to their television sets as the criminal trial of O. J. Simpson unfolded. The real-life murder mystery seemed to upstage anything on the big or small screen, and Judge Ito's courtroom introduced a cast of characters who became household names. In addition to Simpson, who was, of course, a well-known celebrity, members of his hotshot legal team soon achieved starlike status as well. Johnnie Cochran, Robert Shapiro, and Robert Kardashian joined ranks with famed defense attorneys F. Lee Bailey, Alan Dershowitz, and Barry Scheck to form a dream team like never before seen. It seemed that little else was discussed at cocktail parties or across dinner tables during the months of the televised proceedings.

Coinciding with Simpson's trial, Gary Lucchesi was deep in production on a courtroom drama of the fictional kind. Lucchesi had been a successful executive at Paramount Pictures, overseeing the production of hugely popular films such as *Ghost*, *The Hunt for Red October*, *Coming to America*, *The Untouchables*, and *The Naked Gun*—in which O. J. Simpson had starred—among others. By the mid-1990s, he had formed his own production company and had struck a distribution deal with Paramount. This latest project centered on just the type of high-profile trial that was dominating real-world headlines.

Primal Fear is about a gruesome stabbing of a Catholic archbishop in Chicago and the trial of an altar boy who is witnessed running from the murder scene covered in blood. The childlike, nineteen-year-old Aaron Stampler is quickly captured and charged with the crime. Jumping on the chance to fuel his celebrity, a renowned defense lawyer named Martin Vail takes on the case for the publicity it will generate. As the story unfolds, the boy admits to being at the scene of the crime but convinces his attorney that a third person was also in the room, and that he blacked out only to wake and discover the archbishop dead from multiple stab wounds. Shocked and frightened, Aaron flees, a blunder that is misconstrued as guilt.

Lucchesi was thrilled when Richard Gere agreed to play the part of attorney, Martin Vail. The forty-six-year-old actor still had star power, although no big hits since the 1990 blockbuster *Pretty Woman*. This was a good, dramatic part that could reignite buzz for Gere and build moviegoer interest in the picture. He had played arrogant before, and in the wake of the O. J. Simpson case, Gere was just the actor to convince audiences that he was the film incarnation of a Johnnie Cochran–type defense lawyer. Other talented actors would round out the cast, including Laura Linney as the prosecuting attorney, Alfre Woodard as the judge, Frances McDormand as the psychiatrist who is brought in to assess the altar boy, John Mahoney as the district attorney, and Maura Tierney as Martin Vail's secretary. The big hurdle, as Lucchesi would soon discover, was casting the defendant, altar boy Aaron Stampler.

Executives at Paramount, who would distribute the picture, and Lucchesi himself had envisioned a rising young star named Leonardo DiCaprio in the role of Stampler. His boyish face belied his age (twenty-one at the time), and he had undeniable acting talent that had earned him an Oscar nomination for his supporting role in *What's Eating Gilbert Grape*. The studio and filmmakers believed DiCaprio would be perfect as the simpleminded Stampler, who declares his innocence despite the evidence mounting against him. The only problem was that DiCaprio turned down the role. Lucchesi remembered being terribly disappointed.

A flurry of activity ensued as the production team considered other actors for the key role. Lucchesi recalled, "We read every actor in America for the part, including Matt Damon. We simply weren't convinced that we had found our Aaron Stampler."

Among some two thousand auditions, an unknown actor showed up to an open casting call in New York and read for the part with a stammer and a Kentucky twang. Even though he had no résumé to speak of, the casting director Deb Aquila was impressed enough to send him to Los Angeles for a screen test. Lucchesi and the film's director, Gregory Hoblit, liked what they saw. But the studio head remained unsure that the actor, already in his midtwenties, was right for the role. So he was tested again. Finally, at the risk of losing other cast members if production was delayed any longer, the studio and filmmakers decided to take a calculated risk and cast the unknown actor, Edward Norton, in the role that would launch his film career.

The film was shot in Chicago and Los Angeles, and when it was finished, a recruited screening was held in the Studio Theater on the Paramount lot. Lucchesi remembered feeling very eager to see how it would play. He had been through hundreds of test screenings at that point in his career, but this one felt like uncharted territory. The success of the film hinged on catching moviegoers by surprise at the very end.

"What was so exciting about screening *Primal Fear* is that none of us had any idea whether our bet would pay off, if the audience would be able to figure out the ending before it actually happens, especially with a newcomer in that critical role," Lucchesi recalled.

As the test audience watched for the first time, moviegoers seemed to be right where the filmmakers wanted them: sympathetic to Aaron Stampler, a poor boy from Kentucky who escapes an abusive home only to end up living on the streets of Chicago. They learned that the archbishop had rescued him and brought him into a sheltered life at the church. The naive, stammering man-child professes his love for the priest who had saved him and seems incapable of having perpetrated such a vicious attack.

Meanwhile, as he prepares the defense, Martin Vail uncovers information suggesting others may have had motive for wanting the archbishop dead. The overly confident Vail believes he has all he needs to win the case. He enters a not-guilty plea and the trial begins. The audience seemed to be with the story, and on Aaron Stampler's side.

When Vail brings in a psychiatrist to interview his client, the test audience got their first hint that something is terribly wrong with Stampler. As the psychiatrist attempts to understand the boy's episodes of "lost time" and pushes him to remember events from his past, Stampler snaps, and for a minute or two, takes on a much different and more sinister persona, whom he calls Roy. Later in the storyline, when Vail learns that the archbishop had been sexually abusing the boy and confronts Stampler, Aaron again transforms into the violent and foulmouthed Roy and actually admits to killing the archbishop. When the episode subsides, Aaron has no memory of Roy or of the murder.

Vail is in a quandary, because by now he knows that his client has multiple personality disorder and is not guilty by reason of insanity. But he cannot change the plea in the midst of the trial. So he puts his client on the witness stand, hoping the prosecutor will skewer the boy in cross-examination. His strategy works. Aaron snaps and becomes Roy, stunning everyone in the courtroom as he lunges at the prosecuting attorney (Laura Linney), holds her in his grip, and threatens to break her neck. He is eventually subdued and dragged from the courtroom. The judge declares a mistrial and orders Stampler to a mental hospital for evaluation.

At the end of the film, Vail visits Stampler in the holding cell at the courthouse. Stampler is back to being Aaron, with no recollection of the events that occurred moments before in the courtroom. Vail delivers the news about the judge's order and is obviously pleased with the victorious outcome for his client. As he leaves, Stampler calls out to say that he hopes the prosecutor's neck is okay. Vail takes a few steps, and then stops in his tracks. He realizes that if Stampler could remember what happened when he was Roy, he had not really blacked out at all. He turns to face Stampler, who mockingly applauds. When Vail asks, "So there was never a Roy?" Stampler chillingly reveals that there was never an *Aaron*.

In the theater, a weird-sounding laughter erupted and reverberated through the audience. Lucchesi's heart sank. "They didn't buy it," he lamented. In the seats surrounding him, the studio executives were thinking the same thing.

On-screen, Stampler taunts Vail, telling the lawyer that they played off each other perfectly in the courtroom. The astonished attorney looks like he has been kicked in the stomach. In the final scene, he is a lone figure in defeat, an overhead shot showing him leaving the building with the knowledge that he was the pawn and Stampler will get away with murder.

The screen faded to black, and in the theater, there was total silence. By now, Lucchesi could hardly breathe. But then, after a few seconds, the audience broke into huge applause.

Later, during the focus group, the moderator asked moviegoers why they laughed when Stampler said there was no Aaron. The participants admitted they had been shocked. The laughter was almost involuntary, a purely visceral response, as if to say, "You got me!"

What worked so well in *Primal Fear* was its ability to keep moviegoers invested in Aaron right up to the very end when they discovered he was a fabrication. The movie, and a brilliant performance by Edward Norton, had so manipulated its audience that they continued to root for the character even when they knew he was guilty of the crime. The test audience proved that the big reveal worked, and that Norton pulled it off perfectly. They rated the film well above average, a tribute not only to a well-crafted story but also to the big surprise at the end.

"*Primal Fear* scored about an eighty-three [in the top two boxes] on the night of the first screening, even though it was a little long," said Lucchesi. "I was so relieved, especially after hearing that strange laughter at the moment when the audience realized Edward Norton was evil through and through. But it worked. Our gamble paid off."

When focus group participants were asked about their favorite character in the movie, Lucchesi expected them to say, "Richard Gere" or "Martin Vail." Instead, someone asked, "Who was that kid?"

Even before *Primal Fear* opened in April 1996, Hollywood was abuzz over Norton, who would later be nominated for Best Supporting Actor. Although he lost the Academy Award to Cuba Gooding Jr. (for his role in *Jerry Maguire*), Norton won the Golden Globe and several film critic association awards for his portrayal of Stampler. Rumors surfaced that the filmmakers deliberately cast an unknown in the part to throw off audiences, but Lucchesi maintained, "That's hindsight being twenty-twenty. This worked out beautifully."

To this day, *Primal Fear* is considered one of the best "surprise ending" movies of all time.

10.

SPOCK, LADDIE,

AND LESSONS IN MANAGING

HIGHLY EMOTIONAL INDIVIDUALS

I n 1987—one year before he made the bartender flick *Cocktail*— Robert Cort was busy with another film. It was called *Three Men and a Baby*.

Cort knew that *Three Men and a Baby* was most certainly a broad comedy. The question was, how broad would it play? The premise centers on three bachelors sharing a New York penthouse whose carefree lives are turned upside down when a baby that one of them unwittingly fathered arrives on their doorstep. Three popular actors at the time were cast in the roles, two from leading television shows—Ted Danson (*Cheers*) and Tom Selleck (*Magnum, P.I.*)—plus Steve Guttenberg, who had a thriving film career underway with major roles in *Cocoon*, *Short Circuit*, and the *Police Academy* series. The odds were in the film's favor, but the chemistry of the ensemble and the director's comedic abilities were yet to be proven. "We just didn't know at the time," reflected Cort. "It wasn't like we were sitting with Bill Murray and Dan Aykroyd."

Cort was one of the producers of the picture and had traveled to Lake Tahoe at the request of the director, Leonard Nimoy of *Star Trek* fame, who had retreated to the vacation spot to edit the picture after shooting was completed. This was Nimoy's third feature film behind the camera, but the first time he had directed a non–*Star Trek* movie.

In Lake Tahoe, Nimoy put together a first assemblage and arranged for a small test screening at a theater in Incline Village. It was a low-key event, and just 120 moviegoers were recruited to see that first cut, not the usual three-hundred-to-four-hundred-person screening with the studio chiefs in attendance. In fact, Cort was the only executive to travel up from Los Angeles to watch the movie with its first test audience. He was elated when he saw the film, and the audience's reaction buoyed his enthusiasm even further. "It was the longest sustained laughter I had ever witnessed," he recalled. "Moviegoers laughed so hard during the diapering scene, and for so long afterward, you couldn't hear any of the dialogue."

Disney was set to release the picture under its adult comedy banner, Touchstone Pictures, which was headed at the time by Jeffrey Katzenberg. When the screening was over, Cort rushed to a phone to tell Katzenberg that the movie had played extremely well. He remembered Katzenberg replying, "How big? Fifty million?"

"I think bigger," said Cort. "Seventy-five million." The dollar figures they bandied about referred to total domestic grosses, but this was 1987, a time when fewer than ten movies per year hit the $75 million mark, so Cort's estimation positioned *Three Men and a Baby* in the upper echelon.

Now it was Katzenberg's turn to get excited. He told Cort to bring the film to Los Angeles, where it would be screened again before a bigger test audience. Cort returned home and the studio arranged to have the film tested at a theater in Woodland Hills.

On the night of the second preview, Cort was terrified. He had put a stake in the ground, telling the studio that the film would do big business. What if he was wrong? After all, there had been no other executive at the Incline Village screening to corroborate his opinion. Maybe he had just been caught up in the moment.

As the film began to play, every muscle in Cort's body was tense. He sat with Katzenberg and about twenty other people from Disney and Touchstone, his ears closely tuned to the sounds of the audience. To prolong his agony, the baby does not arrive for the first fifteen minutes of the film so there are no big laughs at the beginning. Cort was on pins and needles until the first laugh hit. But from that moment forward, *Three Men and a Baby* played just as it did at its first screening. The Woodland Hills audience loved the picture.

When the movie was over, Cort sensed the studio executives were thrilled with what they had just seen, but he couldn't relax. He was pumped, feeling the adrenaline coursing through his veins. Meanwhile, the focus group was gathered in the front of the theater, and as the moderator prepped them, Katzenberg quietly motioned to Cort and asked if he knew the older gentleman who was seated directly in front of them. The producer didn't recognize the man, who sat quietly writing notes on a pad of paper. Cort leaned forward and said, "Excuse me. Who are you?"

The man answered, keeping his voice low so as not to disturb the focus group. "I'm with the Knight Ridder Press Circuit," Cort heard the man say. Thinking that he was a reporter who had snuck into the theater to get an advance peek at the still-unfinished film, Cort exploded.

"You son of a bitch!" Cort said, reaching for the back of the man's collar and physically pulling him from his seat. "You get your ass out of this theater right now!"

Twenty heads from the focus group swiveled around to see what the commotion was all about. The moderator had just finished telling them that they could be completely honest and forthcoming when expressing their opinions of the film. Now, as they witnessed Cort's outburst, they probably questioned whether they should say anything that would provoke such a reaction. They all stared in horror as Cort hauled the man toward the exit.

Suddenly, Cort heard someone calling his name. "Bob. Bob! He's my publicist," cried Leonard Nimoy, rushing over to save the man from Cort's angry grip.

"In my heightened state of anxiety, I heard, 'I'm from the Knight Ridder Press Circuit,' but what the guy really said was, 'I'm Leonard Nimoy's press agent.' They don't sound exactly alike but there's roughly the same number of syllables," Cort explained.

After apologizing profusely, Cort settled down and the focus group continued. Somehow, the moderator was able to regain control of the group, and Cort learned an important lesson about controlling his nerves. To this day, he often gets up from his seat and paces in the back of the theater to release anxiety when his films are previewed.

The results of the Woodland Hills screening validated the producer's faith in his film. "From the director's cut to the final cut, it was the least number of changes that I have ever seen in a film," said Cort proudly.

However, he was way off in his prediction of box office revenue. As it turned out, 1987 would be a banner year for the movie industry, one that saw the release of *Fatal Attraction*, *Moonstruck*, *Lethal Weapon*, *The Witches of Eastwick*, *Predator*, *Robocop*, *Broadcast News*, *Good Morning, Vietnam*, *Beverly Hills Cop II*, and *Dirty Dancing*. Every one of those films did big business, and three made more than $100 million. But none took in more money than *Three Men and a Baby*. It grossed about $168 million domestically, more than double Cort's estimation. It still ranks among the top revenue-producing comedies in Hollywood history.

There are certain occupations that deal every day with highly emotional people—clinical psychiatrists, divorce attorneys, hostage negotiators, and White House staffers.

You wouldn't think that my job is like any of those. At first blush, "film research" sounds like an occupation for movie buffs—for Hitchcock nerds and Kurosawa obsessives, people who lock themselves in small screening rooms and barely see real human beings at all. You wouldn't expect that the actual job requires diplomatic finesse. That it entails handling individuals sometimes acting like maniacs.

Jonathan Helfgot, who served two stints at 20th Century Fox in top marketing positions and is now at Netflix, remembered a situation where a writer/director was so upset when he saw the low topline scores for his film after a test screening that he actually ate the paper upon which they were printed. "He grabbed the topline and swallowed it," recalled Helfgot.

That particular movie never attracted a broad audience, but the filmmaker went on to make many acclaimed and nominated films.

Emotions can run high on the night of a screening. Filmmakers who have invested years of their lives in a picture, and are about to unveil it for the first time to the scrutiny of the moviegoing public, often arrive at the theater with frayed nerves. Even the coolest of studio executives can show signs of anxiety on the night of a test preview, given the financial stakes and sometimes even career implications that may hinge on whether the audience embraces a film. When a test audience is particularly critical of a movie or rejects it altogether, tempers can flare. On occasion I've actually been in the line of fire, but I know I'm seeing those associated with the film at a moment when they're most vulnerable. I'm sympathetic to their disappointment and frustration, and I understand they need to vent.

Catherine Paura, who gave me my first job in the movie research business and is one of my most cherished mentors, has a plethora of stories about screening-night jitters. Like me, she has been verbally attacked when a film tested poorly. After one particular screening when Paura handed out topline scores, a star director told her that she planned to use the printout as toilet paper. Another director, faced with bad screening results, flung the topline sheets back at Paura.

Not all filmmakers react with such venom, though. Paura also shared a story about Michael Cimino's ill-fated film *Heaven's Gate*. There have been many articles and an entire book written about the film, which has gone down in Hollywood history as one of the greatest financial failures of its time. Cimino, fresh off the success of *The Deer Hunter*, was given latitude to spend what insiders estimated as four times the original production budget. The film was a three-hour-thirty-nine-minute jumble. Without the benefit of any research, it was released by United Artists in November 1980 and was skewered by audiences and the press alike. Vincent Canby (yes, the same *New York Times* critic who panned *Cocktail*) wrote: "*Heaven's Gate*, which opens today at the Cinema One, fails so completely that you might suspect Mr. Cimino sold his soul to the Devil to obtain the success of *The Deer Hunter*, and the Devil has just come around to collect."

In an attempt to salvage the picture, United Artists pulled it from theaters and called Joe Farrell and Catherine Paura, who had founded the National Research Group in Los Angeles just three years earlier. The studio asked NRG to conduct research on the film to see what might be done to fix it, and to do it extremely quietly.

Farrell and Paura arranged a series of out-of-town screenings in Chicago, Boston, and Seattle, and everyone traveled under pseudonyms, which you could do in 1980 before ID was required to fly. Confidentiality was the literal order of the day. No one wanted the word to get out that the film was being tested. "In Chicago, two screenings were conducted, the first one at a theater on Michigan Avenue, where the movie played dreadfully," Paura said. Immediately afterward, she climbed into a waiting limousine that would take her, Michael Cimino, and his producer, Joann Carelli, to the next screening in Calumet City, about twenty-five miles away. The climate inside the limo was somber, and Paura struggled to find the right words to say to the filmmakers following such dismal test results. Suddenly, an idea came to her. Rather than talk about the movie, the ever-gracious Paura pivoted to an entirely different subject. She herself is of Italian descent, so she inquired about Cimino's and Carelli's families. "Before long, the three of us were chatting about our grandmothers and old family recipes." What could have turned into a very hostile situation was actually an enjoyable ride.

Paura doesn't remember much about the Calumet City screening, but despite all efforts to uncover insights that might guide a recut, *Heaven's Gate* never became a commercial or critical success. It was perceived as fatally flawed and ended up destroying Michael Cimino's career and the careers of several executives at United Artists.

This is, of course, an extreme example of a film's outcome, and in today's world, it would be unheard of to get that far along on a major studio motion picture without any research. But there are still nights when I have to deliver disappointing results and face the uncomfortable silences as the scores sink in.

My advice to filmmakers when their films test really poorly is to look beyond the numbers and read the cards. There are always insights to be gleaned from the comments that moviegoers write and the way in which they express themselves. Copies of the surveys are available to them, posted to a secure site for downloading, or delivered digitally to them on the night of the screening or the morning after. I encourage all filmmakers to read them.

Hutch Parker, who is the producer of several *X-Men* movies, agrees.

"What I find most valuable is reading the cards," he has told me. "How did they say what they hated at the end? Their language, their choice for expression tells me a lot."

Of course, there can be glowing praise: "I had goose bumps!" "Oscar-worthy performance." "I laughed so hard, I almost peed my pants." But the cards can also deliver some pretty scathing criticism: "I want my two hours back!" "I'd rather be beat in the face with a donkey penis than watch this film." "Cheesier than nachos."

Yes, these are actual comments from real test preview attendees. And they can be tough to take.

A while back, I was involved in the research on a relatively big-budget studio film that was quite flawed. The movie had been screened once, and although the first test audience had raised issues that suggested the need for additional work on it, the studio people sensed that the director was recalcitrant about making any changes. There was a big investment in the film and the director had not responded to the subtle calls for change that moviegoers had voiced at that initial preview. A second test screening was scheduled to confirm the criticisms that the first audience had registered, with the hope that the director would be enlightened and focus on revisions that were so apparently necessary.

Before the lights went down, the head of the studio pulled me aside and gave me a list of very pointed questions to ask the focus group later in the evening.

After the movie was over and everyone in the audience had filled out the questionnaires, we assembled the standard twenty moviegoers to stay behind and discuss their opinions of the film. We seated the group in the front two rows of the theater, and in typical fashion, the director and studio people sat several rows behind them to listen in on the conversation.

The moviegoers were very vocal about their criticism, and as the moderator, I was pleased that they were so forthcoming. But it was stressful for me because I had to ask certain leading questions that the studio chief wanted me to probe, and for good reason. He wanted to drive the point home. The film needed changes.

As the discussion progressed, the focus group began to skewer the movie. Though their comments were completely valid, it was becoming a bloodbath, which is never a comfortable situation when the filmmaker is sitting right there. And as the head of the studio had instructed, I pointedly asked about specific scenes that he felt needed work, which sparked a flurry of criticism from the participants.

When the group was finished, I thanked the participants and started to make my way up the aisle toward the back of the auditorium. From the corner of my eye, I could see the director leap from his seat and charge up the opposite aisle in the same direction I was headed. He dashed across one of the rows in the middle of the theater and cut me off at the pass. With his face just inches from mine, he screamed at me, "Who the hell do you think you are? How dare you! Who the fuck gave you the authority to ask those questions?"

Although I wanted to retaliate and tell him, "Back off! Why don't you make the changes the audience so desperately wants?" something inside me said, "Just let him rant." I went into a Zen-like state, focusing more on the feel of his angry breath than on the impact of his angry words. When he was finished, I found the studio chief who had instructed me to ask the questions in the first place and relayed what the director had said to me. The head of the studio hurried out of the theater to confront the director, who stood fuming just beyond the front doors. A huge fight ensued, and the studio chief ended it by telling the director that he had made "a piece of shit."

He went on to say, "Don't blame the kid for doing his job."

Test screenings should spark discussion, but no one wants to see an ugly outcome.

Another time I tested a film in Seattle, and the results were neither great nor terrible. I felt that I had a good rapport with the director, so when he invited me to join him and some other production folks for dinner, I went along. Over our meal, we had a lively discussion about the screening, interpreting what the moviegoers had said and implications for the work that still needed to be done on the film. It seemed very amicable, and at the end of the night, we left the restaurant all smiles and hugs.

A few weeks passed, and when there was no word regarding a second screening, I called the studio to inquire. I was told that the director didn't like my feedback on his movie and that he asked to not have me involved in the next screenings for the film. I was floored. I had never expressed any of my personal feelings about the film, but I imagine he had somehow associated me with criticism expressed by moviegoers at that first Seattle screening.

Sometimes I'm blamed for words that don't even come out of my mouth.

About ten years ago, I conducted research on a film that tested dismally. A prominent, Oscar-winning screenwriter, one with an impressive résumé of well-known films, had written the screenplay and was in the audience on the night of the test preview. After the movie, we selected a group of filmgoers to stay behind and talk about the film, and as usual, I moderated the discussion. That early cut of the movie didn't play well at all, and the criticism was free-flowing. Eventually, one moviegoer commented, "It felt like it was written by a twelve-year-old."

The screenwriter, sitting behind the focus group with the production and studio teams, heard every word, and it must have been quite embarrassing for him. Afterward, I was told by one of the marketing executives, who happened to be my buddy, that the screenwriter demanded I be pulled off any and all subsequent research for the film. It bothered me terribly that I was blamed for the negative comment, so years later, when I had the opportunity to work on another one of the screenwriter's films, I confronted him about it. He denied that it had ever happened, which I knew was a lie, and told me that I was the only one he ever wanted to conduct research on his movies.

Welcome to Hollywood.

Perry Katz, who worked for years in top marketing and research positions on the studio side, tells a great story about a film he ushered into theaters at the end of the 1980s, when he was at Universal Pictures. The working title was *Shoeless Joe*, which was the name of the source material, a book by W. P. Kinsella. The film was directed by Phil Alden Robinson and produced by Larry Gordon. Gordon was already an esteemed producer with *Die Hard* and *48 Hours* to his credit.

When the film was finished and previewed, test audiences loved it. But over and over again, Katz and his Universal colleagues heard disparaging remarks about the title. Moviegoers just hated it. They thought *Shoeless Joe* sounded more like a movie about a hobo, not the touching story that they had just seen about an Iowa farmer who builds a baseball diamond in his cornfield after hearing voices.

It was now down to the wire and the studio was ready to start the marketing campaign for the film. They knew they couldn't go out with *Shoeless Joe* as the title. So a big meeting was called in the executive dining room at Universal to try to convince Gordon and Robinson that a change was needed.

"Look, guys," Katz recalled the studio people saying. "We're not going to call the movie *Shoeless Joe*. We've done some title tests and we're going to call it *Field of Dreams*."

Gordon, being protective of his director/writer (Robinson) and in a burst of anger, proceeded to throw over a dining room chair in protest. However, the die was cast, and the title *Field of Dreams* was locked.

Phil Robinson called the author of the book to tell him that Hollywood was intending to bastardize the movie, giving it a different name than the book title. However, instead of being upset, the author admitted that *Shoeless Joe* had never been what he wanted to call his book. His publisher had chosen it. The author's original title was *The Dream Field*.

At which point Larry Gordon and Phil Robinson decided *Field of Dreams* was a perfectly fine title for the film.

This brings me to another story about Harvey Weinstein.

The year was 2015. The movie in question was *Jane's Got a Gun*. It was one of Natalie Portman's minor works, a Western, and I had arranged a "double screening" of it in Sherman Oaks, California, which took place in side-by-side auditoriums of the same theater complex. This test was a "bake-off" to determine which of two versions played better, Weinstein's or the director's cut of the film.

Weinstein was the producer of this particular film, and I had been warned that he was on a warpath that evening. Nobody knew why. All we knew was that by the time he'd entered the theater, he had fired two people, including his head of production.

The screenings that night weren't particularly tricky to organize, but there was one small hitch: one theater had twenty more seats than the other. When conducting a double test of a movie, you want your audiences to be as uniform as possible, for an apples-to-apples comparison. You want the same number of people in the seats and the two audiences to be demographically matched. So in this case, we simply left twenty seats empty in the slightly larger theater and filled 160 seats in both houses.

When Weinstein walked into the complex and asked how the audiences looked, he was told that there were 160 people in the auditorium that held 180. Before it could be explained that there were *another* 160 people in the adjoining theater and both audiences matched in size and demographics, he flew into a rage. He must have thought there were only 80 people in each theater, not the 320 total that were actually there . . . or something. It was hard to tell through the spit flying from his mouth.

"You're trying to fuck me," Weinstein said as he charged toward me.

I shot back, "What are you talking about, Harvey?"

He repeated, "You're trying to fuck me. You want to work with me again?"

I paused, slightly stunned as I tried to make sense of what was going on. Again, he said, "You ever want to work with me again?"

If I had a shred of self-respect in that moment, I would have told him, "No. Go fuck yourself, Harvey." But the truth was, for the good of my company, I wanted the man's business. And so, I said, "Yes, I want to work with you," and allowed him to rant.

Weinstein continued. "So here's what you're going to do. You're going to give me this screening for half price. Then you're going to take the other half of the money and you're going to give it to my charity."

Later on, his head of distribution, Erik Lomis, who is a friend of mine, cleared up the misunderstanding. When all was said and done, Weinstein ended up offering a half-assed apology and, of course, paid for both screenings.

It's perhaps because of moments like these that I consider myself something of an authority when it comes to dealing with angry people and awkward situations. I've dealt with so many of them by now that I had to develop some coping mechanisms and, needless to say, a thick skin.

Here's my secret. When I face filmmakers and studio execs behaving badly, I do so with a simple technique: *I stop, I breathe, and I try to put it all into context.* Then I find something good about that person, or at least some shred of goodness in the situation (there's always something good, right?) to diffuse my own impulse to fight back. It's a reminder to myself to be empathetic and take the high road. I find that empathy is the best weapon against anger and chaos, in any situation.

I'm fully aware that out of context, the anecdotes I've just shared sound like classic Hollywood temper tantrums, tales of individuals who are so used to having their asses kissed that they aren't equipped to handle criticism.

I won't lie: some people are like that in the movie business. Some people are real assholes. They like to dish it out but can't take it. Hollywood can be a place of thin skin. But more often than not, the people who act out on screening nights do so not because they're brats but because they're under intense pressure. It's understandable.

A test screening is judgment time, the moment of reckoning, the moment of truth. For the audience, it's a few hours of their day. But for the people involved in making the movie, it's often the climax of many years of their lives. It can also be their career-defining moment, and the results determine how the next chapter of their career will play out.

I understand the stress that a test screening visits upon a filmmaker. After all, I've been in their shoes. I was an actor for many years and still produce movies. I can relate. So I try to shake off those awful outbursts, sometimes directed squarely at me, and move on.

Which is why I admire the approach that Drew Barrymore and her production partner, Nancy Juvonen, adopt when they test their movies. They take "a great big dose of humility" before entering the theater and, for a few hours, set their own opinions aside and listen to everyone else's. As Drew aptly explains, "It's trying on other people's perspectives while never losing sight of your own gut instincts."

The Barrymore/Juvonen philosophy has helped me redirect my own impulses when our research comes under attack on screening nights. I listen and empathize but stand behind the results.

I've known Drew and Nancy since they were freshman producers, trying to establish themselves as serious filmmakers in a male-dominated business. I was with them when they tested their first big film, *Charlie's Angels* (the one released in 2000, as opposed to the 2019 film that was written, directed, and produced by Elizabeth Banks), and I know for a fact that they were nervous as hell. But on that film, and the many I've tested for them ever since, they remained open-minded and gracious about the feedback. No meltdowns. No rages.

When we sat down over lunch in February 2011, we reminisced about their beginnings as producing partners, and their years-long journey to turn a beloved franchise into a blockbuster hit.

"Dude, someone pretending to be Drew Barrymore left a message for you on the answering machine," Nancy Juvonen recalled her roommate saying when she arrived home one evening in 1995. Juvonen thought for a minute. She had actually met Drew Barrymore three weeks earlier but wondered why the actress would be phoning her.

A striking blonde with a thousand-watt smile, Juvonen was in her late twenties at the time. She was living in San Francisco and had tried her hand at several different jobs, working as a flight attendant for a private jet service, a personal organizer, and assistant to saxophonist Clarence Clemons. (Clemons, who died in 2011, played in Bruce Springsteen's E Street Band and was also an actor and music producer.) Juvonen had recently visited her brother, Jim, in Seattle where he was working on a film called *Mad Love*. The siblings had spent a fun weekend with a group of Jim's friends from the movie set, and Barrymore, who had a starring role in the film, had been one of them. Drew and Nancy hit it off, but after the weekend was over, the two young women had not exchanged phone numbers or made plans to see each other again. Juvonen returned to the Bay Area and her job with Clemons.

Meanwhile, Barrymore had seen something special in Juvonen, and it stayed with her as she traveled to New York for business. She liked

Juvonen's high-octane energy, took note of her intelligence, and admired that she could be "the smartest person in the room without making you feel like she was smarter than everyone else." On a whim, she phoned Juvonen from the back seat of a Town Car on her way to the airport for her return flight home to Los Angeles and left a message on her answering machine. "I dare you to come to LA," Barrymore said. "I want to start my own production company, and I think you'd be a great partner. Why don't you give it a shot?"

Juvonen was taken by surprise, not only by Barrymore's message but by the thought of relocating her entire life. She had attended USC for a couple of years and enjoyed the experience of being in LA, but never imagined that she would return to work there. Yet Barrymore's offer was something she had to consider. Her work with Clemons was winding down, and she was ready to commit to a career path. "I had a lot of energy but it wasn't really being placed anywhere," Juvonen remarked. After talking it through with Barrymore, she decided to take the chance. She packed her belongings into her car and headed south.

It was less of a gamble for Barrymore, who trusted the intuition that she had developed during her years in the movie business. "I had a gut instinct and I followed it," she recounted. "And it changed my life forever." When Juvonen arrived in Los Angeles, Barrymore's hunch proved to be correct. The two women became fast friends and trusted partners.

Under the decidedly feminine Flower Films banner, Barrymore and Juvonen's company was born. The producing partners' first order of business was to assume they had a lot to learn. As Barrymore explained, "We wanted to approach it like college. I had been in the business for nearly twenty years at that point. That didn't make me a good producer. You learn to produce."

Never Been Kissed was Flower Films' first official movie, but Barrymore and Juvonen were unofficially involved in three others before that: *Scream*, *Home Fries*, and *Ever After*. "We were graciously allowed to be involved in those films," explained Juvonen. "Development, casting ideas, director pick, notes, everything. We got to peek behind the curtain and it was a great entry into our own thing. I had no knowledge before those movies. I always liken it to driving a car but not knowing how the motor runs. We opened up the hood and took it apart, piece by piece, to see how it all linked up and worked."

One day in 1998, Barrymore was in her office eating lunch at her desk when Juvonen burst in to tell her that Sony was making a feature film version of *Charlie's Angels*. Juvonen was excited because she had loved the show as a little girl and felt there was a part for Barrymore as one of the Angels. "We've got to get in there," she exclaimed. Barrymore knew her partner was onto something big. She choked down the rest of her lunch and made a call. The two producers learned that the idea to make a *Charlie's Angels* movie had been around for about ten years and had never gotten off the ground. When they received the script, they understood why. They were hugely disappointed.

"I loved that show more than anything," recalled Juvonen. "And I knew the script was all wrong. The story took place in Switzerland, one of the Angels had her head in a petri dish trying to find out if she is pregnant, and they never changed outfits once. It's not just about hair and clothes, but it has to go into that in a fun way. And Switzerland? Cold? Bunny suits? They just didn't get the girl thing."

Juvonen took the initiative and contacted Sony, this time to say that the script was completely unacceptable. She told the studio that Barrymore might be up for taking a role as one of the Angels, but only if major changes were made to it. While on the phone, the studio executive floated the idea of Flower Films producing it. "That took it to a whole new level," said Juvonen.

Barrymore added, "I had a sinking feeling in my stomach because I knew we had stumbled into something big, but also that it would be an uphill battle every step of the way."

The road was indeed bumpy. It took nearly two years to get the film off the ground. Both producers loved the 1978 movie *Foul Play*, starring Chevy Chase and Goldie Hawn, and envisioned the same blend of action, romance, humor, and suspense for *Charlie's Angels*. They admired the work of a young commercial and music video director who went by the single three-letter name, McG, and felt he had a certain talent for coalescing the elements seamlessly. But he had never directed a feature film, so convincing the studio took a lot of work. After months of debate and discussion, the studio relented, and McG was signed on to direct.

Screenwriter John August was also brought in to start fresh on a new script. But casting proved to be very tough, because without a script, actors were hesitant to commit. "That was a valuable lesson for us as producers," said Barrymore. "Basically, we were promising actors that there would be a great script without having seen it ourselves, putting our reputations on the line. Nancy always says that we need to keep our promises. And I love that. So I knew we couldn't go forward unless the script was great."

Barrymore had already decided upon the role of Dylan Sanders, the street-smart Angel. Cameron Diaz was the second actress to commit, taking the part of Natalie Cook, the goofy Angel who is drop-dead gorgeous but still acts like the nerd she was in high school.

Casting for the third Angel was a challenge. Barrymore and Juvonen wanted an actress with a different look, not necessarily another Caucasian and certainly not another blonde. As a girl, Juvonen and her two best friends had playacted the roles of the TV show, and she knew fans would identify most with the character that resembled them physically. So she felt it was important to have different looks in the cast. "I always wanted to be Sabrina Duncan, but I had blond hair. So I played Jill Monroe," Juvonen said. The producers loved the idea of Lucy Liu playing the part of sophisticated Alex Munday, but Liu was in the midst of shooting a season of *Ally McBeal* and was not available, so their search continued.

For the role of John Bosley, they had only one actor in mind: Bill Murray. They had calls out to his agent, but the elusive Murray wasn't responding. Finally, they caught a lucky break. Barrymore was asked to participate in *Saturday Night Live 25*, the twenty-fifth anniversary special commemorating the popular late-night show. She and Juvonen knew that as one of the original cast members, Murray would be there. Barrymore was on a mission.

The night of the *SNL* taping, the audience was packed with celebrities, Drew Barrymore among them. Juvonen commented, "Bill knew we had been after him. And during the live taping, he goes up to Drew and sings 'Don't go chasing waterfalls.' And we're wondering if this is some cryptic message. Don't go chasing you? Or we have you now, and we can stop the chase?"

Whatever Murray may have meant, he eventually signed on to play Bosley. The entire process had taken so long that Lucy Liu was now done with *Ally McBeal* and was also able to commit to the project. The film was underway.

What the producers didn't anticipate was the level of cynicism they would face during production. "It was hell," recalled Juvonen. "This was the beginning of people posting their opinions on the Internet and there was bad press everywhere. Just the idea of a *Charlie's Angels* movie was enough to get criticized. There had been a lot of disappointment in *The Avengers* (1998) and *The Mod Squad* (1999), movies that had not worked. So people were telling us that we were foolish. We wouldn't be able to pull it off. We would fail. On top of that, we had a first-time director, someone who had never directed a feature film, let alone a giant budgeted, hugely scrutinized one. There was a lot of money riding on our little sophomore producing heads."

The Internet chatter was not good, yet the studio remained behind the movie all the way. Armed with a new script, and the vision for a fresh and modern take on the 1970s TV show, the executives were hoping the film would offer something for everyone—action, romance, sex appeal, martial arts stunts, and tongue-in-cheek humor. But no one really knew that it would be a hit—that was the aspiration, but certainly not a sure thing. When the film was finished, Sony arranged an out-of-town preview in Phoenix to keep it as quiet as possible. Flying to that screening, Barrymore and Juvonen were nervous wrecks. Their biggest concern was with the tone of the film, and whether moviegoers would respond to the hybrid genre they tried to channel from *Foul Play*.

"There's so much pressure," explained Barrymore. "You wish you could watch it from behind a glass wall, but you're sitting right there with Amy Pascal [head of Sony Pictures at the time] and all the executives. And you're all thinking the same thing. Does the audience like it? Do they buy the story? Do they like the characters and if not, is that because you intentionally created them that way? Or is it a big problem?"

For all their worry, the test audience loved the movie. A few minutes into the screening, both women had the same thought: it's working! When the topline scores were tabulated, 88 percent of the moviegoers who had previewed the film rated it either excellent or very good.

"Leaving that screening," said Juvonen, "we were both thinking, now it becomes fun. We got a B-plus and it was only the first time anyone had seen it. Let's get those notes and make the refinements. But let's also protect it, because the audience liked it."

Charlie's Angels was released on November 3, 2000, to a $40 million opening weekend. It went on to earn $264 million worldwide, established Flower Films as a first-rate production company, and launched the feature film career of its young director, McG. The 2003 sequel, *Charlie's Angels: Full Throttle*, earned nearly as much as the first installment.

The Barrymore/Juvonen partnership endured, both on a professional and personal level. Their serendipitous beginnings, self-directed education, and years of hard work had paid off. Like most filmmakers, the projects they chose often reflected subjects close to their hearts—strong female characters with extraordinary talents.

To this day, Drew Barrymore and Nancy Juvonen are among the most fun people I've ever worked with in the business. These two soul mates exude positive energy, and despite all the pressures they may feel on screening nights, they always conduct themselves with kindness and elegance.

Speaking of negative word of mouth that can precede a film's opening, one of our biggest concerns in the world of movie market research is that an attendee at an early test screening will post, tweet, or blog something detrimental that lands online for the whole world to see before the film is actually finished. It's a very real problem for studios and filmmakers who are taking an entire theaterful of people into their confidence and asking them to stay silent until the film is finished and released. For that reason, we now have attendees sign nondisclosure agreements, which are legally binding documents that pledge their silence about the film they're about to see. Their signatures are verified against proof of identity, typically their driver's licenses.

"You're walking out naked on stage in front of four hundred strangers, and there's no way that's ever going to feel that comfortable," says Marc Shmuger, former chairman of Universal Pictures. "And what's complicated beyond belief is that a very private process becomes a public spectacle with the Internet. You're going through that process of exposing rough work to an audience and trusting that their judgments about the film and its quality will not end up online."

Before every screening conducted today, I make an announcement asking the audience to respect the process, allowing the filmmakers the opportunity to use their feedback to finesse the movie and make it the best that it can possibly be. For the most part, those who participate in test screenings abide by the rules. But I have had to threaten a few with cease and desists. When the highly anticipated *Blade Runner 2049* was first screened, someone posted comments afterward on a popular sci-fi website. We had signed nondisclosure agreements from everyone who attended the preview, but the comments were anonymous, so our company's attorney wrote a cease and desist letter to the domain owner. The posting was immediately removed.

No discussion about wrangling big Hollywood personalities is complete without mentioning Alan Ladd Jr.

In all my years conducting movie research, I have never heard a negative word about him. "Laddie," as he was known throughout the industry, produced movies on and off for more than four decades. As an independent producer, he is probably best known for the 1996 Academy Award Best Picture film, *Braveheart*. Under the Ladd Company umbrella, he also produced *Chariots of Fire*, *Body Heat*, *Blade Runner*, *Night Shift*, *The Right Stuff*, *Police Academy*, and *Gone Baby Gone*.

But Laddie's notoriety as an admirable leader in an often-cutthroat business began earlier in his career, when he was president of Twentieth Century–Fox in the 1970s and as chairman and CEO of MGM/UA from 1985 to 1993. During his tenure at those studios, he was responsible for dozens of films that have stood the test of time, including *Alien*, *Julia*, *The Towering Inferno*, *The Omen*, *Young Frankenstein*, *Breaking Away*, *Norma*

Rae, The Boys from Brazil, The Turning Point, An Unmarried Woman, All That Jazz, The Rose, Nine to Five, The Rocky Horror Picture Show, Spaceballs, Moonstruck, Thelma & Louise, and *A Fish Called Wanda*. Oh, and *Star Wars*.

Yeah . . . *Star Wars*.

Alan Ladd Jr. has singlehandedly jump-started the careers of some of the most important directors in Hollywood. As impressive, his strong but tempered approach earned him the reputation of being one of the most respected heads of a Hollywood studio in any era.

Oddly, I had never had a one-on-one meeting with Laddie until I interviewed him for this book, but for years I've been hearing stories about him from others in the business. Greg Foster, who shared the *Thelma & Louise* and *Moonstruck* stories in earlier chapters, came up in the business under Laddie's watchful eye and praises his leadership style to this day.

Ladd Jr. is the son of actor Alan Ladd, who played leading-man roles from the 1940s to the early 1960s. In the 1953 Western *Shane*, the senior Ladd portrayed a gunslinger who arrives in a small Wyoming settlement, presumably trying to leave his past behind. At his own peril, Shane fearlessly defends a rancher and his family from a ruthless cattle baron even though he stands to gain nothing personally. Foster describes Laddie as more like Shane than like his famous father.

It isn't difficult to understand Foster's analogy. The fictional Shane is skilled and strong with a restrained manner that belies his willingness to assert himself when he witnesses an injustice. The real-life Laddie is credited with those very same qualities. When I met with him, he was soft-spoken and seemingly quite modest considering the movies he has made and the big studio positions he has held.

Several of the test screening experiences that Laddie shared with me exemplified what I had heard about him from others—that he had a certain skill when dealing with filmmakers, even those with big egos or bad tempers. Sitting in his office, high above the Sunset Strip, he reflected on some of his screening "showdowns."

"I would always preview movies wherever the directors wanted to go," he explained, "because otherwise they'd say it's not the right audience. You're setting me up. So I always let them make the choice regarding location."

This was an easy concession for the former studio head, but he didn't compromise on the bigger, important decisions. In the mid-1970s, while he was at Twentieth Century–Fox, Laddie recalled a screening experience with a star director who didn't want to accept the truth about his movie.

"Peter Bogdanovich had just made three major motion pictures: *The Last Picture Show* for Columbia Pictures, *What's Up, Doc?* with Warner Bros., and *Paper Moon* for Paramount," he recounted. "He had also completed *Daisy Miller*, but no one had seen it yet. It wasn't out. So now he makes this film for Fox, *At Long Last Love*, and it's an homage to 1930s musicals with Burt Reynolds, who was the biggest star in the world at the time."

The film also starred Cybill Shepherd, who was in a relationship with Bogdanovich and had debuted as an actress in his 1971 film, *The Last Picture Show*. Now, four years later when *At Long Last Love* was finished, Laddie arranged for a screening of the movie in San Jose. As he recalled, when the film played and Burt Reynolds first burst into song, moviegoers started leaving the theater in droves. After the showing, Laddie headed over to a hotel across the street where Bogdanovich was waiting to debrief.

As he walked into the hotel room, an exuberant Bogdanovich, who was wearing a cape, greeted him. "Wasn't that a great preview?" the director exclaimed. Ladd was a bit shocked, not only by the director's take on the screening but by his attire. But he didn't mince words. "What are you talking about, Peter?" he replied. "If I had stepped into the aisle during the show, I would have been trampled."

Bogdanovich persisted, telling the studio executive that it had been a better screening than the first preview of *What's Up, Doc?* But Laddie wasn't buying it. "I find that hard to believe," he said to the director. He went on to point out, "Every time Cybill opened her mouth to sing, the audience laughed."

It was a difficult conversation, and Ladd Jr. was well aware that Bogdanovich had final cut. But after talking it over, the director finally agreed to make some changes. Laddie recalled that Bogdanovich did, in fact, take out some of Shepherd's musical numbers. The new version of the film was then taken to Denver, where it screened to better results, although the scores remained mediocre. Still, as Laddie remembered, "There were no walkouts."

"So after that Denver screening, we went back to the hotel and met with Peter, and this time, Cybill was also sitting there. And Peter says that he now knows what's wrong with the picture and how to make it much better. He needs an additional number for Cybill to do. He wanted to put back the old songs and shoot a new one."

Of course, this was all said in front of his girlfriend, the stunningly beautiful Shepherd, whom Bogdanovich was obviously trying to appease. But Laddie had seen the audience responses and he trusted the research. He was not about to sanction more spending on the ill-fated film. Using his characteristic powers of persuasion, he convinced the director that the movie would not improve with more music.

"Peter was a very clever filmmaker," continued Laddie. "But *At Long Last Love* just didn't work. It was fatally flawed."

Thinking back on his dealings with other final-cut directors, Ladd talked about his good friend Mel Brooks. "He knows comedy better than I do," he said. "Before the preview of *Young Frankenstein*, though, he wanted to cut 'Puttin' on the Ritz.' Gene Wilder convinced him to keep it in."

Laddie's relationship with Mel Brooks is one of those long-lasting Hollywood friendships, which Greg Foster had witnessed firsthand. When Brooks made *Spaceballs* for MGM/UA in 1987, Foster had just joined the company. Laddie was a family friend of the Fosters (Greg's brother, Gary, is a producer, as was his late father, David), had known Greg since he was born, and gave him his first big studio job when Greg was just twenty-five years old. But, true to his sense of fairness, he made it clear that it was a probationary period for his young employee, who would have to prove himself.

One of Foster's first assignments was to set up a test preview for *Spaceballs* at the Northpoint Theater in San Francisco. It was Ladd Jr.'s "lucky charm" location, where *Young Frankenstein*, *Star Wars*, and *The Elephant Man* had all first been screened (and all successfully) to test audiences.

It was difficult to recruit enough people to fill the nearly thousand-seat house (auditoriums in today's multiplexes are now much smaller, about two hundred to three hundred seats), but Foster remembered a sense of accomplishment when he saw the crowded theater on the night of the screening. He also recalled that he sat next to Mel Brooks during the preview.

Spaceballs played very well in its first half, but after forty-five minutes, the laughs became fewer and farther between. Accounts of what happened afterward are subject to thirty-year-old memories, explaining why Foster's version differs from Ladd Jr.'s.

According to Foster, Brooks was upset after the screening and felt the audience that he had recruited was wrong for the movie. But Ladd calmed him down by telling him that the film was great in the beginning, that there was some work to do in the back half, but that everything would be fine. He suggested they all go have dinner and talk about it.

In a nearby Chinese restaurant, Foster tried to eat what looked like a delicious meal, but he had no appetite. He was worried not only about taking the fall for what the director blamed on a bad recruit but about seeing his job at the studio come to an end. He tried to placate Brooks and told him he would go back to the hotel, read through the cards, and call him with more detailed feedback the following morning. Brooks was not inclined. He told Foster, "Listen, young man. Don't call me tomorrow morning, don't call me next week, don't ever call me, and best of luck with your career."

But Laddie jumped in and said to Brooks, "Mel, how long have I known you?"

Foster recalled Brooks's reply: "Forever. Twenty-five years."

Then Laddie turned to Foster and said, "Greg, how long have I known you?"

Foster said, "Since I was born."

Using an atypically loud voice, with several other MGM/UA executives who had joined them for dinner within earshot, Laddie proceeded to say, "So you both know me a long time, and I think you both trust me. Mel, Greg is going to go back to the hotel and read the cards, and when he calls you in the morning, what he says will be important. I want you to take his call." Brooks considered what his friend had said and agreed.

Turning to Foster, he said, "Okay, kid. Call me at ten."

And as everyone walked away after dinner, Laddie put his arm around Foster and said, "You're no longer on probation." Foster worked for Ladd for another eight years, until Ladd left the studio in 1993.

Laddie, on the other hand, recalled a somewhat different version. Like Foster, he remembered the film played exceedingly well in the first half but not in the back half. But in Laddie's recollection—and he insisted he remembered the screening clearly—the problem with Mel Brooks was set off when Foster started reading some of the negative comments in the theater right after the surveys were collected.

"We were in the lobby afterward and Greg had seen some of the cards. With any filmmaker, the smart thing to do is to talk about the good cards first. But Greg, being new to the job, told Mel about the bad cards first," recalled Ladd Jr. "So Mel says to him, 'Where are you going to be working next week, kid?'"

In Ladd Jr.'s version of the event, he recalled later pulling Greg aside and telling him that he should always start with the positives and drift into the negatives. "Because otherwise, the director will dislike you right off the bat." He used the situation as a teaching moment.

Regardless of whose version was more accurate, it's indisputable that Laddie diffused what could have been a very volatile situation. He prevailed in terms of standing behind the screening research results, yet he was respectful of both his marquee director and his junior executive. It was a moment that Foster will never forget.

"That was the thing about Laddie," said Foster with admiration. "He led by example. If there was bad news, it was his problem. If there was good news, it was everyone's success."

That statement is not just an accurate description of Alan Ladd Jr. It's also among the most accurate descriptions of what it means to be successful in the movie research business. On the great nights—the *Forrest Gump* and *Titanic* nights—the research company rarely receives credit. The praise goes elsewhere. And rightly so. But on the bad nights, the film research often steps into the spotlight.

To do my job, and do it well, means I often have to make bad situations my problem. It means taking center stage at moments when films and filmmakers are absolute wrecks—and being candid about it, even if honesty causes people to lash out at you. Sometimes that means taking one for the team.

I remember my interaction with a filmmaker who had once been an A-list director with several big hits to his credit. In 2008, he had directed and produced a new comedy, and based on the screening research, this one was going to be a miss. There were two serious problems with the picture. The first was that it had no defined target audience. We'd done three screenings in fact, and the recruit ratio was sky high for each (one person showed up to the theater for every twenty or so invitations that we handed out). This told us it was going to be very challenging to convince moviegoers to pay to see the picture in theaters. It had no big stars, nor did it have a particularly unique concept that could be leveraged in the advertising and publicity to entice crowds to see it. In my business, we identify those assets as "marketability."

Films that have weak marketability can still be successful if they play very well and generate great buzz. It may be difficult to get people into the theater to see them at first, but if they have exceptional "playability" (that is, if the film plays well and is a satisfying entertainment experience), enthusiasm can build. Positive word of mouth is instantaneous in today's environment.

I knew that if this filmmaker's movie was to succeed, it had to somehow overcome its challenged marketability or have terrific playability.

And therein was its second problem. In the tests we conducted, the audiences were not feeling all that enthusiastic about it. In particular, the ending was not satisfying and was one of the lowest-rated aspects. Clearly, the research indicated that the film's playability was not strong *enough* to overcome its weak marketability.

At a minimum, the director/producer had to reshoot his ending, and I told him as much. "Your audience is telling you to do this," I said. "Otherwise it will have very little chance to succeed since you currently don't have marketability *or* playability. You must have at least one of these."

My comment was based entirely on research results, not my opinion.

The filmmaker didn't take kindly to my message, but I had expected that. No one enjoys being told that their baby is really sick, but if they fill this prescription, they can save them. Instead, I was more concerned about the studio heads. They're the ones who commission the research, and generally they're able to look at the results more dispassionately. At first, they thought I had handled my communication with the director well. "You told the truth," was the message I received. "He needed to hear it."

But a couple of days later, I bumped into the executive at another screening. The same executive who had praised my truthfulness days before started to ream me out. "I can't believe you told the director that his movie has no playability or marketability," he said. "You crossed the line. *I* wouldn't even tell him that."

It was as if our prior conversation had never happened. "He wants you off the movie," continued the studio executive.

I wandered in sort of a daze afterward. The snafu had shaken my understanding of my job, which—at its core—was about delivering candid feedback. If the studio, which was also responsible for the quality of the film, couldn't appreciate the harsh but necessary truth, then what was the point?

That weekend, I took a long road trip, up to Yosemite National Park, where my friends were renewing their wedding vows. I was miserable the whole drive, until just near my destination. As I was approaching the Ahwahnee hotel, I received a phone call. It was the chairman of the studio, the boss's boss. He didn't offer praise or criticism. He neither reaffirmed nor apologized for supporting the filmmaker in kicking me off the movie. In fact, he didn't even mention it at all.

He just asked me for help.

There was yet another movie, he said, and it wasn't in good shape. The studio had conducted an initial screening of the film, which clocked in at two hours and fifty-five minutes. They told the director to make it shorter and gave him three months to do it.

"Kevin," the studio chair told me, "he came back with a movie that now runs three hours and five minutes! We know audiences will think it's too long. How can they not? We need you to get through to him to make it shorter. And don't sugarcoat it."

It was an aha moment for me. Only then did I realize the importance of my role as an arbitrator, the person who is challenged to deliver the tough message, often positioning myself as a sacrificial lamb in the process. I can say things that studio executives may not be able to say themselves, for fear of creating an adversarial situation with the filmmaker or even damaging the relationship beyond repair.

I was originally going to title this book *Don't Kill the Messenger*, as a reminder to all stakeholders that I'm not judging their talent or their work but rather eliciting feedback from the very people who will ultimately make or break their movie when it's released. I'm also not about to just state the numbers that we collect on the surveys. In order to fulfill my responsibility to them, I'm providing perspective from decades of experience, interpreting what those numbers mean. I'm connecting the dots, so to speak, focusing not only on the key data measures but the comments written on the cards, the exuberance in the auditorium as the film plays, and the way in which the focus group discusses it afterward, including their implicit responses. I'm observing how fast their hands shoot up when I ask who felt satisfied with the story resolution, or how many heads are nodding when one participant voices confusion, or who in the group is laughing when someone recounts a funny scene.

What I've learned over the years, and I'm fairly certain Laddie embraced this as well, is that there is nothing to be gained by soft-pedaling the truth. And sometimes my candor will be met with screaming and yelling, insults or passive-aggressiveness. I suppose it comes with the territory. But my advice is this: face the truth instead of shooting the messenger.

CONCLUSION

Every movie that I test presents its own unique challenges, and that excites me. And while I have devoted most of this book to big, theatrically released films, I want to mention all the work we do for the streaming services, which also make many, many movies. When we conduct test screenings for a streaming service, the process is quite the same as for theatrical movies, although we will often use smaller theater settings with reclining seats and food service to mimic the home environment, where streamed movies are typically viewed. My company has also developed high-security methods to test online, where participants can watch an early cut of a film right from the comfort of their home, fill out surveys on their own devices, and even participate in Zoom-like focus groups afterward.

Online screenings were initiated out of necessity in early 2020 when theaters closed during the COVID-19 pandemic. But they've turned out to be a happy discovery for many clients, particularly the streaming services, and the perfect way in which to test content for in-home viewing.

The industry is evolving, and movie *consumers* aren't necessarily movie*goers*. An entire generation is comfortable watching a full-length movie on their laptops or tablets or even their phones. This has added a whole new dynamic to my business, and we now include a battery of questions to gauge the level of theatergoing worthiness, identifying films that *must* be seen on the big screen versus those that can be enjoyed just as much at home.

Of course, I still and always will appreciate the extraordinary experience of sitting in a movie theater amid a crowd, the smell of popcorn in the air, my heart beating just a little faster as the lights go down and the sound begins to swell, the crackle of anticipation palpable as another story is about to unfold.

The idea for this book originated with a lecture. Every so often, film schools invite me to speak to their students. I go because I love to talk about what I do. But in my experience only a few students are excited to hear about it . . . at least at first.

They filter into the lecture hall looking dour, which, to be fair, seems to be the standard facial expression for many aspiring filmmakers. It's because of the subject matter. All they know is that their instructor has told them that the guest speaker is some guy named Kevin Goetz, a movie market research expert.

They aren't exactly sure what that means, but they're fairly certain that it involves things like data and analysis, terms like "delta" and "standard deviation," the exact words they've tried to avoid by matriculating to film school instead of getting their MBAs.

Of course, the students are partially right. My job does involve looking at data. Most people in my company have a deeply committed relationship with SaaS (software as a service, a suite for advanced analytics).

But the students never expect the other half of the job. They're surprised when I describe the aspect of film research that is whimsical and thrilling and interpersonal. It's the part that is more art than science, and the one that's kept me driving to theaters across the Greater Los Angeles area for thirty-odd years.

It's also a part that Ed Zwick captured so perfectly, like seeing your lover naked for the first time. It's being there in a moment when no one knows quite what to expect—and watching it unfold.

I'm not talking about all film screenings, of course.

I'm talking about the truly special movies. The *Titanic* nights. The *Forrest Gump* nights. The *Paranormal Activity*, *Top Gun: Maverick*, *Get Out*, *My Big Fat Greek Wedding*, *Deadpool*, and *Wonder Woman* nights. The nights when the audience walks into the theater without any preconceived notions or expectations. There have been no reviews yet; Rotten Tomatoes has yet to pass judgment. In fact, the audience sometimes doesn't even know the name of the movie they're about to see until I step to the front of the auditorium and make an introductory announcement.

"Welcome. Tonight, you will be among the first people to see . . ." I pause for dramatic effect. "*Thor!*" Or "*Minions!*" Or the latest *Mission: Impossible* movie. (Sometimes, if the movie is not already part of a pop culture canon—not a sequel or a comic book—I will say "the new Dwayne Johnson movie!")

I don't watch the crowd at this point. I just listen. It's quiet for a moment, just an inhalation, and then—if the movie is hotly anticipated—an exhalation of applause. A thundering roar that travels across each row of the theater, down the aisle, up to the screen.

I swear, for all the information that we collect, the length and loudness of that applause is also an apt predictor of a movie's success at the box office on the first weekend. I haven't run a study or anything, but anecdotally, after three decades of listening to those moments, I know it to be true. There's something so telling about it. It's a sort of cultural echo, reflecting back the world's interest in a movie, what we refer to at my company as "capability," or the innate intensity level of interest in the film's conceit, and enthusiasm to see it when it's released. No statistic or data point can beat it.

Then, of course, the lights go down and we watch, and in the darkness sometimes amazing things happen. The audience can discover something new.

I was there, for example, on the night an audience saw *Borat* for the first time. No one in that room had seen anything quite like Sacha Baron Cohen's fake Kazakh tourist before—or a movie that was, from start to finish, almost entirely a *Candid Camera*-type affair. The audience wasn't sure what they were watching—whether it was a documentary, a comedy, or both—but the laughs were among the loudest I'd ever heard.

Before *Borat*, there was the Farrelly brothers' raunchy comedy *There's Something About Mary*, which among other things features Ben Stiller snagging his balls and shooting semen into his own hair. In the mid-1990s, no audience had ever seen anything like that on the big screen. Being in the room during its first preview was like witnessing the birth of comedy—or at least a new kind of comedy.

These are the moments I feel privileged to have witnessed.

I was not there on the day when Picasso unveiled *La Guernica* for the first time. Nor was I there when Aaron Copland composed *Piano Variations*, or when Springsteen first sang "Born to Run" at the Stone Pony in Asbury Park, New Jersey, in 1975.

I have, however, been there for the introduction of countless films to the world. Perhaps very few are worthy of comparison to Picasso or Springsteen. But some are pieces of high culture, stories that shock, scare, delight, and inspire millions. And I'm there to experience them at their beginning. Better yet, sometimes I get to help shape them.

A long time ago, when I was in my twenties and building my career in the entertainment industry, I produced my first play in my newly launched theater in San Luis Obispo. When it was over, I went outside and stood on the loading dock, looked up at the stars, and cried. Not out of sadness, partially out of exhaustion, and mostly out of gratitude. Gratitude that I had found a job that left me feeling so satisfied. Gratitude that my labor was my love.

It's been many years since then. I don't cry much at my job anymore. But on some nights—especially nights after a great film screening—I will exit the theater and walk out to the parking lot. And if we're far enough away from the light pollution of Los Angeles, I will look up again and see the same stars.

And the feeling is the same, too. Gratitude that my dream became a reality.

ACKNOWLEDGMENTS

First and foremost, I would like to thank my husband, Neil, the love of my life, who has put up with my demanding schedule and let me off the hook for missing so many dinners as I conducted thousands of test screenings over the past twenty-seven-plus years of our extraordinary relationship.

To Metoka Singletary, my oldest friend, who introduced me to a cool little part-time job at a movie market research company called National Research Group back in 1987.

To Joe Farrell and Catherine Paura, who set modern movie research, and my career, in motion.

To Steve Hayman, for his unwavering support of his beautiful, smart, and talented wife, my cowriter, Darlene Hayman, and the many edits and suggestions that he has offered throughout the years.

To David Meadvin and Ryan Jacobs, for their contributions and guidance on the initial structure of the book.

To Kathy Manabat, my executive assistant for more than two decades, who continues to enable me to put one foot in front of the other.

To my protégé Rachel Parness, who has been by my side for nearly two decades.

To Patrick Goldstein, who initially referred to me as the "Doctor of Audience-ology" (a phrase he also coined).

To the late, great screenwriter William Goldman, who famously said, "Nobody knows anything," and then added, "But you, Kevin . . . you know *a little* bit more because you have data."

To Sherry Lansing, who told me early on that this should be more than just a textbook.

To Theresa DiMasi and Anja Schmidt at Simon & Schuster, for saying yes and for their vision in seeing the great potential of the book and their creative contributions to it.

To Mark Ross, for introducing me to Theresa and Anja after reading an early draft and recognizing its broad appeal.

To Doris Cooper, our editor at Simon & Schuster, for carrying the torch forward.

To Samantha Lubash at Simon & Schuster, for handling the thousands of details from manuscript to publication.

To the talented marketing and publicity team at Simon & Schuster, especially Laura Flavin, Molly Pieper, Nan Rittenhouse, and Jessica Preeg.

To Christine Perakis, for always believing in me and crafting all the original legal documents, and Caroline Mankey, Nick Singer, and Bianca Goodloe, who brought the final contracts home.

To the late Jerry Paonessa, one of my mentors, who continues to guide me from the other side.

To Barbara Moulton and Gene Brissie, our early literary agents, who understood the commercial appeal of the book from the outset.

To Debi Elfenbein, for being an early "go to" resource.

To Shelley Zalis, who gave me the opportunity of a lifetime by setting me up with my own movie screening division at OTX.

To the staff of the Margaret Herrick Library, who were so helpful in assisting in the research for the book.

To Anna Scotti, for her extraordinary attention to detail on an early edit of the manuscript.

To Meredith Parks and Mona Pirnot, for all their work on the transcriptions.

To Jordan and his team at The Shop, for the promotional sizzle reel.

To the handful of friends and colleagues who read drafts along the way: Lauren Schuker Blum, Kari Maxwell Campano, Anet Carlin, Kia Colton, Bob Levin, Claudia Lewis, David Madden, Sheryl Mallory-Johnson, Catherine Paura, Stefanie Powers, Couper Samuelson, Kara Francis Smith, Gail Stocker, and Adam Storke.

To Chris Meledandri, for writing the beautiful foreword.

To the wonderful filmmakers who provided testimonials for this book, including Judd Apatow, Sacha Baron Cohen, Peter Farrelly, Graham King, Nate Parker, Amy Pascal, Tom Rothman, Ben Stiller, and Charlize Theron.

To my other friends and colleagues throughout the industry who contributed to the book, many of whom are quoted within these pages, for their sage words that informed the stories.

To the late Samuel Goldwyn Jr., for sharing his recollections of the Golden Age of Hollywood and for giving my husband, Neil, his very first studio job.

To the memory of so many others who passed away during the writing of this book, including Marvin Antonowsky, Richard Del Belso, Joe Farrell, Arthur Manson, Teri Korban Seide, Tom Sherak, J. C. Spink, Craig Zadan, and Dick Zanuck.

And, finally, to my entire family—especially my dad, Lou, and my late mom, Rhoda, who gave me the greatest gift of all.

A portion of the proceeds from this book will be donated to the Motion Picture & Television Fund, a charitable organization supporting working and retired members of the entertainment community with a safety net of health and social services.

NOTES

CHAPTER 2:
LOCKED DOORS, SEVERED HEADS,
AND THE EARLY HISTORY OF TEST SCREENINGS

1. David Kiehn, "The Navigator," San Francisco Silent Film Festival, 2014.
2. Thomas Wood, "The Backstairs Ritual of Movie Previews," *Coast*, September 1938.

CHAPTER 4:
THE GIRL IN THE BLACK COCKTAIL DRESS

1. Patrick Goldstein, "The Doctor of Audience-ology," *Los Angeles Times*, May 17, 2005, www.latimes.com/archives/la-xpm-2005-may-17-et-goldstein17 -story.html.
2. "Forever Fatal: Remembering *Fatal Attraction*," *Fatal Attraction* Special Collector's Edition DVD, 2002.
3. Ibid.

CHAPTER 7:
SCORES SETTLE SCORES

1. Raisa Bruner, "Here's How They Made *La La Land*'s Extravagant Opening Musical Number," *Time*, December 9, 2016, https://www.yahoo.com/news /made-la-la-land-extravagant-222126724.html.

FILM INDEX

NAME INDEX

NAME INDEX